WOMEN'S ROLES IN THE MIDDLE EAST AND NORTH AFRICA

WOMEN'S ROLES IN THE MIDDLE EAST AND NORTH AFRICA

Ruth Margolies Beitler and Angelica R. Martinez

Women's Roles through History

 GREENWOOD

AN IMPRINT OF ABC-CLIO, LLC
Santa Barbara, California • Denver, Colorado • Oxford, England

Library of Congress Cataloging-in-Publication Data

Beitler, Ruth Margolies, 1966–
    Women's roles in the Middle East and North Africa / Ruth Margolies Beitler and Angelica R. Martinez.
        p. cm. — (Women's roles through history)
    Includes bibliographical references and index.
    ISBN 978-0-313-36240-8 (alk. paper) — ISBN 978-0-313-36241-5 (ebook)
1. Women—Middle East.   2. Women—Africa, North.   I. Martinez, Angelica R. II. Title.
    HQ1726.5.B45   2010
    305.40956—dc22   2010002232

ISBN: 978-0-313-36240-8
EISBN: 978-0-313-36241-5

14   13   12   11   10   1   2   3   4   5

This book is also available on the World Wide Web as an eBook.
Visit www.abc-clio.com for details.

Greenwood
An Imprint of ABC-CLIO, LLC

ABC-CLIO, LLC
130 Cremona Drive, P.O. Box 1911
Santa Barbara, California 93116-1911

This book is printed on acid-free paper ∞

Manufactured in the United States of America

To my parents, Wil and Florence Margolies,
for their constant and unwavering support
and to my three best buddies, Alan,
Eliyana, and Hannah. RMB

To my husband and best friend, Timothy,
and to my loving and supportive family,
Robert, Debbie, Patrocinio,
and Mathilda. ARM

Contents

Series Foreword

Women's history is still being reclaimed. The geographical and chrono-logical scope of the Women's Roles through History series contributes to our understanding of the many facets of women's lives. Indeed, with this series, a content-rich survey of women's lives through history and around the world is available for the first time for high school students to the general public.

The impetus for the series came from the success of Greenwood's 1999 reference *Women's Roles in Ancient Civilizations*, edited by Bella Vivante. Librarians noted the need for new treatments of women's history, and women's roles are an important part of the history curriculum in every era. Thus, this series intensely covers women's roles in Europe and the United States, with volumes by the century or by era, and one volume each is de-voted to the major populated areas of the globe—Africa, the Middle East, Asia, and Latin America, and the Caribbean.

Each volume provides essay chapters on major topics such as

- Family Life
- Marriage and Childbearing
- Religion
- Public Life
- Lives of Ordinary Women
- Women and the Economy
- Political Status
- Legal Status
- Arts

Country and regional differences are discussed as necessary. Other elements include

- Introduction, providing historical context
- Chronology
- Glossary
- Bibliography
- Period illustrations

The volumes, written by historians, offer sound scholarship in an accessible manner. A wealth of disparate material is conveniently synthesized in one source. As well, the insight provided into daily life, which readers find intriguing, further helps to bring knowledge of women's struggles, duties, contributions, pleasures, and more to a wide audience.

Preface

Few subjects can be more complicated to explore than that of women's roles in the Middle East and North Africa. Misperceptions abound portraying women as powerless, hidden, and segregated. Until the 1980s, there was a dearth of literature investigating women's actual role in society, both public and private, especially in the pre-Islamic era (before the seventh century). Due to geography, religion, ethnicity, and social class, the Middle East and North Africa present an area of heterogeneity making discussion of the region daunting. Couple that fact with an exploration of women's roles throughout the region where women emerge from numerous economic and social classes and the topic looms even larger.

Complicating the situation further is the debate over the definition of the "Middle East," since that terminology reflects a colonial assessment of the region. What the region is called depends upon one's geography. Those in India might refer to the Middle East as Southwest Asia. The name "Middle East" revealed the British Empire's perception of India as part of the "Far East" and the area that was closer to Europe as the "Near or Middle East." Clearly, the term is not an indigenous one but is now accepted even by those in the region, albeit begrudgingly. When the British established their Middle East Command during World War II, the term took hold. Since no definitive classification exists for the Middle East, scholars differ as to what countries are included, yet despite these diverse factors, there are key elements that unify the Middle East and North Africa. The majority of people are Muslim and most of the region shares common historical elements, most importantly for contemporary times, such as colonialism. It is in this context of both unity and diversity that we explore the topic of women's roles in the Middle East and North Africa. This book covers the following states: Turkey, Iran, Israel, Lebanon, Syria, Iraq, Jordan, Egypt, Saudi Arabia, Bahrain, Kuwait, Qatar, United Arab Emirates, Oman, Yemen, Libya, Algeria, Morocco, and Tunisia.

To explore these concepts of unity and diversity, this book investigates women's roles throughout the Middle East and North Africa—not just the Arab states—from the advent of Islam to the present day. The Middle East and North Africa have undergone significant social, cultural, economic, and political changes with the introduction of Islam, the subsequent Islamic conquests, the emergence of the Ottoman Empire, the colonial period, the drive for independence, the growth of Islamism, and the impact of globalization. These periods of transformation influenced women's status with regards to work, education, family, religion, law, politics, and culture. To understand the enormous revolution of the political, social and cultural milieu that Islam brought to the region, along with the context in which the new religion emerged, the introductory chapter discusses the role of women in the pre-Islamic Middle East. Understanding what came before Islam sets the stage for a greater comprehension of its impact on the Middle East and North Africa.

The chapters that follow are topical and offer a chronological overview of women's roles in the Middle East and North Africa as they pertain to work and education, religion, family, law, politics, and culture from the advent of Islam to contemporary times. With the creation of the modern nation-state system after World War I, countries in the Middle East and North Africa were searching for self-determination and true independence from colonial powers. As such, each state developed within its own historical and cultural context. To capture these variations, most chapters examine how specific countries approached women's issues after World War I.

A chronology gives a quick rundown of the important events in women's history in the regions. A glossary is offered to help readers understand unfamiliar concepts and terms. The selected bibliography provides the major sources for further reading and research.

ACKNOWLEDGMENTS

Projects of this magnitude always involve more people than just the authors. Bosses cut us some slack, colleagues pick up our slack, and husbands and families learn to do without! Given this, we are indebted to Colonels Michael Meese and Cindy Jebb whose leadership, encouragement, and kindness makes the Department of Social Sciences at West Point an extraordinary place to work. We owe our gratitude to LTC Tania Chacho, LTC Ike Wilson, and Dr. Thomas Sherlock whose support, guidance, and friendship helped us to complete the project on time. We are very grateful to

SooJin Rademacher who was always willing to take on extra responsibilities while we were completing this book. We appreciate the insightful comments and kindness of our editor, Wendi Schnaufer. Most of all, we are indebted to our families whose patience and support motivated us whenever we lost steam.

Introduction

Throughout the Middle East and North Africa, from the advent of Islam in the seventh century until today, women have been subordinate to men. Although their position in society has waxed and waned over the centuries, they rarely held positions equivalent to that of their male counterparts. Despite this, women of all classes have played important roles in history as mothers raising and educating the next generation. They have contributed to the economy in both the formal and informal sectors, although their contributions were not always noted. From early Islam in the seventh century, women participated in religious, political, and cultural activities in both public and private settings. Although Islam brought with it significant changes for women in the realms of work, law, family, religion, politics, and culture, it surfaced in a particular cultural context that affected women's positions in society. As such, it is important to outline the historical context in which Islam emerged.

PRE-ISLAMIC MIDDLE EAST AND NORTH AFRICA FAMILY AND WORK

In pre-Islamic society, family organization was linked as much to the relations of production as to culture. Among other features, lifestyle type, sex ratios, and the availability of land shaped familial organization.[1] As such, a woman's role in the family depended upon her community's daily life. In nomadic societies, men and women shared the burdens associated with physical labor, warfare, and other activities outside the home. Hence, in places where women were active in public life, there was much less gender segregation. This factor changed after the discovery of agriculture and the domestication of animals; these events caused a marked transformation in gender roles, as women increasingly assumed domestic duties, while men focused on external matters in the public sphere. This shift in gender responsibilities intensified as people accumulated wealth. In an effort to keep resources within the family, men assumed control of women's sexuality and mobility in society.

Between 10,000 and 12,000 years ago people primarily hunted and gathered food. Until the discovery of agriculture, nomads living in groups of about 20 to 60 followed herds for sustenance, limiting the number of children that women could bear while constantly mobile. Women's roles in the Middle East and North Africa were affected by elements that also influenced women's status across the globe. The advent of food production through settled agriculture and the domestication of animals significantly altered the social and economic structure of many societies. With the ability to grow food, as opposed to gathering and hunting for sustenance, women's functions in economic activity changed. When agriculture replaced hunting as the primary source of food from the Nile Valley to Mesopotamia, populations increased as villages converged around fertile fields with access to water.

As people domesticated animals and farmed land, new gender roles in the family emerged. Rather than work alongside men, women performed light agricultural work in addition to completing their traditional responsibilities raising children, cooking, carrying firewood, and weaving textiles. Some groups lacking access to arable land resorted to nomadic pastoralism, the practice of herding animals seasonally and moving when required to new grazing pastures. Food production also freed up segments of the population to specialize in other areas, including handicrafts. As cities grew, trade with other communities expanded requiring travel. Since childcare can be incompatible, or at least much more challenging, with long-distance travel and longer workdays, women were usually relegated to home activities. Intensive agriculture and the plow's introduction created an even greater divide between a woman's ability to provide childcare and work outside the home. Overall, the domestication of food production transferred women to the home and, as such, lowered their status in many societies. They lacked the opportunity to create outside contacts and external obligations, thereby decreasing their power in society.

More than any other factor, economics modified women's roles in the family. In ancient times, a woman's most important function was to have and raise children, thereby increasing the labor pool. As people shifted from nomadic lifestyles to more settled environments, this function became critical as more children were required for agricultural labor. As women were not expected to live beyond their childbearing years, it was critical for them to produce large families. To do so, women married at a much younger age than men. If a married woman was infertile, her husband could take another wife to have children. Male heirs were desirable because they could better support the family since women usually moved to their husband's family once they married. Religious literature and poetry reflect women's positions in society and illustrate that, in addition to reproducing, women fed their families, participated in agricultural work, and cared for domesticated animals.[2]

Once a family settled, women raised children without the burden of constant mobility. Frequent pregnancies kept women closer to home where they could best tend to young children. This stability gave rise to steady population growth and, eventually, more urban communities. In more settled home environments, women supported the family by weaving, cooking, doing light agriculture work, and child rearing. In some cases women had important roles both in and out of the home, especially in smaller communities where men and women worked fields together, but overall, once people settled in more urban environments, gender roles shifted, leaving women with few opportunities to interact with others outside the home.

Women's responsibilities in economic activities varied according to their status in society. Some poorer women worked in addition to completing domestic chores and raising children. A result of this arrangement was that women worked at their jobs for fewer hours than men and earned considerably less money from jobs outside the home. Already in the third millennium B.C.E., there was a documented gap in the wages that men and women earned for the same job. Historical evidence also from that time reveals that women of the lower classes made up the majority of workers in textile factories and held a variety of jobs in textile manufacturing, breweries, and bakeries. Wealthy and royal families usually had female slaves who performed menial tasks associated with running a large household. In some temples, women were allowed to be priestesses and even scribes.[3] Affluent women were permitted to own land and maintained wealth independent from that of their male relatives through inheritance or earnings. During the Sumerian period (3500–2000 B.C.E.), some rulers' wives were able to participate in the production of textiles, regional trade, and the handling of real estate. Wealthy women outside of royal households also engaged in commercial activities. Seals used to certify contracts from the second millennium B.C.E. reveal that women also participated in international trade and other business deals.

Likewise, in a study of ancient Egyptian monuments and statues (3150 B.C.E.), scholars explored both the role and perception of women during that period and found that "even female workers are usually portrayed with grace and dignity." Tomb inscriptions provide insight into the professional lives of women from the elite class in ancient Egypt. In one case,

Native method of cooking on clay stoves, using charcoal for fuel, Palestine, ca. 1906. (Courtesy of Library of Congress)

a woman discussed her position as the overseer of physicians, while other inscriptions used honorific titles such as vizier and judge when referring to women.[4]

Although pre-Islamic societies were culturally diverse, the primary social unit in much of the Middle East and North Africa was the tribe. The basis of the tribe was the family, which traced its descent through male bloodlines. Throughout Arabia, the tribal system consisted of a group of kindred clans that made up an encampment of multiple goat or camelhair tents with each tent representing a family. Other settled tribes lived in mud huts similar to adobe houses. Nomadic and settled peoples traded with one another and occasionally fought for limited resources. The tribe's elders selected the sheikh, who led the tribe and arbitrated internal conflicts. Tribal loyalty and group solidarity were of the utmost importance because tribal affiliation protected members from external threats. People had a profound emotional attachment to their tribe since it offered them survival, protection, and identity. Tribal warfare frequently erupted over water and grazing rights among other limited resources. There was little gender or social stratification in nomadic tribes because life required constant interaction between the sexes to perform tasks associated with survival. Hence, there were few distinct realms for men and women. Later, as people settled into more urban communities, women's external activities were curtailed.

Tribal and nomadic life gave rise to diverse marriage patterns. The threat of conflict was always present as tribes fought for limited resources. During intertribal conflict, it was not uncommon for women and children to be abducted. Abducted women and children could be held for ransom, sold as slaves, or subsumed by their abductor's tribe. Marriage, as a result of capture or sale, rendered a woman the property of her husband. Other marriages were arranged between tribes to cement alliances. Often the arrangement included a dowry, which could be paid directly to the bride. In many places, the dowry was viewed as the price for exclusive sexual rights.[5] Some women simply married a relative within her own the tribe to retain resources within the family with the added benefit of remaining close to her family. Of course, many women married into a different tribe, bolstering an important alliance between tribes. Upon death, some men willed their widow to a male relative who could then marry the woman himself, give her away for a dowry, or forbid her to marry again.[6] Many of these marriage practices were later abolished under Islam.

The manner and patterns with which people settled the Middle East shaped family patterns and influenced values that exist today. In part, the rise of the Arabs was due to the domestication of the camel, which enabled bands of people to cross the vast deserts of Arabia, eastern Persia, and North Africa. Some people became sedentary while others left settled areas after they outstripped the means of subsistence in well-endowed areas like the Fertile Crescent. Many chose to herd sheep or goats in lands where crops would not grow. These nomadic pastoralists migrated from one desert oasis to another for seasonal water and vegetation for their flocks. Those who mastered the camel could move farther away. In the Arabian Peninsula, a place lacking vegetation and water, people moved constantly to locate water for themselves and their animals. Because of this seasonal nomadic lifestyle, urban centers did not flourish. Rather, clans and tribes of extended families migrated from place to place together, holding property in common. These families had to defend themselves against others, leading to the concept of "family honor," as tribes battled one another in defense of their families. Each sheikh or elder who represented the family in the local council was chosen either for his bravery or family heritage. The council decided on issues of war and peace among the different tribes and clans. Although men seemed to be the most important members of the tribe and family, women had significant roles in maintaining the tribe and sustaining the family. In adverse conditions, tribal strength was critical, thus giving women the important role of bearing children to increase the tribe's relative power. Since men primarily provided for the tribe's security against rivals, male offspring were viewed as more desirable than females. Men were also associated with their potential to possess needed attributes, such as bravery in battle, the insistence on revenge for ills committed against the tribe, and strength under pressure. In some instances, women were not considered part of a tribe until they produced a male heir. In addition to raising children, women attended to every need of the tribe by feeding both people and animals, cleaning and making clothing and tents, and teaching children survival skills in challenging climates and dangerous conditions. Women also inculcated children with tribal culture and traditions, thereby establishing the centrality of family and tribal loyalty for future generations.

WOMEN AND THE LAW

As mentioned, for many tribes, a code of honor was fundamental to the functioning of society and had crucial ramifications for women in society. In the pre-Islamic Middle East and North Africa, tribes incorporated this code into customary laws that, at times, doled out harsh sentences for alleged adultery or even the perception of illicit activity. According to some interpretations, the Qu'ran elevated the status of women relative to what it was in pre-Islamic times. Women were considered chattel that could be sold into marriage and retained no legal standing.[7] Some Islamic scholars, and particularly Islamic feminists, have argued that some later interpretations of Islamic law actually veered from early Islam and the scriptures by incorporating tribal practices that were not part of Islam. In some extreme cases, women were treated no better than slaves. By going back to a literal reading of the Qu'ran, Islamic feminists seek to put the issue of women's equality and rights in context. Modern Muslim writers emphasize that, during the Prophet's era, women were accorded a more respected place in society and more rights than they had prior to Islam. But other scholars claim that in pre-Islamic Arabia, women did not need to live under seclusion (*harem*) and could select their husbands. From pre-Islamic poetry in Arabia, it is clear that women interacted with men and were not completely separated in society. Women were also allowed to be religious leaders, as evidenced by the existence of female soothsayers and temple priestesses. In some cases, women were also arbiters and judges and participated in warfare either by leading armies or accompanying and assisting their husbands in battle.[8]

Perhaps the dichotomy of views of women's status exists because, prior to the Prophet's revelations, a woman's position in Arabia on the eve of Islam had declined from an earlier period, and for some scholars, the Qu'ran rectified this worsened situation.[9] One reason why women's positions in society deteriorated is connected with the increase in urban living. As previously mentioned, after the agricultural revolution and the introduction of a plow that required more strength to use, women were relegated to the home.

Like Islam, the culture of the pre-Islamic Middle East and North Africa put a premium on marriage and children. Evidence from Neo-Babylonian times suggests that women married in their mid to late teens, whereas bridegrooms were closer to their 30s, giving women more time to have children by taking advantage of their most reproductive years.[10] Although polygamy was allowed, early laws such as that of the Law of Eshnunna in the second millennium B.C.E., made it more difficult for men to take other wives. The law stipulated that the second wife needed to be of a lower status than the first so as to protect the first wife's primacy. The law also decreed that a man could not divorce a wife with whom he had children. While men were free to have sex with slaves, a man could not sell a female slave if he impregnated her. Also, causing a woman to miscarry was punishable with a fine. With time, the laws of marriage became less stringent and men were able to marry many women and have concubines. In the Code of Hammurabi, which emerged about 200 years after the Law of Eshnunna, a man's right to divorce was simplified.[11]

While men were superior to women in pre-Islamic tribal society, the extent of their control varied according to tribal customs and traditions. Men, especially elders, were privileged and viewed as more valuable members of the tribe. Evidence suggests that, in some areas, women were considered burdens with no real social status. Lacking inheritance rights or parental rights over children, some tribes seem to have subjugated women almost entirely. Although female infanticide in pre-Islamic Arab culture emerged as a result of the harsh living conditions of the desert, the practice also implies that women were expendable. In some cases, men feared the disgrace associated with the capture of their female children and practiced infanticide to avoid this situation. Infanticide and the perception of women as property, however, were not endemic to all tribes in the pre-Islamic Middle East and North Africa. In certain places, women had social status commensurate with their vital role in raising and maintaining the family. Evidence of a few ancient matriarchal cultures suggest that, in certain tribes, a woman married and remained in her kin's tribe, as did her children and inheritance.[12] But, clearly the patriarchal family structure was more prevalent during the rise of Islam.

In the northern empires, where Sumerian society flourished (from 3500 B.C.E. until 2000 B.C.E.), two important changes shaped women's roles in the family and society. One was the effort to maintain wealth and resources within the family, and the other concerned a shift from a clan-based organization to a more nuclear family structure. These structural changes resulted from the formation of a class system that emerged as some families accumulated more political and economic power than others. During the rise of agrarian-urban culture, especially in the southern half of the delta between the Tigris and the Euphrates rivers, Sumerians took advantage of the rivers to irrigate their fields yielding a crop surplus. Rather than only having enough food to subsist, families now had a surplus that provided access to wealth and led to a stratification of society. The emergence of a class system impacted women in a variety of ways. To maintain wealth in the smaller nuclear family, men controlled women's sexuality by limiting their contact with the outside world. The concept of paternity is crucial in the Middle East and North Africa and its importance can be traced to the concern for keeping resources in the family and passing them along through male bloodlines. This interest in a pure lineage gave rise to endogamous, or cousin, marriage.

This Sumerian period marks a clear sexual division of labor and social stratification according to gender. Over the next 7,000 years, social and political institutions grew more complex as populations expanded and wealth increased. The underlying economic conditions that gave rise to the Sumerians—a surplus of agricultural and specialized craft production—led to a woman's role becoming focused inside the home.

While men specialized in trade, crafts, and professions to earn a living, women often shared domestic responsibilities with other female members of the extended family. The emphasis on a woman as wife and mother and the emergence of different standards for male behavior was clearly reflected in religious teachings and legal codes. The social and cultural pressure to have multiple children also affected men and how society perceived them. During the Sasanian period (226–651 C.E.), a married man who died childless could be considered the father of the first child that his wife had by another man, so that someone would pray for him.[13] Another pre-Islamic custom meant to produce offspring included the tribal practice of wife lending, whereby a man permitted his wife to live with a "man of distinction" to produce noble children. Among the Semites, who practiced polygamy, childless women would care for their slaves' offspring if her husband fathered the children. Female slaves, common in the Middle East, were bought and sold and could even be used as prostitutes to generate income. Even Mecca, the place of Muhammad's birth, had a market where women, captured in various conflicts, were sold.

RELIGION AND POLITICS

Since the earliest periods of recorded history, women have fulfilled important roles in religious practices and activities. During times when ancient gods were mostly tribal and local, their adherents were defined by place or descent. At some times, the pre-Islamic people of the Middle East and North Africa believed in several gods, and during other times they believed in one supreme God controlling other gods.[14] As such, ancient women had numerous associations with all things divine. In fact, much of what is known about ancient women comes from religious artifacts clearly associated with female influence and involvement in society and divinity. From these artifacts, scholars have been able to understand more about the lives and roles of women in religion. For example, women were particularly active in celebrating religious rituals and rites of passage. Across the region, women composed and performed various lamentations, poems, dances, and songs to mark important holidays and events. Several women also worked in the service of the gods. For instance, Sumerian women who worked in temples were called *naditu* and, because of their occupation, although they were permitted to marry, they were not allowed to have children.[15] Across the Levant, or Eastern Mediterranean, women served deities in temples as priestesses, often performing official religious functions. Women also mediated between the mortal and divine in their role as sages and prophetesses. Some women even committed themselves entirely to their beliefs by taking special vows and serving as caretakers for important temples and other sacred religious sites for the majority of their adult lives.

In Mesopotamia, gods and goddesses were associated with some of the most fundamental aspects of human life, such as creation, reproduction, and survival. Goddesses, in particular, were linked to water and agriculture, signifying a mortal woman's role in the provision of basic necessities. For example, the goddess Bilulu was associated with rain and thunder, and the goddess Nammu was associated with the sea. According to Mesopotamian mythology, the most important goddess, Inanna, was linked with the storehouse where people kept all of their most valuable items, including meats, grain, wool, and dairy products. In Sumerian cities, temples marked the place where people paid homage to their respective gods. Those who worked in the temple were viewed as divine servants, many of whom were women. Temples built to honor Inanna lined the Tigris and Euphrates rivers, signifying the importance of water and women's function in providing water in an arid environment. Despite Inanna's prominence in earlier times, her name and gender were later changed to Ishtar, reflecting a diminished role for women's in religion and society.

Other examples of deities associated with important aspects of ancient life abound. These deities and the religious rituals provide scholars with clues about the roles of women in the ancient Middle East. For example, evidence suggests that some goddesses had political and economic influence, as indicated by their participation in the assembly of gods. In addition, Uttu served as the goddess of weaving, perhaps a reflection of women's important role in this vital economic activity.[16] Some female deities were associated with farming, like Nissaba who was the goddess of cereal and grass.

The ample presence of deities connected with agriculture implies an emphasis on women's role in feeding their families and the community before the introduction of the plow. Female deities also had a recurring presence in creation myths. According to one interpretation, the goddess Nammu conceived the first two deities, one male and one female, who subsequently had all of the others.[17] This reflects a woman's crucial role in society as wife and mother. Much of women's religious influence and power concerns fertility, creation, and motherhood.

Another indication of women's role in religion and power in society is reflected in their service to gods. Women who served in the temple were called the high priestess of the temple. A renowned poet and writer, Enheduanna, served in the largest Sumerian temple. Generally, priestesses were the daughters of rulers, but common women also worked in the service of important temples. Scholars contend that women were later excluded from key temple positions as their overall status deteriorated. By the first millennium B.C.E., women were almost completely excluded from prominent positions in the service of deities. This move to eliminate women from roles associated with religious practices might have been part of an effort to restrict women's access to the world outside of the home.[18]

People of the ancient Levant believed in several gods and goddesses associated with both natural and manmade phenomena. Levantine goddesses were closely linked with women's traditional roles in society as wives, mothers, workers, and public servants. While many goddesses were simply viewed as counterparts or wives of gods, others were empowered with typically male enterprises, such as war and the military. Scholars contend that the presence of certain female deities reflects a societal belief in certain divine qualities of women. Also of note is the manner with which gods and goddesses shared tasks, reflecting a societal belief that men and women should apportion burdens in daily life. This is important because, with the shift to monotheism, society would later make a clear preference for limiting women's roles to the private sphere while excluding them from the public realm.

Women were essential practitioners of their respective religions across the Levant. For instance, Israelite women were active in worshipping Tammuz, a Sumerian god. During the sixth century B.C.E., women participated in elaborate mourning rites at the north gate of the Temple of Yahweh in Jerusalem. Each year, women sang dirges accompanied by a flute and engaged in self-laceration while chanting over an image of Tammuz. The women who participated in this annual mourning rite were later criticized for their continuing practice of polytheism. In fact, Ezekiel attacked women who performed religious rites for polytheistic gods and for their disloyalty to Yahweh. Jeremiah also scolded women who continued to worship deities other than Yahweh. Scholars contend that Levantine women's role perpetuating polytheism further undermined their future participation in religious practices.[19] Hebrew scripture also recognizes women's work in the service of various temples, performing functions ranging from housekeeping to assisting priests in their daily duties.

WOMEN AND CULTURE

Religious literature, poetry, and artifacts portray women's important positions in the artistic expression of human thought. Before the rise of agriculture, women worked alongside men, constantly moving in search of sustenance. With the rise of settled communities, people developed more complex cultural practices and institutions. As they gained access to more resources, such as food and shelter, religious practices developed, as did women's role in establishing the cultural identities of their local communities. Women had an important responsibility in passing the spoken and written word to their children and marital families, since women often left their birth family behind upon marriage.

Ancient women also actively participated in celebrating and commemorating special occasions and important rites of passage. Community members composed songs and poems about romantic relationships between men and women. Some compositions, through metaphors, described a woman's physical attractiveness.[20] Marriage, a key rite of passage, was often the subject of literature, hymns, art, and cultural traditions. An interesting ancient cultural tradition that persists in some parts of the Middle East and North Africa concerns the verification of a bride's virginity. On a couple's wedding night, after the union is consummated, the groom's male friends would display the bloody sheet to assure the new bride's purity. The birth of a child was also steeped in cultural traditions and practices involving women. If the birth was difficult or complicated, men and women prayed to the gods for comfort and strength. If the child cried in excess, women sang lullabies to prevent the infant from disturbing the gods. Women also took part in funerary rituals, which included the preparation of the body, gift giving, and a ceremony to send the deceased forth into the next world.[21]

In the earliest civilizations of Mesopotamia and Egypt, social class and environment often shaped women's cultural experiences and roles in society. Women of lower classes had more contact with people outside the home and more interaction with people of various cultures, especially in urban areas heavily engaged in long-distance trade. Non-elite women also worked as servants throughout the region. In ancient Egypt, female servants served as entertainers, singers, and dancers, perhaps using their position as an outlet for artistic expression.[22] Egyptian women also actively participated in cultural events, mostly during religious rituals and services. Women in the service of Egyptian temples put on instrumental performances to bring the dangerous aspects of the divine under control so that humans could safely contact deities.[23] Social class also shaped pre-Islamic women's outward appearance, an obvious sign of one's culture and role in society. For instance, elite women frequently wore a veil, indicating their status as an individual who did not need outside employment. Conversely, slaves, prostitutes, and concubines were forbidden from veiling, shaping their outward appearance and letting others know their place in society.

Evidence suggests that women in ancient societies fulfilled cultural roles closely associated with their sexuality. For instance, in Mesopotamia, men and women served as diviners, sorcerers, and exorcists, often performing rites and rituals for a variety of reasons. The "potency" ritual involved spells and instructions to rekindle passion in a relationship. Women's sexuality was also reflected in Mesopotamian art, as demonstrated by the discovery of clay, terra cotta, and pierced metal renderings of naked women or of couples engaged in sexual intercourse.[24] Egyptian art also highlights women's role in fertility and reproduction. Scholars believe that the use of the color red on male Egyptian figurines is associated with potency. When female figurines are colored in red, it suggests female receptiveness to this potency. Female figurines are normally smaller than males, and, if depicted in a scene, women are often in a secondary place, away from the central position reserved for males. This artistic depiction of men and women reflects the senior-subordinate relationship between men and women in ancient Egypt.[25]

Levantine women were known for their communication with and artistic expressions of divine worship. Prophetesses of the Levant frequently received divinely inspired messages and at times went into trance-like states of ecstasy while receiving and delivering them. Ancient Israeli prophetesses also served as sages or intercessors with divinity, although the Hebrew Bible alludes to more prophetesses than sages. In terms of artistic expression, women were heavily involved in the composition and performance of songs, poems, and lamentations. The Hebrew Bible attributes numerous poems and songs to women such as Miriam, Deborah, and Hannah among others. In times of sorrow, women frequently wailed in public, with their hands above their head, to lament the passing of a loved one. Women also sang in times of triumph and thanksgiving, often after a military victory. Like sages, many women spent time training to write and sing, honing their skills to perform important rituals and ceremonies.[26]

WOMEN IN EARLY ISLAM

During the rise of Islam in the seventh century, similar to pre-Islamic times, women held critical roles in society advancing culture and traditions for both tribe and family. Although women were excluded from positions of authority in the major monotheistic religions, during the formation of the Islamic community, they remained important for their role in inculcating successive generations with religious values, practices, and beliefs. The Prophet Muhammad's wives, daughters, and granddaughters were especially critical in spreading his message and recounting his words and deeds. Some women in Arabia participated in the lucrative trade industry that developed around the holy city of Mecca. Meccan women owned property, served as employers, and traveled with trade caravans across the Arabian Desert. Meanwhile, women in rural and agricultural communities continued to work alongside men. In early Islam, women and men prayed together inside mosques. While families with access to wealth and resources increasingly secluded women to assure their children's paternity, the exigencies of daily life required many women to carry on active roles in society outside the home.

Additionally, women were expected to express cultural and religious beliefs artistically by composing and reciting poetry and oral folklore. Women also preserved important spiritual and cultural traditions by marking special rites of passage such as weddings, funerals, and circumcisions. For women, marriage marked an important transition in their roles, from daughter to wife and mother. While few women selected their marriage partner, women's rights and responsibilities in Muslim families increased. As Islam spread out of Arabia, different societies adapted their unique cultural traditions to fit their practice of Islam. These beliefs and practices had significant implications for women's roles in society after Muhammad's death in ca. 632.

WOMEN IN THE AGE OF THE RIGHTLY GUIDED CALIPHS AND BEYOND

Women's roles in society changed as Islam spread throughout the Middle East and North Africa under Muhammad's first four successors, also known as the Rightly Guided Caliphs, who ruled from ca. 632 until ca. 661. While the first caliphs shared Muhammad's mandate to serve as the Muslim community's leaders, they held more conservative views on women's place in society. Eventually, women were increasingly secluded in their homes and excluded from the public sector. They were prohibited from sharing public spaces with men, including places of worship. While emulating conquered peoples, successive caliphs built large harems of secluded women. As communities transitioned from rural to urban ones, women's positions also shifted. Since they did not need to work, elite women remained at home. If families employed domestic servants, women were not required to leave the house, yet if they did, they wore a veil to mark their social status. As states formed, societal beliefs about women's roles were codified in institutions that kept women subservient. While nomadic and pastoral communities afforded women more opportunities to engage in public life amongst their kin group, urban women were increasingly restricted to domestic activities. The Turks' arrival in the 9th century, followed by the Mongols in the 13th, did little to alter women's position in society, as both conquering groups generally adopted the prevailing views of those they subjugated.

WOMEN IN THE OTTOMAN PERIOD

During the Ottoman Period, which lasted from the end of the 13th until the beginning of the 20th century, women's roles underwent significant transformations. Records indicate that women owned property, were active in commercial real estate, and had the right to argue freely in courts on matters dealing with inheritance. In marriage, women's rights were detailed in marriage contracts and in many cases were upheld by judges, especially with issues pertaining to property rights. Women were also granted guardianship of their children in divorce. Despite these apparent freedoms, many women remained constrained by Islamic legal interpretations that relegated them to subservient positions in society.[27] As the Ottoman Empire's control declined and Europe encroached on its territory, critical changes in the Empire's political and economic power impacted women's status throughout the Middle East and North Africa. Growing European domination in Ottoman areas in the 18th and 19th centuries shifted the power structure of the region. Agriculture became commercialized and rural women who worked in the fields and produced handicrafts at home were forced to compete with cheaper European goods flooding the markets. As men left home to seek employment elsewhere, women remained to tend to family plots and run the households. Although the pace of change differed throughout the Middle East and North Africa, there was almost no escape from European encroachment. It was during this period of Ottoman decline that missionaries arrived and established schools for both men and women. In response to the missionaries, and out of fear that the missionaries' goal was to convert the population, the Ottomans built their own schools for boys and girls. As girls' education expanded so did the number of women's organizations promoting a more public presence for women in society.

WORLD WAR I AND ITS AFTERMATH

The aftermath of World War I witnessed the growth of national movements as countries in the Middle East and North Africa worked toward independence from foreign domination. Women became important participants in these national organizations, aspiring to gain increased rights after independence. In many cases, women were disappointed to discover that, despite their participation in the national movements, the patriarchic structure of society endured. Notwithstanding this fact, in some countries women began to make significant inroads in education, employment, and political positions. In countries less impacted by colonialism, such as the Gulf States, reforms for women came at a later stage of national development.

It was not until after World War II that most states were granted independence, although several small Gulf countries such as Bahrain, Qatar, and the United Arab Emirates did not achieve independence until much later. As countries grappled with state formation, they also confronted the question of women's roles in both the public and private realms. Most countries adopted personal status laws that restricted women to varying degrees with regards to marriage, divorce, inheritance, and property rights. States such as Turkey, Iran, Israel, Egypt, Tunisia, and Iraq emphasized secularism, thereby instituting more liberal policies for women. As women were educated and entered the workforce, family relationships changed. In some cases, women gained more power within the family structure, although women were burdened with juggling the stresses of domestic life and work.

In the 1970s, the region underwent a resurgence of Islam, the culmination of which was the Iranian Revolution in 1979. A religious cleric, Ayatollah Ruhollah Khomeini, overthrew the secular leader and instituted Islamic law in Iran. This event had a momentous impact on countries throughout the Middle East and North Africa, forcing leaders to confront growing opposition to any Western or secular tendencies. Even in countries such as Saudi Arabia that had already instituted Islamic law, opposition groups arose contesting what they perceived as government laxity in religious enforcement. In many Middle Eastern and North African countries, women's roles in society were reassessed. Using violence and social force, religious groups pressured women to wear a veil, leave their jobs, and return to the home.

By the 1990s, increased globalization and a push toward democratization were affecting the Middle East and North Africa. Governments, even the theocratic Iranian regime, began to reconsider women's positions in all realms of society. Although exceptions exist, almost every country in the Middle East and North Africa now permits women to vote and participate in politics. Even so, women's participation rates remain well below those of men, but most countries across the region have been making progress in women's rights. This book provides an overview of these women's roles throughout the Middle East and North Africa.

NOTES

1. Guity Nashat and Judith Tucker, *Women in the Middle East and North Africa* (Bloomington: Indiana University Press, 2006), xli.
2. Nashat and Tucker, *Women in the Middle East and North Africa,* 16.

3. Nashat and Tucker, *Women in the Middle East and North Africa*, 22–26.

4. Barbara S. Lasko, "Women's Monumental Mark on Ancient Egypt," *The Biblical Archaeologist* 54 (March 1991): 4–5.

5. Nikki R. Keddie, *Women in the Middle East: Past and Present* (Princeton, NJ: Princeton University Press, 2007), 21.

6. W. Robertson Smith, *Kinship and Marriage in Early Arabia* (London: Adam and Charles Black, 1903), 105.

7. Javaid Rehman, "The Sharia, Islamic Family Laws and International Human Rights Law: Examining the Theory and Practice of Polygamy and Talaq," *International Journal of Law, Policy and the Family* 21 (2007): 113.

8. Nabia Abbott, "Women and the State on the Eve of Islam," *American Journal of Semitic Languages and Literatures* 58 (July 1941): 260–63.

9. Jane Smith, "Women in Islam: Equity, Equality, and the Search for the Natural Order," *Journal of the American Academy of Religion* 47 (December 1979): 520.

10. Nashat and Tucker, *Women in the Middle East and North Africa*, 22.

11. Nashat and Tucker, *Women in the Middle East and North Africa*, 30–31.

12. Muslim Women's League, "Women in Pre-Islamic Arabia," (1995). http://www.mwlusa.org/topics/history/herstory.html.

13. Nashat and Tucker, *Women in the Middle East and North Africa*, 24.

14. Bernard Lewis, *The Multiple Identities of the Middle East* (New York: Schocken Books, 1998), 25.

15. Nashat and Tucker, *Women in the Middle East and North Africa*, 23.

16. Piotr Bienkowsik and Alan Millard, *Dictionary of the Ancient Near East*, (Philadelphia: University of Pennsylvania Press, 2000), 321.

17. Samuel Noah Kramer, *Sumerian Mythology: A Study of Spiritual and Literary Achievement in the Third Millennium B.C.* (Philadelphia: University of Pennsylvania Press, 1972), 74.

18. Nashat and Tucker, *Women in the Middle East and North Africa*, 28.

19. Mayer I. Gruber, "Women in the Ancient Levant," in *Women's Roles in Ancient Civilizations*, ed. Bella Vivante (Westport, CT: Greenwood Press, 1999): 121–23.

20. Karen Rhea Nemet Nejat, "Women in Ancient Mesopotamia," in *Women's Roles in Ancient Civilizations*, ed. Bella Vivante, 110.

21. Nejat, "Women in Ancient Mesopotamia," 90–97.

22. Gay Robbins, "Women in Ancient Egypt," in *Women's Roles in Ancient Civilizations*, ed. Bella Vivante, 182–83.

23. Robbins, "Women in Ancient Egypt," 163.

24. Nejat, "Women in Ancient Mesopotamia," 105–9.

25. Robbins, "Women in Ancient Egypt," 184.

26. Gruber, "Women in the Ancient Levant," 131.

27. Nashat and Tucker, *Women in the Middle East and North Africa*, 71–72.

Chronology

625	Battle of Uhud between the Meccans and Medinians, in which a woman, Nusaybah bint Kaab, is credited with saving Muhammad's life
632	Death of Muhammad
632–634	Abu Bakr succeeds Muhammad
634–644	Umar succeeds Abu Bakr and places tighter controls on women's movement and expands the Islamic Empire
644–656	Uthman succeeds Umar as caliph; Uthman is murdered by one of his followers
656	Ali succeeds Uthman as caliph, but is confronted by Uthman's Umayyad tribe. Aisha, Muhammad's youngest wife, opposes Ali's ascension as caliph and organizes the Battle of the Camel. Ali is victorious
680	Ali's son Husain dies in the battle of Karbala and Zaynab brings his head to Damascus
705	Caliph Walid pushes for the seclusion of royal women in Syria; the veil becomes accepted for royal women
717–801	Rabi'a Al' Adawiya emerges as an important female Sufi saint in what is now Iraq
750	Abbasid dynasty comes to power; Islamic cities expanded
763–809	Abbasid caliph Harun-al-Rashid is born to a Yemeni slave women
Ninth century	Turks are brought to the Middle East as slaves to serve in the military, but they eventually gain control of the region
909–902	Fatimid Empire expands in North Africa
940–1020	Abo'l-Qasem Ferdowsi writes the Shah-nameh, or "Book of Kings," over the course of 30 years
Early 1000s	Islam splits into Sunni, Shia, Isma'ili, and other sects
ca. 1000s–1200s	Jewish women are excluded from the study of Scripture
1200s	Sufism becomes a mass religious movement throughout the Middle East and North Africa
1225	Mongol Genghis Khan enters the Middle East and eventually conquers most of North Africa
1249	Mamluk Dynasty is founded in Egypt by Turkish mercenaries

1258	Genghis Khan's grandson, Huluagu, captures Baghdad, ending the Abbasid rule; Mongols hold women in higher esteem than in the conquered lands
Late 1200s	Beginning of Ottoman Empire founded by the ruling family of Osman Turks
1453–1924	Ottoman Empire rules from Anatolia, to the central Middle East and North Africa, later expanding to east and central Europe
	Women are active in real estate and own shops and houses
1501–1722	Safavid Dynasty in Persia adopts Shi'ism as its official religion
1700s	Merger between a staunchly religious leader, Muhammad Ibn Abd-al Wahab, and a local tribal leader, Ibn Saud, eventually leads to the creation of Saudi Arabia
ca. 1735	Wahhabi movement begins in Arabia
1750	Hindiyya Ujaymi founds the first exclusively women's order in the Maronite Church in Lebanon
1798	Napoleon invades Egypt and tries to introduce unveiling for women and a Western approach to women's rights
1805–1849	Muhammad Ali rules in Ottoman-controlled Egypt; he forces peasants to work on large infrastructure projects, with men leaving women in control of the family plot
1842	Medical school in Istanbul allows women to be trained as midwives
1844	Qurrat al-Ayn assumes a leadership position among the Babis of Iran
1858	Turkey establishes a vocational school for girls
1863–1879	Khedive Isma'il rules Egypt and modernizes the education system
1881	Egyptian authorities prohibit Sufis from using musical instruments in women's presence during rituals
1882	Britain invades Egypt
ca. 1890	In Damascus, Syria, about 5,000 women are employed in their homes unreeling silk and yarn
Late 1800s	Women participate in the entertainment industry, especially in cities like Cairo
1906	Constitutional Revolution in Iran calls for more rights for the people

1906	Afifa Karam writes the first novel in Arabic
1907	First girls' school opens in Iran
1911	Sufi orders develop in Libya, providing women with a spiritual outlet
1914	Ottoman government creates school in Basra, Iraq, where girls learned the Qu'ran, hadith (sayings and teachings of Prophet Muhammad), and needlework
1915	Decree in Turkey allows women to work unveiled
1923	Mustafa Kemal Ataturk becomes the president of Turkey and implements far-reaching reforms for women; Ataturk's government subsequently drives Sufi orders into private homes
1925	Reza Shah Pahlavi rises to power in Iran, ending the Qajar Dynasty, which assumed power in 1779. The Shah forces women to remove their veils
1926	Turkey adopts the secular Turkish Civil Code based on the Swiss model
1932	Saudi Arabia gains its independence and implements sharia law; a strict segregation of the sexes is enforced
	Sultan Said Bin Taymur assumes power in Oman. He fears modernity and closes his country off from the outside world
1936	Women gain access to university education in Iran
1941	Shah of Iran abdicates the throne to his son, Mohammed Reza Pahlavi, who emulates Ataturk's secularization program in Turkey
1946	Jordan gains independence from Britain; Lebanon and Syria gain independence from France
	In Lebanon, workers at a tobacco factory strike, with women playing key roles in the protests
1947	The United Nations partitions the area of British-mandated Palestine into Jewish and Palestinian states
1948	State of Israel is created; Israel's War of Independence begins
1950s	Numerous immigrants of Asian and African origin come to Israel with family structures and perceptions of gender roles that differ from those of the country's Europeanized founders
	Israel implements family-friendly policies to encourage Jewish women to have larger families

1950s–1960s	Feminist authors begin to challenge the patriarchal system through their publications
1951	Libya gains independence from Italy; women's roles have been dictated by interpretations of the Qu'ran
1952	Free Officer's Revolution in Egypt; one participant, Gamal Abdel Nasser, becomes president in 1954
	Iraqi Women's League is founded to champion the rights of women and children
1956	Gamal Abdel Nasser nationalizes the Suez Canal, precipitating the Suez Crisis; Britain, France, and Israel attack Egypt
	Tunisia and Morocco gain their independence from France; Tunisia passes liberal gender laws and completely abolishes polygamy
	New constitution in Egypt gives women the vote and calls for gender equality
1957	Morocco adopts a new family law, or *Mudawwana*, that continues support for polygyny but ends forced marriage
1959	Iraq enacts one of the most liberal personal status laws in the region
1960s	Ba'ath party assumes power in Iraq, encouraging women's participation in the economy
1960	Saudi Arabia opens public schools for girls
1961	Kuwait gains its independence from Britain
1962	Iranian women are given the right to vote
	Algeria gains independence from France
1964	Jordan passes the Compulsory Education Law, but cultural factors prevent some girls from going to school
1966	Kuwait University is established
1967	Iranian government passes the Family Protection Law that curtails polygamy, allows women to divorce, and broadens custody rights
1969	Libyan King Idris is overthrown by Colonel Muammar al-Qaddafi, who implements a compulsory nine-year education for all Libyans
1970s–1980s	Several Middle East states shift from agricultural to industrial economies, especially in places like Iraq where the oil industry has developed

1970	Nasser dies and Anwar Sadat assumes power in Egypt
	Sultan Qaboos bin Said ousts his father from power in Oman and begins to modernize the country; he implements a universal education program, improving prospects for women to enter the workforce
1971	Qatar and the United Arab Emirates gain independence from Britain
1972	In Libya, the minimum age for marriage for girls is raised to 16 and women are allowed to select their husbands
1975	Iran appoints its first female judge
	Union of Libyan Women forms and makes progress in advancing rights for women in employment, childcare, and maternity leave
	General Women's Union is founded in the United Arab Emirates to monitor women's groups and dealing mostly with charitable and business organizations
1975–1990	Lebanon's civil war
1977	Qatar University opens with seven separate colleges for women and men
1978	Libya opens its Military Academy and allows women to attend
1979	Iranian Revolution removes the Shah from power, and Ayatollah Ruhollah Khomeini implements strict sharia law
	Saddam Hussein assumes power in Iraq and endorses women's rights, in an effort to deal with a labor shortage
	Grand Mosque takeover in Saudi Arabia by Islamic militants leads to even more stringent policies for women
1980–1988	Iran-Iraq War strains women and families in both states
1980s–1990s	Growth in Islamist movements across the Middle East and North Africa
1984	Algeria drafts the Algerian Family Code, permitting women to work, but strengthening male control of women
1985	Egyptian President Hosni Mubarak passes a law that places the burden on the woman to prove that a polygamous marriage is harmful to her, reversing more liberal policies toward women

1987	First Intifada, or Palestinian uprising, against Israel
1989	Ayatollah Khomeini of Iran dies; Ali Akbar Rafsanjani becomes president and improves the status of women
1990	Iraq invades Kuwait, precipitating an international response led by the United States to remove the Iraqi military from Kuwait
	North and South Yemen unify into one state; North Yemen's more conservative laws toward women prevail
1991	In Algeria, Islamists win the first round of legislative elections, prompting the government to cancel the next round of elections
1992	Social and Cultural Council of Women is established in Iran to deal with women's employment issues
1997	In Iran, reformist candidate Mohammad Khatami is elected president on a platform of civil and women's rights. He is reelected president in 2001
	Women in Oman are given the vote and can run for office
2000	New law passes in Egypt allowing a woman to divorce, provided she repays her dowry
2001	More than half of all students in Iranian universities are women; by 2005, women make up more than half of the student population
2002	Justice and Development Party (AKP) assumes power in Turkey, changing parts of the constitution to increase gender equality
2003	United States invades Iraq and overthrows leader Saddam Hussein
	Women are given the vote in Qatar
2004	New, more liberal family code is passed in Morocco increasing the age of marriage, allowing women to inherit family assets, and allowing judges to decide whether divorce is valid
2005	Conservative Mahmoud Ahmadinejad is elected president in Iran, negating many gains that women have made during the Khatami reform period
	Iraqi women go to the polls to elect political leaders
2007	In Libya, under pressure from Islamic groups, Qaddafi requires women under 40 to have a male relative accompany them when traveling

2008	In Israel, women hold only three out of 26 cabinet positions, although these are high profile positions
2009	In Iran, Ahmadinejad is declared president after what some believe are fraudulent elections
2010	Iranian authorities crack down on opposition groups including many women's organizations

1

~∞~

Women and Work

Women in the Middle East and North Africa have played significant economic roles, both in and outside the home, from the sixth century through present times. There has been a tremendous amount of variation in the types of jobs women perform, depending on their social status. A look at nomadic, village, and urban women reveals different functions in diverse social structures, and also discloses some interesting similarities among the groups, including the effect of a patriarchal structure on women's place in society. This cultural system of male dominance has constrained the type of work that women can do outside the home. Islam is just one explanation for why the level of female employment is lower in the Middle East and North Africa than in many other parts of the world. Segregation of the sexes in the workplace, coupled with other cultural restrictions placed on the types of work that seem appropriate for women, have made it challenging for them to boost their employment numbers.

Women in the Middle East and North Africa are becoming more educated, and this factor is influencing a change in the type of jobs that they are pursuing. Before there was significant research in the area of women's studies, it was assumed that women were invisible in the Middle East labor force. Although it is obvious now that women's roles in the workforce were not sufficiently appreciated, it is also clear that cultural and religious values kept them on the margins of the economy.

As women became more important economic figures in the family, both their freedom and decision-making capabilities within that unit began to increase, changing some of the traditional values that a woman's place was only in the home. Despite this, women's growing employment in the Middle East and North Africa has been a double-edged sword. Women who are employed are empowered by having more control over spending and decision making in the household, leading to an increase in children's welfare, as expanded education and employment for women leads to lower fertility rates that benefit both women and society. However, the types of employment women find in developing countries with mostly authoritarian regimes exposes them to exploitation and harsh working conditions. As such, the question becomes whether paid employment has actually benefited women. This chapter explores women's work and education throughout the Middle East and North Africa, along with the consequences of globalization there.

THE ISLAMIC PERIOD

Many scholars debate whether women in pre-Islamic Arabia had more or fewer rights than after the advent of Islam. In the pre-Islamic Bedouin society of the Arabian Peninsula, some argue that women were afforded a large role in the public sphere, and that changed during the Islamic period. The more egalitarian nature of pre-Islamic tribal life, as in most nomadic existence, was due to the lack of surplus since groups did not amass wealth. As such, there was little stratification in society and, although a division of labor occurred according to age and gender, women played large roles in domestic and public life. Additionally, since women contributed greatly to food collection, this factor played a role in their fairly equal status in society. In Bedouin society, when the men were absent from the community due to trade or warfare, the women took charge of the camp. During these periods, in addition to performing tasks traditional to men, women continued their domestic activities including spinning, milking, food preparation, and childcare. Despite the view that society was more egalitarian prior to Islam, other scholars contend that the Qu'ran afforded women explicit privileges that were lacking in pre-Islamic times, such as inheritance rights and the payment of a dowry directly to the woman as opposed to her guardian.[1] Countering this view is the argument that, although the rules regarding women might not have been as well-defined in pre-Islamic times as in the Qu'ran, women did not require a guardian's approval for all aspects of their lives, including mobility and marriage selection.

What is clear to all is that women's roles in most aspects of society changed after the revelations that Muhammad received in 610 C.E. in Arabia. Born in 570 C.E., Muhammad was orphaned at six years old and raised by his paternal uncle, Abu Talib, from the Quraysh tribe in Mecca. Mecca had become a key center of trade due in part to the fact that it was home to the Ka'bah, an important shrine for many deities, and that it sat at the crossroads between trade routes of the Mediterranean and Indian Ocean. As the tribes of Mecca became wealthier, women's roles shifted. On one hand, more elite women were able to engage in trade in part because slaves freed up time for them to do so by taking on some of their domestic chores. On the other hand, urbanization strained Mecca's tribal life, and this fact impacted the family structure by placing more emphasis on the nuclear family rather than the extended one. In the nuclear family structure, stricter regulations were placed on women's mores, since they lacked the extended family to keep an eye on them.

Having married a wealthy widow, Khadija, Muhammad became a well-respected and successful businessman in Mecca. According to Bedouin custom, women could choose their spouse and, true to form, Khadija proposed to Muhammad. Arabia at that time was polytheistic, and several powerful tribes made money on pilgrimages to the pagan shrines in Mecca. After Muhammad began receiving revelations, he preached his new faith based on monotheism and generosity to his neighbors. Since he upset the social and economic order of the times, many Meccans opposed Muhammad and his teachings. People from a neighboring town, Yathrib (Medina), who had heard of Muhammad's ability to negotiate, invited Muhammad to their city to arbitrate disputes between various tribes. In 622 C.E., Muhammad and his closest followers left Mecca to begin a new life in Medina. Moreover, after the death of both Khadija and Abu Talib, Muhammad lost his benefactors in Mecca and pressure against him was building.

Muhammad's new faith had an enormous impact on the role of women in society and their place in economic activity.

As previously mentioned, tradition holds that, during Muhammad's time, women's status actually improved from previous tribal laws. Islamic modernists argue that the Qu'ran provided for gender equality and that Muhammad elevated the status of women. Several women close to Muhammad played key roles during crucial periods of his life, especially during his reception of the revelations. Khadija gave Muhammad his start as a trader and supported him during the early revelations. His decisive act of faith, and his later declaration as a prophet, put him squarely against other interests in Mecca, especially economic ones.

During Muhammad's lifetime women were still active in public life and, in some cases, even assumed combat roles, though this was not the norm. During the battle of Uhud in 625 between the Meccans and Muhammad's followers, Nusaybah bint Kaab, also known as Umm Umaya, is credited with saving Muhammad's life. According to the Qu'ran, the Muslims were winning the fight against the Quraysh tribe in Uhud, but when the enemy camp was opened, some of Muhammad's followers began to leave their posts to loot the camp. The tide of battle began to turn and the archers who were left in place to protect the prophet abandoned their posts. During the fight, Nusaybah was one of 10 warriors who protected the prophet with her own body from the enemies' arrow. During that same battle, Muhammad had an impressive female foe. Hind bint Utbah, the wife of Mecca's leader, Abu Sufyan, screamed encouragement to Meccan troops by disparaging the prophet. In many battles, women would follow the troops and yell encouragement, tend to the wounded and carry water to the soldiers. In a particularly gruesome story, as the Meccans defeated the Muslim fighters, Hind searched for the man who had killed her father in the battle of Badr in 624 and, when she found his corpse, bit into his liver. In another battle, Muhammad's aunt, Safiyah, was the first woman to kill an opponent in battle. In the battle of Yarmouk in 636 against the Byzantine Empire, Asma bint Yazid played a role in killing nine men and is considered one of the best reporters of hadith, the sayings of Muhammad, with 81 connected with her name. In another event showcasing the public roles of women during the beginning of Islam, Muhammad consulted with Umm Salamah when he negotiated the Treaty of Hudaibiya. Muhammad's daughter Fatima also played a key role in the early social and political development of Muslim society.

THE GOLDEN AGE OF ISLAM

Women's roles in Islamic society slowly began to change in the Golden Age of Islam, which refers to the period after Muhammad's death in 632 and the successful spread of Islam across the Middle East, North Africa, Spain, and India and the growth of technology and culture. His first successor, Abu Bakr, led for only two years, most of which was spent contending with internal revolts by those who believed that the death of the prophet signaled the end of the new religion. Under the second caliph, Umar (634–644), tighter controls were placed on women's movements and impacted women's ability to work in more public positions as they had in the past. These more stringent limitations on women may be attributed to the conquest of lands outside of Arabia and contact with other cultures. As the Muslims acquired land that had been under Byzantine control, the Christian empire influenced its new conquerors. The impact of these new restrictions, however, was not immediate and some scholars contend that the seventh century was a positive one for women. According to Muslim treasury registries, women were included among those who received a cut of taxes given to the Arabian conquerors.[2] The third caliph, Uthman (644–646), continued the conquests into other lands, but was murdered by one of his followers after his second year in power. Aisha, Muhammad's youngest wife, opposed Ali's rise to the caliphate and organized a group to counter his power in the Battle of the Camel. Ali's victory against his opponents in that war and his ascension as caliph energized those who held that women's roles in the public arena should be curtailed. They used Aisha's failure to mobilize effective support against Ali as proof that women should be kept out of politics.

By 705, under the leadership of the caliph Walid, women's status in society began to decline. Walid pushed for the seclusion of the royal women in his household due, in part, to his increased contact with foreigners. Although most rural women continued to live unveiled, the veil had become accepted for the royal women in Walid's time.

The growth of urban culture impacted the role of women in society, and especially the seclusion of women. This is due to the fact that, with the large economic expansion during the Abbasid period (750–1258), which led to the growth of Islamic cities, female slaves were available to do work outside the home, thus allowing middle and upper class women to remain in their homes. Many of the slaves originated from outside the Middle East and once the Islamic conquest occurred and the region was under Islamic rule, Islamic law dictated that non-Muslims, especially Jews and Christians, should be protected from enslavement. The most beautiful slaves were educated and trained in music, singing, and literature. Although upper class women were veiled outside their homes and in the presence of men other than their immediate family, slaves were permitted to roam freely and uncovered.

TURKISH AND MONGOL PERIOD

Turkish influence in the Middle East began around the ninth century as Turks were brought as slaves to serve in the military. Eventually, these Turkish slaves acquired more power through their military service and eventually grew to control the region. Female slaves served as concubines for members of aristocratic families. The Turkish lifestyle was mostly pastoral nomadic, and women played important roles in the Turkish economy. They milked cows, made cheese, spun rugs and clothes, and tended to the children. When the tribes migrated, women shared responsibility for the movement of people and goods. Women's important roles in the economy affected their political status, as illustrated by their appointment to tribal councils.[3]

The Mongols' arrival in the Middle East followed closely on the heels of the Turkish influx. They were predominantly a pastoral nomadic group. In 1225, Ghengis Khan entered the Middle East and by 1258 his grandson, Huluagu, had captured Baghdad. This conquest put an end to the Abbasid Dynasty; under both the Turks and Mongols, women were held in much higher esteem than in the lands they conquered. A group of Turkish mercenaries eventually founded the Mamluk Dynasty in Egypt in 1249 and did not immediately assimilate with the indigenous population. They married women of Central Asian origin and perpetuated the roles that women played in the Turkish lands. The women were able to control estates, serve as guardians for their children, and hold important positions in charitable institutions. Eventually, after the Turks and Mongols converted to Islam, the role of women changed to reflect more closely the traditions of Muslim society, especially in the urban areas. Those who remained nomadic, however, continued to hold on to more freedom and women served the community as they had in the past.

As seclusion and the veiling of women became more prevalent for urban women, much information about women during the 14th century comes from literature as opposed to the chronicles of Islamic scholars. Upper class women stayed mostly in the home, but used their wealth to deal in real estate. Few women were involved in commerce, since that would require them, in the course of doing business, to come into contact with men who were not their relatives. In the 15th century, elite women who wanted to get an education were permitted to do so, and this impacted upon their work opportunities. They studied a variety of religious topics including sharia, Qu'ran, and hadith. Since women such as Muhammad's wives and other female relatives transmitted many hadith, this fact opened the door to women studying and teaching the traditions. Although men usually studied with male scholars, some men did study with the most renowned female scholars.[4] Women also pursued an education in literature, philosophy, economics, and artistic topics.

Some lower class urban women of this period did work outside the home. The intention for some of the single women was to earn enough money to enter into a good marriage by working as midwives, peddlers, and domestic servants. Many widows spun cloth at home while caring for their children and simultaneously being paid for the number of items that they produced. Most women were not involved in the large-scale production of textiles, as this would have entailed significant amounts of contact with men outside their families.

In contrast to urban women, rural women filled a larger public role in their communities. According to the 14th-century historian Ibn Battatu, during his travels across the Middle East, even most rural women were veiled. However, some scholars believe that rural women adhered less to the requirement of veiling in order to execute their agricultural tasks and because they lived in small villages where they were acquainted with most people. As such, they did not perceive themselves as among strangers and were less inclined to veil. Although women worked in the fields outside the home, in many rural areas throughout the Middle East where plows were used, men conducted the majority of fieldwork due to the difficulty and weight of using the plow. Plowing also requires the extensive clearing of fields prior to its use; this was arduous work usually performed by men.

Women, however, had some key roles including planting seeds, participating in the harvest, caring for the animals, and milking. In Iran, Anatolia, and Central Asia during this period, women and children made rugs in shops that were established by entrepreneurs.[5]

THE OTTOMAN PERIOD

The Ottoman Empire stemmed from the ruling family of Osman Turks in the 13th century. By the height of its conquests in the 17th century, it controlled most of what is now the modern-day Middle East and expanded through Eastern Europe to Hungary in the west, although the Ottomans were repelled from entering Vienna. A key finding of the Ottoman period was a large number of documents detailing economic and social issues of the areas that they controlled; these include discussions of women's roles. Although records confirm that veiling hampered women from working in many areas, they also illustrate that some women found ways to better their financial situations. For example, in some places women were active in real estate, and in 17th century Aleppo, a few Syrian women worked as moneylenders. Although women owned less than men, records show that they were quite active, comprising a third of dealers in commercial real estate between 1750 and 1751. Many women were also property owners.[6]

Likewise, in the Anatolian city of Bursa (in modern-day Turkey), in the 17th century, the Ottomans retained extensive records of deceased people's estates. These records illustrate that women were involved in selling and buying village real estate and owned shops, mills, and houses. They also had the ability to argue freely in court in matters dealing with inheritance. In one case in Bursa, Imhani bint Mehmed Celebi left an enormous estate to her children, but there was no husband listed in the inheritance. This finding implied that she was the head of the household. As in Aleppo, some of the records reflect women's heavy involvement in money lending.[7]

As the Ottoman Empire declined, its leaders sought advice from European powers for technological advancement. Although the Ottomans perceived the European culture as "backward," they recognized the advances that Europe had made in military technology. Through military contacts, Europeans slowly began to encroach upon the Ottoman territories. The 18th- and 19th-century Middle East ushered in a period of imperialism and foreign control. The colonial powers significantly influenced the social, economic, and political structure of the region during this time, but the changes occurred at various rates in different parts of the Middle East and North Africa. Consequently, the roles of women and the types of work that they were permitted to do was also altered. Colonization impacted rural and urban women differently. Prior to colonization, rural women were important members of the agricultural society, since they worked in the fields and also produced handicrafts at home. When agriculture was commercialized in the 19th century, many traditional crafts had to compete with European products. In Egypt and Syria, peasants usually worked on family plots for both subsistence farming and to sell surplus crops at the market. In addition to their household chores, women worked in the fields during harvest time, tended to the animals, and dealt with pest control. They also made yarn that they sold to weavers.

When Napoleon invaded Egypt in 1798, he tried to introduce unveiling for women in Cairo coupled with a more Western approach to women's rights, but experienced a backlash against these policies by the local population. After Napoleon's departure in 1802, although Egypt was under Ottoman direction, an independent and strong leader took control. During Muhammad Ali's rule (1805–1849), the state forced peasants to work on infrastructure projects, such as building canals and dams to hasten Egypt's commercialization of agriculture. Many of these projects involved travel and extended periods away from home. As men made up the majority of laborers, the women left behind were forced to tend to the family plot.[8] Occasionally, women worked in new factories that were expanding in the region. Muhammad Ali also implemented military reforms, the most notable of which was male conscription, leaving women at home with more responsibility in the fields. The commercialization of agriculture also took men away from home, since it led to the growth of cash crops in Egypt, with men forming the bulk of labor for these crops. Again, due to these changes, women took control of the household plot. The aforementioned factors set the stage for a changed perspective on women and work in these areas.

Muhammad Ali's modernizing policies increased education opportunities for women. He set up new technical and medical schools, one exclusively for women. Although the school had trouble attracting free women at first, it eventually became one of the first schools to give women a modern education.[9] Syria underwent a similar adjustment in its peasant structure, although the changes occurred more gradually due to Syria's lesser dependence on cash crops. In more rural areas and ones less affected by commercialization, such as rural Iran and the Gulf states, few changes occurred in regard to women's role in the economy.

In the 19th century, Damascus was a center of agriculture, manufacturing, and trading, but was also increasingly influenced by changes in the world market and European colonialism. By the 1850s, the infringement of European textiles into the Damascus market threatened to destroy the local economy. Simultaneously, the growing demand for commercial agriculture brought great wealth to some Damascus landholders who emerged as a new, elite class in the latter part of Ottoman rule. Through a reorganization of trade networks, Damascene merchants were able to prosper despite some of the negative effects of the global shifts in markets. During the 18th and 19th centuries, middle to upper class families strengthened their economic positions by acquiring property that they registered in the Islamic law courts. According to these records, women also acquired residential, commercial, and agricultural properties. With regards to residential properties, women bought houses from non-family members and sold houses at least as often to non-relatives as to family members. This shows that women were concerned with market advantages and not just family consolidation. Noblewomen and those from the Ottoman aristocracy bought and sold properties more often than the middle class women did.[10]

Women also bought and sold commercial properties. Some of these properties were inherited, but many were straightforward commercial transactions. Women bought and sold a variety of shops, including coffee houses, groceries, perfume stores, lumber warehouses, and others. In Damascus, aside from women who owned property, a majority of urban and poor women worked in production and services. In production, women worked predominantly in the textile and craft industries. In 1890, about 5,000 women were employed in their homes unreeling silk and yarn. They did this work in addition to their other housekeeping chores. To compete against the growing number of European imports, manufacturers exploited their laborers forcing them to work long hours in challenging conditions.[11] In North Africa, which was mostly rural, women produced a variety of items including tents, linens, mats, rugs, and cooking utensils. They also made items for warfare, including gunpowder.[12]

In the service industries across the region, all work that was connected to childbirth and childcare fell into the exclusive sphere of women. Women worked as midwives learning the necessary skills from their mothers. Other poor women became wet nurses to more affluent women's children. In Damascus, another domain where women provided important services was in body decoration with henna before a marriage.

As the Middle East became more integrated into the global market, traditional craft industries were destroyed. Since Europe exported cloth to the Middle East, women who spun for the textile industry no longer had a livelihood. Some of them went to work in textile factories, but were usually paid less than men. Algeria, which had been under direct French influence since the early 1800s, experienced a profound transformation in its weaving and craft industries. When the French came to Algeria, they expropriated land from peasants and settled Europeans on those lands. This land grab led to the destruction of the pastoral-nomadic economy, which had produced raw materials for the craft industry.[13] Additionally, with the European influence, tastes were changing and traditional crafts and clothing styles were no longer in high demand. The handicraft industry in Algeria was almost completely destroyed. In contrast to Algeria, women in Lebanon found expanded labor opportunities in factories producing silk during the 1800s as the European demand increased.[14] Likewise, women found more opportunities in Iran as European demand for carpets grew. In many cases, however, increased labor opportunities did not translate into political power, as women were still saddled with the bulk of child-rearing and household chores. As such, they did not have the opportunity to use the earnings and create outside obligations. Even if women earn money, unless they can participate in the public arena and foster mutual obligations, they will most likely remain less powerful than men.

Economic changes in the 19th century, especially land consolidation and population growth, led to more urban migration. In the cities, it was difficult for women to find work, as they were closed out of many of the craft and trade industries, yet worked on the margins of the economy by spinning yarn for weavers. Making the situation more challenging was that, with European military victories, the Ottoman Empire was forced to accept the entry of European goods into areas under their control along with low tariffs. These two factors severely harmed the handicraft industries and many lower class women's livelihood.[15]

Other than textile and handicraft production, there were certain trades that were also associated with women. In 19th-century Cairo and other cities, women sold food items, were musicians, soothsayers, and bath attendants. Furthermore, an interesting interconnection developed between elite and lower class women. Many women in the seclusion of the harem hired lower class women as entertainers, midwives, and peddlers. Not only did the women in the harem gain services, but they also profited from a vital connection to the world outside the harem walls.

Another important transformation in the 19th century Middle East was the outlawing of the slave trade. Since people could no longer use slaves, they hired domestic servants who were paid a low wage. As such, lower class women were able to get jobs in elite households. Not only were the lives of lower class women affected by colonization, the increasing pace of modernization impacted upon the role of upper class women in the economy as well. Historical records of sales and purchases show that upper class women owned a significant amount of land and were involved in a variety of businesses.[16] Women mostly provided the capital to invest in particular businesses and built a variety of social projects.

The impact of the West on the women of the Middle East has been interpreted in a variety of ways. Some scholars perceive the influence as mostly positive, while others find that view simplistic. Clearly, Western influence positively impacted education, medical care, and the public role of women, but under closer inspection, the breakdown of the more traditional, extended family placed more burdens on women who worked outside the home yet also needed to attend to their domestic responsibilities. Most societies remained traditional, and domestic chores were deemed "women's work." As such, women ended up working both inside and outside the home.

Westernization in the Ottoman Empire, Egypt, and Iran also brought with it increasing education for both genders. Missionary schools were established, stressing modern education for both men and women, and many elite girls received Western educations at home. Local Muslims viewed many of the missionary schools suspiciously because they believed the missionaries' goal was to convert Muslims. In Egypt, this perception spurred a movement to improve state schooling for both boys and girls. Under Khedive Isma'il (1863–1879), a committee was established to modernize education. Although several primary and secondary schools were created, the British invasion of 1882 slowed the process. Several women's groups, such as the Society of Advancement of Women, were created to improve opportunities and conditions for women. In Istanbul, the Ottomans also made strong advancements in female education. By 1842, the Medical School was accepting women to be trained as midwives. Secondary schools for girls were established in 1858, followed by a vocational school and a teaching training school by 1870. After World War I, Turkey, Egypt, and Iran established universities that allowed women to matriculate. Also, during this time period, women's organizations became more active in promoting education, domestic skills, and hygiene. Middle and upper class women participated in these groups that worked overwhelmingly toward philanthropic goals. As the women's groups expanded, their influence aided women in gaining a more public presence in society.

WORLD WAR I AND ITS AFTERMATH

After World War I, most countries in the Middle East and North Africa developed national movements to gain their independence from the colonial powers. Although most states did not see their independence until after World War II or much later, countries prepared for their self-determination with women playing large roles in national movements. Although there are some similarities among the countries in the region with regards to their development, the directions that each country took differed significantly. The following section will highlight several countries' development and their policies toward women and work.

TURKEY

The demise of the Ottoman Empire and clear encroachment of European powers on most of the Middle East affected women's role in the workforce in a variety of ways. Powerful socioeconomic changes emerged during the period of World War I. With the Ottoman Empire's extended phases of war, including the Balkans, World War I, and Turkey's War of Independence, men were absent for long periods of time forcing women to support the household. In Turkey, the need for women to enter the workforce during wartime elicited contradictory responses. For example, a public decree in 1915 allowed women to unveil at work, while in 1917 the police posted an announcement objecting to the more modern women's dress.[17] Although the government retracted the 1917 decree, its initial declaration reflects the push and pull between tradition and modernity regarding women's issues.

Mustafa Kemal, also known as Ataturk and the father of Turkey, pushed hard for gender equality, as he believed it was the correct approach to secularism and modernization, two key goals of his rule. Ataturk set the stage for many future changes with regards to women. He offered women the opportunity for public roles in both politics and work. Ataturk's view toward women was influenced by his experience in the Balkans and World War I, where women served as nurses on the front lines and had filled positions in all realms of society. Ataturk believed that education was the route to gender equality. His elimination of Islamic courts and his undermining of the religious organizations' power by implementing more secular education curtailed access to the more gender biased texts. As time progressed, many women participated in the legal profession to an extent much greater than in other Middle Eastern countries. After Ataturk's death in 1938, his political party continued his liberal policies toward women. Despite Turkey's more open policies toward women, its agrarian sector and the fact that Turkey sought to export agriculture left many women as unwaged workers. Some studies have found that, when women participate in the formal wage sector, their status in the home increases. Many women in the agricultural sector became mired in the traditional patriarchal structure. Additionally, for Ataturk, the most important element of his program was creating a national identity. As such, he pushed for gender equality in the economic and education realm, but was less inclined to allow independent women's movements to flourish.[18]

Women entered the labor market in large numbers during the early years of Turkey's independence, and this fact has influenced the gender-neutral laws and employment opportunities that women there have today. Yet, in 1993, the labor force participation rate of urban women was only 17 percent. This number reflects the continued tension between modernity and traditionalism evident in Turkey, as many urban women are housewives. Likewise, women remain concentrated in agriculture, making up 65 percent of all "economically active" women.[19] In many cases, women remain unwaged family laborers. Turkey's quest to join the European Union has prompted the government to improve its labor laws specifically with regards to gender. In 2001, the Ministry of Labor and Social Security formed a committee to explore and prepare a new Labor Act, which was adopted in 2003. The law contains improved provisions on maternity leave and the creation of nursing rooms in places employing from 100 to 150 women and for workplaces with more than 150 female workers, a nursing room, and a nursery.[20] The law also provides for equal pay and treatment of both genders.

IRAN

Under the Qajar Dynasty in Iran, which held power from 1779–1925, several key changes with regards to women's role in society occurred. A constitutional revolution took place in 1906 calling for more rights for the population. Reform for Iran's women came later than for women of the Ottoman Empire. The first girls' school was opened in Teheran in 1907, followed by a teacher training college in 1918, and, ultimately, access to university education in 1936. At the end of the Qajar Dynasty, Reza Shah Pahlavi assumed power in 1925 and sought to create a modern, independent state by implementing broad social reform. The Shah forced women to remove the veil and supported women's employment in most occupations. He established a state controlled women's organization that pushed for women's emancipation while simultaneously directing the pace and amount of change. Organizations independent of the state were prevented from forming, since the Shah wanted to limit any type of opposition.

Reza Shah abdicated the throne to his son Mohammed Reza Pahlavi in 1941. The new Shah was enamored with Ataturk's modernization and reform plan in Turkey. Like his father, he outlawed the veil and implemented Western dress for both men and women. Women were educated and allowed to work alongside men in most occupations. In 1962, under the Pahlavi regime, women were given the vote, and, in 1967, the government passed the Family Protection Act that curtailed polygamy, allowed women to divorce, and broadened their custody rights after divorce, yet the Shah himself was not particularly wedded to the idea of women's rights. The Pahlavi regime believed that granting women real power and independence would have some broad implications for society and, as such, the Shah advanced a state-sponsored women's movement that he could better control.

Other key changes were occurring in Iran during the 1960s and 1970s that affected women's status in society. A new movement stressing cultural nationalism was closely aligned with Islamic modernists. When, in 1961, the major religious leader Ayatollah Borujerdi died, other clerics, including Ayatollah Ruhollah Khomeini, began to acquire their own followers. They disseminated literature on a broad range of topics, including the role of women. These groups found an opening to push for traditional values in family life in Iran because the Shah had concentrated his efforts for reforms

Iranian women militia volunteers march at a parade on 20th anniversary of the outset of the Iran-Iraq war (1980–1988). (AP Photo/Vahid Salemi)

in civic aspects of society, including women's education, unveiling, and de-segregation, and not in familial ones. As such, Islamic groups were able to fill in the gap in this area.[21] After the revolution in 1979, many of the rights that women enjoyed under the Shah were dissolved. In 1975, Shirin Ebadi, a lawyer and human rights activist, became Iran's first female judge. After the revolution, she had to step down from that position, since women were prohibited from being judges. Certain women, despite the constraints of the new regime, protested the changes implemented by Ayatollah Khomeini. Many of these political activists were imprisoned or killed, as was most opposition under the new regime.

The constitution promulgated after the revolution defined women as mothers and citizens and advocated increased male control over women in the home and family while permitting women to participate in public life. To mobilize the population, the new theocracy used Islam and connected its ideals with those of nationalism. To solidify women's support for the regime, the clerics redefined women's social roles in education, employment, and political participation. Since the regime wanted the women's cooperation, they allowed them to participate in politics and public life, necessitating a transformation in the relationship between women and men outside their family members. To do this, the regime implemented strict rules about wearing the hijab and segregating the sexes. To counter the secular feminist movement, the regime encouraged the growth of an Islamic women's movement. By controlling this movement, the regime was able to manipulate women to participate in mass protests against secular and other opposition groups, which were driven underground.

The Women's Society of the Islamic Revolution (WSIR) was founded after the revolution and sought to create an authentic gender identity based on Islam and Iranian culture.[22] With the war raging with Iraq beginning in 1980, the regime recognized the need for women's participation in the labor market and allowed them to work. This also increased women's support for the Islamic regime. The first parliament after the revolution, however, concerned itself with women's issues occurring in the private, rather than the public, sphere, and because of this the needs of employed women were overlooked. The Social and Cultural Council of Women was established in 1988, and it, along with the Office of Women's Affairs, created in 1992, dealt with these issues. A major issue facing employed women was the absence of adequate childcare, yet the pervasive view held even by the few female parliamentarians that a women's place was at home with her children lent little urgency to the problem. One parliamentarian, Azam Taliqani, was concerned with issues of social justice and took up women's causes. She started a political group called the Women's Society and published the magazine *Payam-I Hajar* in 1979. *Payam I-Hajar* discussed family issues and urged a reinterpretation of Islamic laws with regards to women.

After the Iran-Iraq war ended in 1988, the Iranian population began to voice its economic and political grievances, something that was viewed as unpatriotic during the war. To respond to the discontent, the government allowed some freedom of the press and a variety of journals and magazines flourished during the period following the war, including women's magazines. Secular women, who were relegated mostly to the domestic sphere during the revolutionary period, began their return to the labor force. The challenging economic situation propelled women back to their jobs to provide a second income for their families. By 1993, women's participation in the labor force was 18 percent, up from a low of 6.1 percent after the revolution in 1979. Most of the women who returned to the formal economic sector were educated, urban women.[23]

The period of the 1990s reflected an era of change. A growing young population began to push for reform and liberalization. In 1992, although the government reiterated the important role of women in the family, it simultaneously encouraged women to enter certain scientific fields such as pharmacology, gynecology, midwifery, and laboratory work. Women were also permitted to become legal consultants and assistant judges. Many women entered the public sector and, by 1995, 33 percent of public sector jobs were held by women. By 1996, women comprised 12.5 percent of the labor force, a number that reflected improvement in Iran, but was low by international standards.[24] The movement for reform continued, and in 1997 and again in 2001, a reformist, Mohammad Khatami, was elected president by a wide margin. He campaigned for civil rights and the rule of law and promised women more of a role in the political system. A reformist parliament was elected in 2000, leading many observers to believe that true change was underway in Iran. The structure of Iran's government where the president is elected, yet the Guardian Council retains the power to reject laws and disqualify candidates that it deems "un-Islamic," led to a reversal of liberalization. Conservative elements of society managed to stem reformist progress by disqualifying candidates in the 2004 parliamentary elections, thus leading to a more conservative government and the eventual election of the conservative Mahmud Ahmadinejad as president in 2005 and again in a hotly contested election in 2009. During this new fundamentalist period, any gains that women achieved during the reform period were negated. Non-governmental organizations that were recognized and sought out for advice during Khatemi's regime have been weakened severely. Women who campaign for women's rights are attacked as "immoral and Westernized."[25]

ISRAEL

The role of women in the labor force in Israel differs significantly from that of the Arab countries that surround it. Israel is a democracy and, although religion is an important part of the Israeli culture, women under Jewish tradition have fared quite differently from those under Islam. Despite the fact that 80 percent of Israeli citizens are Jewish, as an immigrant society, it is an ethnically heterogeneous state. Consequently, women in different groups, including religious and secular Jews and Arabs, retain various views about women's roles in society. Although Jewish women participated in large numbers in the settlement of the land, they were not always given equal access to jobs, political participation, and economic opportunities. In many cases, the story of women's important roles in the War of Independence and other aspects of settling the state were excluded from the literature and have only recently been incorporated into the historical narrative.[26]

Because of pogroms in Eastern Europe in the 1880s, many Jews immigrated to Palestine to settle the biblical land and establish a homeland for the Jewish people. Since Jews immigrated from many different countries and cultural backgrounds, their knowledge of health care and their own personal levels of health differed significantly. Early on, women were publicly involved in the assistance and settlement of the refugees. A voluntary women's organization, Hadassah, raised money to provide nurses to deal with the absorption and care of these new immigrants along with health care education.[27]

Israel's birth in 1948 was surrounded by controversy and violence. In 1947, the United Nations partitioned Israel into Palestinian and Israeli states. The Arab states rejected the partition, holding out hope that all of modern day Israel would remain under Arab control. The Israelis reluctantly accepted the boundaries of the new state, and when they declared their independence many Arab states attacked the new country to regain land that they believed was rightfully theirs. Despite its rough beginning, Israel became the only democracy in the Middle East. Settled mostly by European Jews known as Ashkenazis, education was an important aspect of the Jewish culture. In 1955, the Israeli education system implemented a pre-vocational training program in the seventh and eighth grades that concentrated on both crafts and agriculture. By the 1960s, 15 percent of students in Israel were enrolled in the vocational program. Israel's goal in implementing this program was to benefit the state by making it economically self-sufficient by training its citizens in a variety of skills. It was found that the pre-vocational program implemented in the Israeli educational system to benefit girls as well as boys ended up reinforcing both ethnic and gender stereotypes in society and thus affecting female labor patterns. However, the program actually ended up benefiting girls from Asian and African origin, known as Mitzrahis.[28]

In the 1950s, large waves of Mizrahi immigrants began coming to Israel with ideas on family structure and gender roles that differed significantly from those of the European Jews. Mizrahi Jews had larger families than Ashkenazis, and women were usually less educated than men and participated less in the labor force. As time progressed, fertility rates for Mizrahi women declined, reflecting an influence of the dominant European culture. Both Ashkenazi and Mizrahi began entering the workforce in greater numbers and, by 1995, almost 61 percent of second-generation Mizrahi women worked, while 66 percent of Ashkenazi women did.[29]

In all societies, women face the traditional pressure to be nurturing mothers and wives, while new demands push women to be self-sufficient. These views have an important impact on the role of women in the family and workplace. In Israel, although traditional family values remain strong, the nature of the democracy's stressing gender equality and rights has impacted the traditional cultural structure. Additionally, Israel has a strong work ethic, and this factor increases tension with the traditional family structure. The early pioneers who came to the area prior to the establishment of Israel possessed a strong work ethic and espoused gender equality in the workplace. The socialist ideology of the Kibbutzim—communal agricultural settlements—offered childcare in the form of communal child rearing and allowed women to work unencumbered. A 2003 study revealed that over 50 percent of working Israeli women surveyed found work and family equally important. This finding illustrates several important factors. First, although Israeli society places a premium on family and childrearing, this finding suggests a value shift that says work is also important. Second, the large number of women who find both work and family equally important should signal to employers women's motivation to work coupled with a strong commitment to their jobs.[30] Interestingly, Israeli women who value both family and women gravitate to "female type" jobs, such as teaching, nursing, and secretarial work, perhaps because these jobs give them the most flexibility to raise a family.

The Israeli government recognizes the tension between traditional and modern values and supports working women with special tax exemptions, child allowances, and other types of benefits. Despite these incentives, Israel still lags behind the United States and Europe with regards to women's participation in the labor force. It is possible that traditional values constrain the number of women who work outside the home. Women in Israel do compulsory military service for two years, although men serve for three years. In certain cases, women can get exemptions from service in the Israel Defense Forces if they are married or have children. In the army, women do not serve in combat positions, although recently women have been allowed to join combat units.

EGYPT

Prior to World War I, textile and sewing factories, oil press plants, and flourmills hired women. As trade unionism began to grow in Egypt, a special committee was established to explore the labor issues of women and children. In the 1930s, as international companies became interested in Egypt for its cheap labor, the manufacturing sector continued to expand. Peasants, including women, moved into Cairo and other Egyptian cities to find work. With the increase in female labor, new laws were enacted to curtail working hours and provide improved conditions. These laws were continued and broadened under Gamal Abdul Nasser's tutelage.[31]

When Nasser came to power in Egypt after the Free Officer's Revolution of 1952, he expanded the public sector and nationalized several industries, including banking, trade, and manufacturing. The most publicized of these was the nationalization of the Suez Canal. Along with state ownership of industry, Nasser wanted to expand the number of jobs available in these areas. The government promised to employ all high school and university graduates, which had the effect of bloating the bureaucracy in the long-term. However, in the short term, women perceived their opportunities as expanding and many took advantage of the government's free public education. Although Nasser pushed for free education and increased the number of women in the labor force, he discouraged independent women's organizations. This aspect is not surprising, since Nasser limited many types of independent organizations due to his concern that they would challenge his leadership. In 1954, a labor law facilitated women's participation in the labor force by guaranteeing equal wages and rights and offering special provisions for working mothers. The 1956 constitution not only gave women suffrage, but also called for gender equality before the law and in employment. Despite these legal changes, tradition held strong in the family as men continued to dominate both the home and workplace. Although change was slow, Nasser's policies demanding more gender equality continued into Anwar Sadat's government, which assumed power in 1970 after Nasser's death. Under Sadat's leadership, the public sector became the largest employer of women.

During the 1970s, Sadat pursued a new policy of economic liberalization necessitating the removal of extra workers from the bloated bureaucracy. By 1986, unemployment reached over 15 percent and a recession was underway. Coupled with some harsh economic times affecting women's employment in significant ways, a resurgence of Islamic ideals gripped the Muslim world. The perceived failure of secular ideologies such as Pan-Arabism and socialism to ameliorate the ills of society led to the broader appeal of Islam throughout the region. President Sadat encouraged the growth of Muslim groups such as the Muslim Brotherhood as a counterbalance to his leftist opposition. A return to Islamic ideals affected women and their ability to work in a variety of ways. Traditional Islam dictates that a woman's main role is as wife and mother, and therefore, as Islamic groups attracted more people in society, women were pressured to remain in the home. Those women who continued to work oftentimes opted to wear the hijab.

In 1976, Sadat amended the constitution calling for Islamic law to be the main source of Egyptian law. This constitutional modification allowed Islamists to curtail women's rights. However, after Islamists killed a government minister in 1977, Sadat broke his affiliations with the Muslim groups and began to improve conditions for women. Although women managed to overcome certain barriers by entering traditionally male jobs in universities, administration, industry, and business, economic downturns made women in the Middle East the first victims. Egypt's economy was in decline in 1977 and Sadat requested assistance from the International Monetary Fund (IMF). As in most cases, the IMF required structural adjustment programs to reform the economy and placed conditions for loans on actions by the government. Some of the measures called for the government to decrease subsidies on staples such as flour and to cut other key government programs. In Egypt, as the economy worsened and public sector jobs were cut, female unemployment rose.

Although Egyptian women have begun to hold more liberal views toward gender roles, some segments of Arab societies still adhere to the traditional values that a women's primary function is in the home and with the children. This is reflected in the fact that many Arab societies support educating boys rather than girls, as boys are perceived as a greater economic asset in the future. In 2001, the *Economist* published an article concluding that patriarchy is the strongest institution in the Arab world. Patriarchy refers to male domination in the political, social, and economic spheres, yet scholars have found that as a society moves from an agrarian to an industrial focus with increases in urbanization and education, traditional attitudes may change. Additionally, as people are exposed to new ideas through education and media, they might also influence others to alter their beliefs.[32]

TUNISIA

In Tunisia, rural women have participated in agriculture for a long time, although they have been limited in the types of agricultural work they could do. In the 18th and 19th centuries, peasant populations maintained a sharp division of labor, with men responsible for plowing and harvesting and women relegated to domestic chores and jobs that could be executed close to home. Some scholars argue that women in Tunisia have played an important role in the agricultural sector although their contributions have often been ignored or denied. Some women worked as farm laborers even though this was considered a dishonorable job for a woman. As male migration to find other work increased, women assumed a larger role in the Tunisian agricultural sector. In certain parts of Tunisia, male migration occurred even prior to 1881, the year when Tunisia became a French protectorate. In the area of Nefza, 10 to 15 percent of men migrated to numerous regions to find employment. Women were required to fill in for the men in all aspects of agricultural labor. This trend has continued and, by 2002, in certain peasant villages, 83 percent of men between the ages of 21 and 45 left their villages to find work in the Tunis region and returned home occasionally. Women make up 90 percent of those working on farms. In the rural areas, this phenomenon has had significant implications for the role of women in society, not least of which is their acquisition of traditionally male tasks. Out of necessity, women have acquired greater decision making power in the domestic realm.[33]

When Tunisia gained its independence in 1956, the secular government under President Hagib Bourguiba pushed for women's integration in all aspects of social, political, and economic life. Additionally, the implementation of a civil code allowed women the same rights as men, outlawed polygamy, and gave women the right to divorce. In 1960, the government began to offer women maternity leave in some economic sectors and eventually offered social security to all workers, a benefit that helped both women and men. By the 1980s, women were working in all sectors of society, including agriculture, manufacturing, teaching, medicine, and politics.

Following the Iranian Revolution in 1979, similar to many other Muslim nations, segments of Tunisia's population turned toward Islamist groups, precipitating a reactionary growth of women's groups. The government encouraged the development of women's groups to oppose the expanding influence of the Islamic organizations. In the 1989 parliamentary elections, although Islamist groups won 14 percent of the vote, Zein el-Abedin Ben Ali, who replaced President Bourguiba, continued his policies incorporating women into the social, political, and economic structure. Women now make up 30 percent of the workforce and continue to have important rights in Tunisian society. Although women persistently face high unemployment rates, Ben Ali's policies have allowed women to thrive in many occupations.

ALGERIA

Algeria was a French colony from 1830–1962 and fought a long and protracted battle for independence from 1954–1962. Before Algeria's independence, women were almost completely excluded from public life in part because only 4.5 percent of women were literate.[34] Women participated in the struggle for independence in a variety of capacities, including as nurses, fighters, and teachers. Clearly, due to their participation in the war for liberation, most women expected to gain equal rights in an independent Algeria. The country's first constitution did ensure equal rights for the sexes, and 10 out of the 194 representatives elected to the first National Assembly were women.

Houari Boumedienne took power in a military coup in 1965 and led the country until his death in 1979. Under President Boumedienne's leadership, the number of women in the workforce grew and more girls enrolled in school.[35] The situation in Algeria, however, was changing as the country struggled to find its post-independence identity. The Front de Liberation Nationale (FLN) led the country's war for liberation and became the only party after independence. After it held its first congress in 1964, some delegates were pushing for Islamic values. By the time of the second National Assembly elections, only two women gained seats. Unlike Tunisia, the Algerian government took a much less liberal approach to women in the workforce. By 1980, women made up only 8.8 percent of the employed population in Algeria. They were much more likely to work in the public sector than in the private sector, and they earned much less than men. This was due to the leadership's conservative view of the role of women, high overall unemployment, and an emphasis on heavy industrialization. Men were usually better trained for the types of industrial jobs that were available in the new steel and petrochemical plants.

As the Islamist movement in Algeria grew in the 1980s, President Chadli Benjedid's government agreed to draft the Algerian Family Code in 1984, which permitted women to work, but strengthened male control of women by depicting them as "economic dependents."[36] As the Islamists' status grew and disillusionment with the incumbent regime increased, Islamists won municipal elections in 1990. The Islamist victory concerned women who believed that their rights would be curtailed even more than they were under a secular government. Likewise, the government was alarmed that it might be voted out of office as the Islamist groups were growing in popularity. The Islamic Salvation Front's (FIS) program called for segregated schools and wanted to forbid women from teaching boys. The election of the FIS to the municipal councils opened up another violent chapter of Algeria's history. Women who did not dress modestly were assaulted and women-owned businesses were attacked. In one particular case, in 1989, FIS members surrounded the dormitories at the University of Bilda and assaulted women who broke the curfew.[37]

In 1991, after FIS won the first round of legislative elections, the government feared it would lose control of Algeria. To combat this, the government prevented the next and deciding round of legislative elections by cracking down on FIS and declaring a state of emergency. Although the government entered into negotiations with FIS and other Islamic groups in 1995–1996, there has been no resolution of the conflict.

LIBYA

Many areas of North Africa, including Libya, were mainly rural areas with many pastoral, nomadic communities into the 20th century. Women participated in making tents, rugs, clothing, mats, and many other goods that were crucial for their community's survival. Libya gained its independence from Italy in 1951 and was a traditional, patriarchal society where the role of women was dictated by interpretations of the Qu'ran and traditions. Prior to 1951, women were segregated and they required a male relative to accompany them when they left their homes. Women's main role was as wives and mothers. King Idris, who was overthrown in 1969 by Colonel Muammar al-Qaddafi, ruled the country. Although girls were permitted to get an education after 1951, since 1969, a nine-year education has been compulsory and free for all Libyans. In 1972, the minimum age for marriage was raised to 16, and women were allowed to choose their husbands.[38] In reality, however, fathers still have a significant role in selecting husbands for their daughters. Although, many village schools educate boys and girls separately, classes in cities and the universities are mixed.

By 1999, girls' participation in primary school was 99.9 percent, equal to that of boys' participation.[39]

In the 1970s, when Qaddafi began to accept a socialist agenda and declared his country a socialist republic, he supported more equal rights for men and women, especially in the realm of education and employment. Women could work in all fields and serve as judges, doctors, lawyers, politicians, and other professions. Women could also serve in the police force and army and are famous for providing Qaddafi with his all-female group of bodyguards. In 1978, Libya opened its Military Academy, which has trained over 7,000 women since its inception.[40] Despite support from Qaddafi in his quest to narrow the gap between men's and women's rights, women are still underrepresented in high-level positions of government or businesses and many women remain homemakers. Qaddafi has to balance some of his revolutionary views with the opposition that he faces from Islamists in Libyan society. As such, he allows for unwed mothers to be jailed if the children's fathers do not marry them.

In 1975, the Union of Libyan Women was formed and made progress in getting certain rights for women. With regards to improvements for employment, day care centers were established and women gained access to maternity leave. Additionally, women were allowed to divorce and get custody of their children. They were also exempt from working night shifts or performing any type of work that would put them in danger. Although women have made progress in Libya with regards to rights, their labor participation rates remain low. Additionally, there are significant wage differentials between men and women due to discrimination in the workplace. Although women have been gaining rights through legislation in Libya, cultural factors have hampered their complete integration into the labor force.

In the 1990s, under pressure from Islamic opposition, Qaddafi reversed some of his previous decisions regarding women. This trend continued and, in 2007, Libya banned women under 40 from traveling unaccompanied by a male relative. This decision elicited harsh criticism in Libya's press, countering that the government did not have the right to make this change without consulting the national and legislative bodies.

IRAQ

In April 1920, Britain gained a mandate over Iraq until it was prepared for its independence. Women were not given the right to vote, although the country was a constitutional monarchy. The tribal nature of much of the population also subjected women to a variety of traditional rules. Although there were some primary schools in urban centers, many girls remained uneducated. King Faisal I recognized the importance of education in the quest for Iraqi independence and pushed for women's inclusion into the labor force as well.[41] The status of women in Iraq in the 1920s was heavily influenced by several factors, including the battle for Arab independence from foreign intervention and the fact that a segment of the population was educated in Egypt, Lebanon, or Turkey.[42] In each of these countries, the elites were engaged in a debate about the role of women, and women's groups had already pushed for increased education and rights. As Iraq gained its independence in the 1930s, women participated more in the public sphere.

When the Ba'ath party ascended to power in the 1960s, it encouraged women's participation in the economy in order to increase loyalty to the state and weaken tribal and familial ties. When the government conducted a census in 1977, it determined that 70 percent of illiterate Iraqis were women. To combat this problem, the government mandated literacy courses, put women through public education. and recruited them into state-run agencies. When Saddam Hussein assumed overt power in 1979, he endorsed women's rights in order to deal with a labor shortage. Instead of importing foreign labor, he believed that women could satisfy economic roles in society.[43] The government implemented programs to give women equality in the workplace and to ease their transition from the home to the workplace. The government enacted maternity benefits and subsidized day care and transportation to employment. The Ba'ath party promoted a variety of employment choices for women who, by the late 1970s, comprised 29 percent of Iraq's medical doctors, 46 percent of dentists, and 70 percent of pharmacists. Aside from the medical professions, women were prevalent as teachers, government servants, and agricultural workers.[44] By the 1970s women filled 60 percent of the civil service jobs. These changes coincided with the beginning of the eight-year-long Iran-Iraq war, which that necessitated men join the battle. As such, women were needed to fill economic roles while the men were off fighting. However, as men returned from the battlefield, women were fired to employ the returning soldiers. Additionally, the government began a campaign to increase the size of Iraqi families, in hopes of catching up with the more populous Iran. As the war continued, Hussein's policies toward women changed in several ways. Although women were told that they should have at least five children to lessen the population disparity between Iran and Iraq, they were also prodded to fill jobs vacated by men who went to battle. During this period, birth control became more difficult to find in Iraq; this factor had an enormous impact on women, since increased fertility rates have been shown to have a negative effect on their status. When men began to return home in 1988, women were encouraged to return to their roles as wives and mothers.

Iraq invaded Kuwait in 1990 and the world responded with a United States-led coalition to remove Iraqis from Kuwait and return the Kuwaiti

Al-Sabah family to power. Due to sanctions imposed on Iraq by the international community, women and girls were affected more than men and boys in the realm of education and healthcare. As such, the first victims of the economic crisis were women, who continued to be released from their jobs. By 1998, all female secretaries in government jobs had been dismissed.[45]

In 2003, the United States invaded Iraq for a variety of complex reasons, but the result of the invasion was the removal of Hussein and the attempt to establish a more democratic government. Although a new constitution guarantees equal rights for women, one source of legislation is sharia law, leaving Islamic judges with the right of interpretation in certain cases. As Iraq fights to establish a working democracy, the security situation remains somewhat precarious. This has also affected women's ability to go to school and to work.

JORDAN

Prior to World War I, the British promised the Arabs an independent state if they helped them fight against the Ottomans. Between 1915 and 1916, British officials communicated this to Sherif Husein, who controlled the Hejaz, the eastern portion of modern-day Saudi Arabia. The Husein family controlled the Muslim holy sites of Mecca and Medina, and therefore the British considered their participation in overthrowing the Ottomans important. While the British were negotiating borders for post-World War I boundaries with the Arabs, they were also plotting with the French as to what areas would become British or French protectorates. When the war ended and it was time for the British to fulfill their promises, there was some question as to what areas would be considered part of an independent Arab state that the Husein family would control. To appease the family, Britain created the state of Transjordan, which later became Jordan. Abdullah, Sherif Husein's son, was placed in control of that new state. Although heavily supported and subsidized by the British, Jordan gained its independence in 1946. Jordan was and remains a monarchy with a parliament. Just two years after independence, Jordan faced its first crisis when Israel became a state. Jordan invaded the Jewish state along with its Arab neighbors and seized control of the West Bank. An area that was supposed to be part of a new, independent Palestinian state under the United Nations' 1947 partition of Palestine.

With regards to women and work in Jordan, the Arab Women's Federation was created in 1954 to expand literacy and push for legal reforms, yet women's participation in the labor force was low, with women making up only 3.3 percent of the labor force in 1961. From 1961–1975 there was an increase in women's participation in non-agricultural sectors of the economy, although women in rural areas comprised a large percentage of workers on farms. Women worked in manufacturing, the second largest employer of women; however, as women became more educated, there was an increase in women entering the professions, such as teaching.[46] Women made up 51 percent of all teachers by 1981, although the higher the level of education, the lower the percentage of female teachers.[47] By 1976, the number of female workers in the professions doubled. Part of the reason for the changes in the labor structure is connected to modifications in the educational system. In 1952, girls made up only 25 percent of all students, but by 1981, they made up 46.3 percent. In the 1952 constitution, education was made mandatory for nine years, and although the Compulsory Education Law of 1964 was passed, mandatory education was not enforced because of cultural factors. Some families did not permit their daughters to attend school. Even so, girls benefited tremendously from this law and made up 48 percent of the school enrollment by 1984.[48]

In 1981, Jordan suffered from a labor shortage due to the fact that technicians and skilled manual laborers were working abroad. Government officials recognized that they needed to incorporate women into the labor force to make up for the labor deficit. However, rural migrant males and foreign workers took many jobs that urban women could have filled. Other than the agricultural sector, women worked in five major areas, mostly in the service sector: public administration, education, clerical, textile production, and finance. Jordan also began vocational training programs in the 1970s where women could learn dressmaking, spinning, and childcare, yet the number of women engaged in these programs was small. In order to encourage women to enter the labor force and close the wage differential between the genders, the government introduced wage controls according to skill level.[49] Despite these efforts, cultural restrictions affected Jordanian women's work patterns in interesting ways. In the 1970s, during the oil boom, the migration of men to work in other countries did not lead to a growth of women's employment, as many remained in the informal sector. To make up for the loss of male labor, Jordan imported workers from neighboring countries such as Egypt. As male unemployment rose, the government and cultural patterns discouraged women from entering the workforce and women remained concentrated in the teaching profession and as textile workers.

Although the female employment rate remains low in Jordan, young women have begun to participate more in its workforce. This participation has serious ramifications with regards to both the economy and structure of Jordanian society. Jordan experienced strong economic growth during the oil boom of the 1970s because many Jordanian men worked in the oil rich states and sent home remittances. Jordan's relatively liberal regime fostered stability within the country and led to increased foreign investments. Likewise, broad regional instability also led businesses to relocate to

Jordan. Notwithstanding these positive developments, other economic factors have worked against Jordan. During the oil boom, Jordan accrued an enormous debt because of its spending habits. When the economic downturn of the early 1980s occurred, many Jordanians who worked in the oil producing states lost their jobs and Jordan forfeited the income that those workers sent back to Jordan. Additionally, when Saddam Hussein invaded Kuwait in August 1990, many Jordanian workers returned to Jordan. After riots in Jordan in 1989, due to a structural readjustment program imposed on Jordan by the IMF, the king attempted to liberalize the political system and endorsed the National Charter in 1991. The National Charter espoused democratic rights and equality, particularly that of gender equality.[50]

As the economic crisis deepened, unemployment grew and women, who had fewer opportunities than men in the workforce, suffered from 28.5 percent unemployment, as compared with 11.7 percent for men. Yet despite these unemployment trends, the growth rate of women entering the workforce exceeded that of men in 1997. From 1979 to 1997, women's employment almost doubled, from 7.7 to 14 percent of the female population. Women's literacy has also increased, allowing them access to better employment. Despite their increased education levels, family members

Turkish Foreign Minister Tansu Ciller is embraced by Toujan Faisal, the only woman member of the Jordanian Parliament, in Amman, 1996. (AP Photo/Yousef Allan)

Jordanian princess Aisha Bint-Al Hussein, commander of the Jordanian Army Women's Corps, inspects an Israeli military guard on a visit to Israel to learn about the service of women in the army. (AP Photo/Nati Harnik)

still expect women to find work that does not challenge traditional gender roles.[51] Parents remain concerned with women's reputations and many insist that their daughters work in segregated environments and return home before dark. Parents also place restrictions on their daughters' travel, since using public transportation would entail traveling with men. In some cases, women in Jordan have found ways around this by commuting with other women. The women of the royal family have taken on an enormous role in promoting women's causes and pushing women into more positions of power. In 1992, King Hussein's sister, Princess Basma, headed the National Committee for Women, which developed a National Strategy for Women. As a result of this strategy, 99 women were appointed to local and municipal councils and eventually one woman, Toujan Faisal, was elected to the Jordanian parliament in 1993. By 2003, Jordan had 19 female judges. Women now make up about 14.7 percent of the workforce and laws have been passed mandating equal pay for them. Slow progress is being made for both women's rights and employment in Jordan.[52]

SAUDI ARABIA

Founded in the 18th century by a merger between a staunchly religious leader, Muhammad Ibn Abd-al Wahab, and a local tribal leader, Ibn Saud, Saudi Arabia is one of the most conservative states in the Middle East and North Africa. Although under Ottoman control in some parts of Saudi Arabia, the country was mostly left alone from foreign intervention until recently. As such, some of the Western values regarding women have not influenced the kingdom as much as other states in the Middle East. Saudi Arabia gained its independence in 1932 and was predominantly a nomadic and tribal society. In Saudi Arabia, cultural norms and tribal customs dictate that women remain in the home, and a stringent segregation of the sexes is enforced. Although the percentage of women who worked outside the home was 10 percent in the 1990s, Saudi Arabia retains the strictest policies in the Middle East with regards to segregation of women. Unlike other Middle Eastern countries, where women entered the workforce alongside men and lessened the space between them, in Saudi Arabia, women have joined the public sphere but the boundaries between men and women remain strong.[53]

Prior to 1960, Saudi Arabia had several private schools for girls but very few girls were literate. Although conservative from its founding, Saudi Arabia underwent an Islamic revival in the 1960s. This revival led to increased pressure to separate women and men in the public sphere. The Islamic revival, coupled with Saudi Arabia's growing economic strength from oil revenues, led to a decrease in women's jobs. With the growing imports of crafts and food, rural women who worked in fields or made crafts no longer had work, and increased standards of living allowed men to provide for their families without a second income. As such, women were relegated to the home and their position in society was presented to the rest of the world as a reflection of the moral nature and economic success of Saudi society. Obviously, segregation plays a large role in women's ability to work. With regards to the segregation of women and their relegation to the home, there is no direct mention of it in the Qu'ran. "For men is the benefit of what they earn. And for women is the benefit of what they earn." This Qu'ranic statement clearly alludes to the fact that women can work and should be able to retain money they earn. The more conservative interpretations of these statements reflect the intersection of Islamic law with a particular historical context. In certain eras, such as both the Byzantine and Persian periods, which were highly feudalized, Islamic law was heavily influenced by theorists who clearly were products of the times. In the Qu'ran, men are required to take care of their wives and in return the wife will take care of the children. This does not negate a woman's ability to work, so long as she can fulfill her requirements at home and maintain a certain level of modesty in the workplace. In reality, the level of female segregation is dependent upon the role a woman plays in the economy. For example, rural women who are responsible for gardening, herding, and farming will have more freedom of movement and less segregation than wealthier women who do not need to work outside the home. As such, segregation acts as a "status marker" for a woman's family.[54]

In 1960, the government opened public schools for girls, and by 1990 girls were more successful than boys in school and were graduating at higher rates. Interestingly, in 1980, half of the students who received scholarships to study abroad were female, but that fact changed after 1982 when government restrictions prohibited women from traveling abroad without a chaperone. The period after the Iranian Revolution in 1979, along with the Grand Mosque takeover in Saudi Arabia by militants during that same year, led to more stringent policies regarding the segregation of women. Today there are very few women's groups in Saudi Arabia to fight for women's rights, for they appear to challenge the stringent control that the regime holds over women. The only organizations that are permissible are the ones formed by female members of the royal household. These groups deal predominantly with philanthropic issues.[55]

For some scholars it is oil, not Islam, that bears responsibility for the lack of women's progress in the region and in other countries outside of the region where oil and mineral production are important factors in economics. Women are less likely to work in oil production, and thus in countries where oil is a significant part of the economy women are underrepresented in the workforce. When women do not work, other significant consequences follow such as higher fertility rates, lower levels of education, and less influence in the home. With these social aspects come political ramifications, such as fewer women in the political realm and an inability for women to mobilize, resulting in a strong patriarchal structure of the society.[56] Although some scholars and organizations such as the World Bank contend that economic development writ large leads to progress for women in society, others argue that the type of economic development is crucial as to whether or not women's role in society and the labor force progresses. As such, when oil and mineral production is the leading factor of economic growth in a country, then gender inequalities will be greater than in countries where economic expansion leads to more women entering the labor force.

In the Saudi case, due to the economic growth stemming from the oil boom in the 1970s, work conditions have become more favorable to women relative to what they had been prior to that period and have begun very to gradually undermine some of the more stringent patriarchal values. Although still constrained by cultural factors such as the inability to drive or to leave the country without permission from a male relative, by 1990,

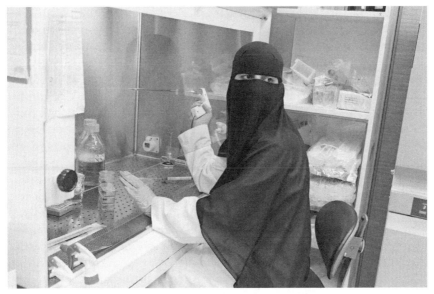

Women work at the Department of Pathology and Laboratory Medicine of the King Faisal Hospital in Riyadh, Saudi Arabia, 2003. (AP Photo/Franco Pagetti/VII)

women made up 7 percent of the workforce and were employed in a variety of jobs. According to one study, women now own about 10 percent of businesses in the kingdom.[57] Interestingly, the Internet has influenced women's work by allowing them to conduct business with men without violating the principle of mixing with unrelated men. Consequently, some women are starting web-based businesses and, although unconfirmed, unofficial data show that women make up two thirds of those using the Internet.[58] Aside from aiding in employment issues, the Internet provides women a venue to discuss usually taboo subjects such as the prohibition on driving, segregation, and the lack of women's rights. Modern technology has facilitated the government's ability to retain the barriers between the sexes, while allowing women to participate in public life. At universities, video-conferencing has granted women access to the male sphere without requiring them to enter their realm physically. Despite women's segregation, the public sphere is actually expanding for women in schools, government offices, charitable institutions. and universities, while simultaneously retaining the boundaries between the sexes.[59] During the 1960s, free and compulsory education was established for both boys and girls, although the schools were strictly segregated. The effect of this was twofold. Segregation was institutionalized, yet at the same time, the government was clear that women had a role in the public realm. Interestingly, a woman's guardian—usually her father or husband—retains the right to allow her to work or attend a university.

Cultural factors have also restricted the type of work that Saudi Arabian women can do. For the most part, Saudi Arabia imported expatriates to work as nurses because of a cultural stigma that deems nursing servants' work. Additionally, nursing necessitates working long hours, and this can infringe upon women's key roles as wife and mother within Saudi society. In a 2001 survey carried out in male secondary schools, 69 percent responded that they would not marry a nurse because they perceive the work as socially unacceptable. Recently, however, more women have been attending nursing courses since there is a shortage in the profession. In Saudi Arabia, specifically, the nursing and labor shortage is related to many foreign workers' fear of the increased terrorist risk in Saudi Arabia.[60] Due to the labor shortage, the government has decreed that Saudis train in all spheres of employment, and this proclamation has led to more women entering the labor force. Consequently, women also began training as doctors, pharmacists, and in the social sciences. Due to the strict gender segregation laws, more women are encouraged to become doctors to avoid the problem of having a male doctor examine a female patient.

In some cases, wealthy Saudi Arabian women own businesses, although male relatives usually administer the companies. By 1995, women owned 40 percent of Saudi Arabia's wealth.[61] While most workplaces are completely segregated, there are some regional variations. Where women do work with men, there is a strict enforcement of wearing the abaya (the traditional black cloak). The Saudis themselves have begun to recognize the need for change with regards to women's status, but prefer modifications that fit the context of Arab-Islamic civilization. In Saudi Arabia, the process of integrating women into the workforce has been difficult due to cultural factors and nebulous laws regarding women's status. Even though Saudi Arabia is moving toward equality in the workplace, women have retained their secondary status in the family context.[62] This ambivalent approach to women has made progress in women's development challenging, and the number of women in the workforce remains limited. The Saudi Arabian government has also been influenced by international pressure, as evidenced by the Beijing Women's Conference in 1995. Due to the emphasis on universal human rights, and women's rights in particular, many Arab states remain on the defensive when it comes to explaining their policies toward women. Rather than explain their position on women, the Saudis did not go to Beijing realizing that they would face intense questioning of their gender policies.

There has been a backlash toward any liberalizing policies regarding women by the most conservative elements of Saudi society. The Committee for the Promotion of Virtue and the Prevention of Vice is responsible for maintaining proper decorum within the kingdom. The group represents a type of religious police that enforces the strict rules, particularly those

Flight attendant of Emirates, 2009. (AP Photo/Daniel Roland)

regarding women's dress and the segregation of the sexes. An intensely egregious case involving the religious police occurred in 2002 and led to some changes regarding women's rights. During a fire in a girls' school, religious police prevented girls who did not wear their abaya correctly from leaving the building. This resulted in 14 deaths.[63]

In 2000, the government of Saudi Arabia signed the United Nations convention eliminating discrimination against women, yet the Saudi Deputy Foreign Minister, Prince Turki Bin Mohammed, explained that the government is dedicated to promoting women's rights as long as it respects a country's traditions and beliefs. More females than males are enrolled in humanities courses in universities, and the number of women graduating from universities has increased dramatically. Despite the fact that Saudi Arabia has made great strides in women's education, only 78 percent of women were literate in 2005. Women still cannot drive or walk around unaccompanied by an appropriate male relative. They must wear a black abaya, and police circulate to enforce a strict adherence to modest dress. If, in the future, Saudi Arabia's welfare state declines due to lower oil prices and an inability to diversity its economy, women will be forced into the workforce in greater numbers. This reality will have an impact on attitudes toward women's roles in both the workforce and their domestic lives.

UNITED ARAB EMIRATES

The United Arab Emirates (UAE) gained its independence from Britain in 1971. It is made up of a federation of seven different states, or emirates, that select a president from among them every five years. Until oil was discovered in the UAE in the 1950s, most of the population made a living as nomads, in fishing, and pearl cultivation. Britain made the UAE its protectorate in the 1800s to secure its route to India.

Although women make up only about 20 percent of the labor force, they comprise about a third of all doctors, technicians, pharmacists, and administrators. Over 80 percent of those employed in the Ministries of Health and Education are women. Despite the growing trend toward women in the workforce, traditional values encourage women to remain homemakers. Women in the UAE can control their own money, and men are expected to pay the household expenses. Women are allowed to own property and may contribute to household expenses if they desire. The General's Women's Union was founded in 1975 and monitors other women's groups dealing mostly with charitable and business organizations.

Education in the UAE is free to all citizens through the university level and has been the main driving force in women's progress in the UAE. Women make up 75 percent of students at the National University; this high percentage is caused partially by the fact that many men study abroad. By 2002, women made up more than 57 percent of university chairs.[64] In a departure from most countries in the region, the literacy rate for women in the UAE exceeds that of men. Despite this high level of education, the number of women in the labor force remains fairly low.

YEMEN

In 1990, North and South Yemen unified to become one state. Prior to that, it was divided between South Yemen, which had been under British control since they seized the port city of Aden in 1839, and North Yemen, a conservative tribal society run by a hereditary Imam or religious leader. As separate entities, each country dealt with women very differently, and unification has led to some tensions. Overall, Yemen is an extraordinarily poor country, but it is surrounded by very wealthy Arab states, such as its neighbor to the north, Saudi Arabia. As such, many Yemenis work in the Saudi oil industry, and this factor has affected the role of women in Yemeni society.

After World War I, the Ottomans who had controlled parts of Yemen left the region and the British granted control to Imam Yahya, a descendent of the religious tribe that ruled the northern Yemen Arab Republic (YAR) until 1962. Due to its conservative nature and the fact that sharia law was in place, most women were veiled and practiced seclusion. After the death of the Imam in 1962, a republic was born and new legislation gave women more rights, including pregnancy leave, voting, driving, and land owner-ship.[65] Tradition, however, held strong and many women in the north con-tinued to wear a veil and adhere to more traditional values, while much of the new legislation was rarely enforced. Although rural women worked in agriculture and herding, a taboo remained against urban women work-ing in factories, offices, or markets. The perception was that only desperate economic situations would push women into these types of work.[66] After oil was found in Saudi Arabia in the 1930s, many men left to work in the oil industry, so women assumed some traditional male roles in the household and in agricultural communities. This phenomenon is also found in several other countries where men leave to find more lucrative work. By 1986, al-though still low, women's participation in the workforce was 22 percent and the number of girls getting an education was on the rise. By 1988, 22 percent of girls were in primary schools, up from only 8 percent in 1969. By 1981, women even outnumbered men in the Faculty of Medicine.[67]

The People's Democratic Republic of Yemen (PDRY) in the south dif-fered from North Yemen due to its adoption of Marxist policies that led to a secular constitution in 1970. The constitution stated that the govern-ment would work toward state-sponsored childcare to encourage women to enter the labor force. In 1974, the government passed a new family law that supported women's employment. Yemen was sparsely populated and many men worked abroad, so women were needed in the workforce. Ad-ditionally, the socialist nature of the new regime pushed religion aside and worked toward equal rights for all citizens. The modified constitution of 1978 promised to balance female employment and family life, most nota-bly by providing childcare. In the South, many women worked unveiled in the medical field, teaching, and in factories. A small minority became lawyers and some even served as judges, a profession that some religious leaders contend is closed for women. When the states merged in 1990, the rules of the North prevailed and women's issues received short shrift. The more conservative religious leaders of the North wanted Islamic law to remain the main source of legislation, and therefore the new family law of 1992 held that women needed to have their guardian's permission to work outside the home. In 1993, two women won seats in parliament in the mul-tiparty elections. By 1997, women's groups had become more established and advocated for women's rights. Despite this trend of increased activism, by 2001 female literacy will still extremely low, at 28.5 percent. Women gained independence and work experience since many men left to work in Saudi Arabia's oil industry, yet when the men returned home during peri-ods of economic decline, they brought with them a conservative brand of Islam that hampered women's ability to gain more equality.

OMAN

Oman holds an important strategic location for the world because its sits on the Straits of Hormuz, through which a large portion of the world's oil passes. Additionally, Oman began producing oil in the 1960s and, as such, became more important to the rest of the world. However, prior to 1970, Oman had been a country relatively closed to the outside. Sultan Said bin Taymur, who ruled Oman from 1938–1970, only permitted a small number of people to leave the country for work or education. Those who left and were educated abroad, however, were not allowed to return home to Oman. This was a particularly challenging law, as women could not accompany their husbands abroad.

The population of Oman was and is very heterogeneous, with urban merchant classes, fishing communities on the coast, and farming communities in the valley and mountain areas. Since Sultan Taymur was suspicious of modernity, he kept his population fairly uneducated and confined to Oman. Due to a lack of infrastructure, travel within Oman was extremely difficult and most Omanis were isolated from one another. Very few modern schools existed in Oman, leaving the majority of the population uneducated, though some families smuggled their children out of the country to matriculate. Although the British had established a hold on Oman in the 1830s, the British government did not interfere much in the internal dynamics of Oman. The British interest in maintaining access to India and forestalling foreign influences was the main goal of the British protectorate.

In 1970, Sultan Qaboos bin Said ousted his father in a bloodless coup in order to modernize Oman. Sultan Qaboos's commitment to modernization was reflected in changes employed with regards to women. A universal education program was implement in 1970, which improved the prospects for women entering the labor force. Sultan Qaboos invited the return of Omanis who had left the country to be educated but were refused reentry, and many men and women returned to Oman to assist in the modernization efforts, believing that their education abroad would be beneficial. Women participated in this modernization program as active members in the military, police force, civil service, and education. Most of the women who entered the labor force were recently returned exiles. By the 1980s, Omani society was transformed by expanded an infrastructure; most importantly, new roads greatly facilitated travel and commerce throughout the country. Due to the high price of oil in the 1970s, Oman was able to fund vast infrastructure and modernization projects. As the number of people returning to Oman increased and jobs became scarce, however, women were the main victims. Whereas women had played a large role in nation building after Sultan Qaboos's coup in 1970, by the 1980s, women's role in society was being reassessed.

The Oman Women's Association, formed in 1971 to help poor women and supported by the Sultan, was eventually taken over by the government in 1978 and subordinated to the Ministry of Social Affairs and Labor.[68] This ministry determined that women should participate in certain types of work and steer clear of others. In the 1980s, the government encouraged women to engage with the disabled. Government-run women's groups established day care centers for handicapped children, and elite women were persuaded to volunteer their time at these centers. Under the auspices of the Ministry of Social Development, women learned about health issues, education, and handicraft-training programs.[69]

As time progressed, the government placed restrictions on women's activities. One area where the government began to crack down was on the organization of women's groups. Independent groups were prohibited, and some educational programs and occupations were closed to women. A particularly telling story regarding cultural views of women in public occurred in 1990, during a ceremony in front of the sultan of the first graduating class of the College of Medicine. The professors had instituted an "outstanding student" award that was selected by secret ballot. The international faculty was uncomfortable when a woman won and did not know how the sultan would accept this outcome. The faculty decided to extend the prize to two students, but, again, a woman took second place. Finally, in the third vote, a man emerged and he stepped forward during the ceremony to accept the award on behalf of the three winners. This story reflects a belief that men might be more "intellectually deserving in public than women."[70]

Despite these setbacks, in 1997, Sultan Qaboos allowed women to vote and run for office. By March 2004, a woman was appointed a ministerial position, while other women served in the government in a variety of capacities. Education was another area where there was significant improvement for women. By 2001, girls and boys could be found in equal numbers in primary education and were permitted to study abroad. Women also made up 54 percent of students matriculating in Sultan Qaboos University and worked in a variety of fields including business, government, and media. By 2002, women comprised 33 percent of the civil service. As the largest employer of women, the government has mandated that women receive equal pay and get maternity leave.

Oman has been advocating a move to rely more Omanis than on foreigners in the labor force. Clearly women, who make up 50 percent of the population, can move into jobs formerly held by foreign workers, yet, as in many Middle Eastern countries, cultural factors emphasizing the woman's primary role as wife and caregiver make it difficult for women to enter the labor force.[71] Although educated women in Oman work in many occupations, such as medicine, engineering, and economics, only 8.6 percent of women are considered "economically active." This statistic, however, fails to take into account jobs that women perform in agricultural production and sheep herding. According to the Omani Census Committee, women involved in this type of work are categorized as "housewives," and therefore are not counted as part of the workforce.[72] As in many other Middle Eastern nations, Oman is making progress in women's education and coming to a slow realization that women are necessary in the workforce.

QATAR

Qatar is a small, wealthy country that achieved independence from Britain in 1971. Unlike some of the other Arab Gulf states, Qatar has a fairly homogenous society, the majority of whom are Sunni Muslims. This fact has contributed, along with the discovery of oil, to Qatar's stability. Oil allowed the Qatari regime to offer material and economic benefits to its citizens in return for compliance without complete political participation, yet as Qatar attempts to diversify its economy and oil revenues decline, significant changes have been occurring. In an understated and quiet fashion, Qatar has been moving toward democracy with the opening of the Al-Jazeera television network, which is fairly free from government interference. In Qatar, the role of women in the economic, social, and political realms is transforming. In 2003, women gained the vote and the first female minister was appointed to the government. Qatar's ruler, Sheikh Hamad bin Khalifa Al Thani, has pushed Qatar as a key player in the region and supported top-down women's reforms, hoping that these changes can sprout deeper roots within the population.

In Qatar, both men and women have experienced extraordinary changes in the last few decades. In the late 1800s, wealthy families hired tutors for their sons to learn the Qu'ran and other aspects of Islam. Very few girls had this luxury and those who did only studied from ages 6 to 12 and then awaited their marriage. In early times, although women were uneducated, they mended nets for the fisherman in the pearl and fishing industries, wove cloth in their homes, sold produce in the local markets. And. in the desert, helped herd camels. Girls' education was transformed in the 1940s when Amnah Mahmud al-Jiddah, a female tutor, opened a private school for girls. As Qatar gained wealth from the nascent oil industry, it began to offer more social services to its population. By 1955, the government opened the first public school for girls and, along with a free education, offered free books and other equipment, although schooling was not mandatory. Girls took advantage of education, and by 1978 girls surpassed boys in graduating high school.[73] By 1977, Qatar University opened with seven colleges that consisted of a branch for each gender, although faculty of either gender could teach at both branches. The seven colleges included education, humanities, sciences, law and sharia, technology, economics, business administration, and engineering. Women were able to participate in all programs but engineering.

In Qatar and several other Gulf states, women comprise a larger proportion of the university population than men. In Qatar, for example, 70 percent of the students are women. There are several explanations for this phenomenon. First, some of the best male students are sent overseas to study. Second, Qatar is still a conservative society that rejects the idea of sending women abroad unaccompanied, so their only option is to remain in the country to study. Third, in many cases, men are expected to work after high school, so a percentage of men defer their university education to enter the labor force. Almost 95 percent of women who complete secondary school, versus 55 percent of men, attend university.[74]

In 2003, a reform minded woman became the president of Qatar University and tackled some key issues that benefited both men and women there. Dr. Shaikha Abd Allah al Misnad pushed for new teaching methods to promote critical thinking and to distance teaching from the more traditional techniques that emphasized memorization. To improve pedagogy in Qatar, the government asked the Rand Corporation—a United States-based think tank—to help reform its education system from K-12. The government also created a Supreme Education Council to oversee and implement these changes. Women are playing a large role in this effort as both teachers and administrators. An important role model for Qatari women is the Emir's wife, Sheikha Mozah bint Nasser al Misnad, who has begun to take a more public role in Qatar by supporting important charities, heading several institutions, and giving public speeches.[75] The Qatari "first lady" has been instrumental in establishing Education City, which allows Western universities to open branches in Qatar and educate both Qatari and non-Qatari students. Girls are also being educated in private schools that offer the International Baccalaureate degree.

The growth in female education has fostered changes in the Qatari labor force. In Qatar, as in many other places in the Middle East, it is the lower class women who need work to survive. Over the last 25 years, employment options for women have broadened, coupled with a gradual change in society's attitude toward working women. Whereas in 1999 women comprised 39 percent of the workforce, by 2002 they made up 41 percent. In government work, women continue to close the gap with men and now hold 49 percent of jobs in that field.

Clearly, changing perceptions in a traditional society can be challenging and there are still groups that resist women in the workforce or in jobs perceived as traditionally in the male domain. For those who oppose women entering the labor force because they will mix with unrelated men, the concept of the seclusion comes to the forefront. In many places, separating men and women in the workplace can be a logistical challenge. Others hold to a more tribal explanation of why women should not work by explaining that, in families with enough wealth to survive, men should be the bread-winners. Women who work in this situation bring shame to the family. Many younger women who do work contend that, although their families are financially secure, two incomes are necessary to maintain a quality of life in a society where the cost of living continues to rise. Additionally, un-married women who have a university education would like to make use of that education. Furthermore, some women want to relieve some of the boredom that comes with staying at home. In some cases, when women marry, their husbands expect them to remain at home to care for them and the children.

Women hold a variety of jobs in Qatar, working mostly in positions that are considered socially acceptable for them, such as teaching, secretarial work, and nursing. In Qatar between 1996 and 2001, almost 90 percent of teachers in primary and secondary schools were women.[76] Women are entering the labor market in high rates and delaying marriage, thereby re-stricting the number of children they have. In 1969, a nursing school for women was established and women continue to dominate in that field. As a conservative society, women who work with men usually cover their hair and some go so far as to cover their faces.

Recently, Qatari women have ventured into jobs that have not previously been open to them. Some have become customs agents, policewomen, or passport controllers at Doha Airport. Education has propelled some women into key positions of authority, including the head of the Children's Depart-ment of Hamad Hospital, a leading hospital in Qatar.

LEBANON

Women's associations influenced the type of work that women selected in Lebanon. Early associations stressed charitable and social work, usually addressing women's issues, poverty, education, and vocational training. Lebanon has always been a bit of an anomaly in the Middle East due to its large Christian community and the extraordinary French influence in the country. After World War I, France was granted a mandate over Lebanon solidifying a relationship and influence in that country that began much earlier with the Christian community. Lebanon was one of the Middle East's early democracies, while its religious diversity and heterogeneous society has made stability challenging. Although foreign influence in early years led to a more open education system for women, external influences hampered Lebanon's ability to develop into a liberal democracy. The in-flux of Palestinian refugees, Syrian troops, and Israeli invasions have also made Lebanon's political development difficult. To incorporate the vari-ous religious groups in Lebanon's heterogeneous society, the structure of its government is such that the President is Maronite Christian, the Prime Minister is Sunni, and the Speaker of the Chamber of Deputies is Shia.

After World War I, many rural women in both Syria and Lebanon were active in the production of handicrafts, including silk, cotton, and wool products, and most of their work was done at home. This afforded them the opportunity to tend to their cultivation and domestic chores. As European influence grew, women went to work in difficult conditions as factory workers. By the 1930s, as textile factories continued to increase, more women were supplementing their family's income by working outside the home. Some peasant women became domestic servants. In the urban setting, many male artisans lost their jobs because of the factories that produced cheaper goods and this factor altered the division of labor within a family. In 1946, the government passed some labor laws, several of which limited when and where women could work. A law in 1948 prohibited women from working at night, although some exceptions existed if a woman worked in a family business or was in music, art, or theater.

In 1946, workers at a tobacco factory owned and managed by a French-Lebanese consortium in Beirut threatened to strike if their demands for better conditions were not met. Although Lebanon gained its independence in 1941, French influence over the government continued. The workers organized protests and circulated leaflets urging other workers to support the strike. What was most interesting about the strike's organization was that women made up the majority of workers calling for the demonstrations. This fact was ignored by most of the news media at the time, reflecting how women were disregarded when it came to public activism. Factory management described these women as "unruly" and "dare devils" because they defied conventional public behavior for women.[77] The event ended tragically when police used live bullets to force the opening of the factory; this event shaped future labor movements in Lebanon. What this event also reflected was the various views about women in the workforce. Many bourgeois women wanted men to respect their domestic contribution and remained committed to "women's work," such as charitable organizations and teaching. Working women, in contrast, pushed for a better status in society. When men began migrating to the oil rich states for jobs in the 1970s and 1980s, some women assumed jobs in non-traditional areas. Despite this, in the 1970s, many women remained clustered in teaching, nursing, and administrative positions. Key decision making positions continue to be occupied by men. Even though women make up over 90 percent of bank workers, they make up only 19 percent of managers or general managers of banks.[78]

Women have had access to education since Lebanon's independence and they have participated in intellectual and social organizations. Prior to Lebanon's civil war, which began in 1975 and raged until 1990, Lebanon boasted one of the freest presses in the Middle East. The civil war, however, had mixed effects on the status of women. Whereas prior to the civil war the more socially liberal Maronites held most of the power in the country, as Shia power increased, their socially conservative views also proliferated.

The challenges leading to the civil war, however, were in place long before it actually erupted. Changing demographics made the Shia one of the largest confessional groups in Lebanon, yet they were also one of the more socially and politically dispossessed. The Lebanese American University opened an Institute for Women's Studies in the Arab World in 1973 just two years prior to the outbreak of Lebanon's long civil war. The Institute conducts research and publishes the *Al-Raida* journal, which tackles controversial issues regarding women. One of the Institute's key goals is to assist women who have been harmed by the war to find employment. The Institute also explores questions such as domestic violence and professes the belief that a high level of violence against women in a community reflects a severe problem in society. Eliminating violence against women will elevate the level of society as a whole. This theme was echoed by the Lebanese Council to Resist Violence Against Women (LECORVAW), founded in 1997 to combat increasing incidents of violence against women. The Council informs women of their rights and provides them with legal and psychological support. Like other women's studies programs in conflict regions, the program in Lebanon tries to help women in their local community survive the hardships of everyday life with the women playing a role in policy-making.[79]

Iraq's invasion of Kuwait in 1990 sparked the Gulf War in 1991, which brought U.S. troops to the region. The war led to economic hardship throughout the region and pushed the United Nations to explore ways to alleviate the economic pressures. In 1994, the United Nations Development Fund for Women (UNIFEM) in West Asia was established to assist in the development of women-owned businesses in Syria, Jordan, and Lebanon.[80] UNIFEM's goal was to integrate women from the informal sector into the formal one to encourage economic development. In their quest to balance family and economic life, many women were and are constrained from entering the formal economic sector and rely on the informal sector to make money. The informal sector, however, provides few if any benefits and pay is usually very limited. UNIFEM attempts to increase the availability of financial services to female entrepreneurs to help them jumpstart their businesses. After some research, UNIFEM found that formal financial institutions supplied credit support to very few women. To ameliorate this problem, UNIFEM organized a gender-awareness workshop that was attended by 26 non-governmental organizations and some representatives from the banking sector. The goal was to provide institutional support to micro-enterprises. For the most part, women were mainly found in the less profitable sectors in Lebanon since they produced food items and handicrafts, items that are more traditional women's domains. What UNIFEM concluded was that one of the main impediments for women is a lack of credit hampering their ability to start businesses. Couple this lack of financial support with a government overwhelmed by internal and external strife and the issue of women's employment was not a priority.

In many ways, the discussions on gender in Lebanon followed the discourse in Iran. The year 1989 was an important one for both Iranians and Lebanese. For the Iranians, the death of Ayatollah Khomeini ushered in a period of reform and the search for a new Iranian identity after the revolution. For the Lebanese, an end to the civil war in 1990 led to an assessment of their society. Both Iran and Lebanon explored the question of women's role in society, but Lebanese clerics sought to differentiate themselves from the Khomeini era in Iran. The Lebanese religious authorities who wrote on women's issues were mostly reformist in their outlook. They believed that Islam argues for gender equality and holds that Islam and modernity are compatible.

In the Shia world, Muhammad's daughter, Fatima, has been portrayed as a model for women. She is important to Shias because she married Ali, who became the fourth caliph in Islam but is believed to have been the rightful caliph after Muhammad. Ayatollah Muhammad Husein Fadlallah, an important Lebanese cleric, recognizes Fatima as a model not only for women, but for men as well. Fatima participated in social and political life and after her father's death, and was involved in the discussions as to who would follow him. She also defended her right to inherit land from her father. For Fadlallah, her actions represent a person who was politically active and, as such, justify women's participation in the public realm in contemporary times.[81]

Another Lebanese cleric, Ayatollah Shams al-din, believes that all women should wear the hijab, but that total segregation was only meant for the Prophet's wives. Women should cover their body and hair, but can expose their hands, face, and feet. He also contends that women can meet with males who are not relatives in social, work, and political settings. For Fadlallah, the hijab is meant "to neutralize the perception of the woman as a female in order to prioritize her status as a person." He holds that the hijab is neither an obstacle nor an attempt to destroy a woman's dignity. The clerics contend that women have the right to an education and employment and that nothing in Islamic teachings prohibits these from occurring. Education is crucial for propelling women from the backwardness that is not innate to Muslim society but which is a part of neglect in developing their minds. The clerics also believe that women should have a profession to make them more independent and that they should do so without the permission of either their father or husband.[82] As for politics both Fadlallah and Shams Al-Din believe that women have a right to run for and serve in political office. However, since the priority in Islam is for women to be wives and mothers, they can be active in the social and political world as long as their work does not interfere with their primary mission.

NOTES

1. Nikki R. Keddie, *Women in the Middle East: Past and Present* (Princeton, NJ: Princeton University Press, 2007), 19.

2. Guity Nashat and Judith Tucker, *Women in the Middle East and North Africa* (Bloomington: Indiana University Press, 2006), 46.

3. Nashat and Tucker, *Women in the Middle East and North Africa*, 57.

4. Jonathan P. Berkey, "Women and Islamic Education in the Mamluk Period," in *Women in Middle Eastern History*, eds. Nikki R. Keddie and Beth Baron (New Haven, CT: Yale University Press, 1991), 153.

5. Nashat and Tucker, *Women in the Middle East and North Africa*, 67.

6. Abraham Marcus, "Men, Women and Property: Dealers in Real Estate in Eighteenth Century Aleppo," *Journal of Economic and Social History of the Orient* 26 (1973): 138.

7. Haim Gerber, "Social and Economic Position of Women in an Ottoman City, Bursa, 1600–1700," *International Journal of Middle East Studies* 12, no. 3 (November 1980): 233–34.

8. Nashat and Tucker, *Women in the Middle East and North Africa*, 75–76.

9. Keddie, *Women in the Middle East: Past and Present*, 61–62.

10. James Reilly, "Women in the Economic Life of Late-Ottoman Damascus," *Arabica* 42 (March 1995): 79–81.

11. Reilly, "Women in the Economic Life of Late-Ottoman Damascus," 93–94.

12. Julia Clancy-Smith, "A Woman Without her Distaff: Gender, Work and Handicraft Production in Colonial North Africa," in *A Social History of Women in the Modern Middle East*, eds. Margaret L. Meriwether and Judith E. Tucker (Boulder, CO: Westview Press, 1999), 27.

13. Clancy-Smith, "A Woman Without her Distaff: Gender, Work and Handicraft Production in Colonial North Africa," 29.

14. Nashat and Tucker, *Women in the Middle East and North Africa*, 78.

15. Keddie, *Women in the Middle East: Past and Present*, 62.

16. Nashat and Tucker, *Women in the Middle East and North Africa*, 80.

17. Keddie, *Women in the Middle East: Past and Present*, 82.

18. Metin Yüksel, "The Encounter of Kurdish Women with Nationalism in Turkey," *Middle Eastern Studies* 42, no. 5 (September 2006): 781.

19. Valentine M. Moghadam, "Feminism and Islam in Iran," in *Modernizing Women: Gender and Social Change in the Middle East*, 2nd ed. (Boulder, CO: Lynne Reinner, 2003), 43.

20. A. Nurhan Süral, "Legal Framework for Gender Equality at Work in Turkey," *Middle Eastern Studies* 43 (September 2007): 816.

21. Parvin Paidar, "Feminism and Islam in Iran," in *Taking Sides: Clashing Views on Controversial Issues in Cultural Anthropology*, eds. Robert L. Welsch and Kirk M. Endicott (Guilford, CT: Dushkin McGraw Hill, 2003), 203.

22. Paidar, "Feminism and Islam in Iran," 205.

23. Azadeh Kian, "Women and Politics in Post-Islamist Iran: the Gender Conscious Drive to Change," *British Journal of Middle Eastern Studies* (1997): 80–83.

24. Paidar, "Feminism and Islam in Iran," 210–11.

25. Mehrangiz Kar, "Focusing on Women in the Internal Politics of Iran," *Brown Journal of World Affairs* 15, no. 1 (Fall/Winter 2008): 83–84.

26. Paula Kabalo, "Leadership Behind the Curtains: The Case of Israeli Women in 1948," *Modern Judaism* (February 2008): 15.

27. Peri Rosenfeld, "Women in Green: The Contributions of Hadassah Nursing to Immigrant and Refugee Health in Pre-State and the Early Years of the State of Israel," *Nursing History Review* 13 (2005): 102.

28. Yossi Yonah and Ishak Saporta, "The Wavering Luck of Girls: Gender and Pre-Vocational Education in Israel," *Journal of Middle East Women's Studies* 2 (Fall 2006): 72.

29. Ephraim Ya'ar, "Continuity and Change in Israeli Society: The Test of the Melting Pot," *Israel Studies* 10 (Summer 2005): 101–3.

30. Nina Toren, "Tradition and Transition: Family Change in Israel," *Gender Issues* (Spring 2003): 71.

31. Gahda Hashem Talhami, *The Mobilization of Muslim Women in Egypt* (Gainesville: University Press of Florida, 1996), 26.

32. Mohamed M Mostafa, "Attitudes Towards Women who Work in Egypt," *Women in Management Review* (2003): 260.

33. Martin Latreille, "Honor, the Gender Division of Labor and the Status of Women in Rural Tunisia-A Social Organizational Reading," *International Journal of Middle East Studies* 40 (2008): 601–2.

34. Danièle Djamila Amrane-Minne, "Women and Politics in Algeria from the War of Independence to Our Day," *Research in African Literatures* (Fall 1999): 62.

35. Karima Bennoune, "Between Betrayal and Betrayal: Fundamentalism, Family Law and Feminist Struggle in Algeria," *Arab Studies Quarterly* 17 (Winter/Spring 95): 51.

36. Moghadem, *Modernizing Women,* 62–63.

37. Bennoune, "Between Betrayal and Betrayal," 37.

38. Ann Mayer, "Developments in the Law of Marriage and Divorce in Libya Since the 1969 Revolution," *Journal of African Law* 22 (Spring, 1978): 30–49.

39. G. Reza Arabsheibani and Lamine Manfor, "From 'Farashia' to Military Uniform: Male-Female Wage Differentials in Libya," *Economic Development and Cultural Change* 50 (July 2002): 1009.

40. Judith Miller, "Libya's Women: Era of Change," *New York Times,* February 3, 1986, B.5.

41. Orit Bashkin, "Representations of Women in the Writings of the Intelligentsia in Hashemite Iraq, 1921–1958," *Journal of Middle East Women's Studies* 4 (Winter 2008): 56.

42. Orit Bashkin, "Representations of Women in the Writings of the Intelligentsia in Hashemite Iraq," 54.

43. Judith Colp Rubin, "Women in the New Iraq," *Middle East Review of International Affairs* 12 (September 2008): 35–36.

44. Moghadem, *Modernizing Women,* 61.

45. Rubin, "Women in the New Iraq," 37.

46. Ali S. Zaghal, "Social Change in Jordan," *Middle Eastern Studies* 20 (October 1984): 57–60.

47. Zaghal, "Social Change in Jordan," 71–72.

48. Moghadem, *Modernizing Women,* 63.

49. Linda Layne, "Women in Jordan's Workforce," *MERIP* 95 (March/April 1981): 19–20.

50. Glenn E. Robinson, "Democratization in Jordan," *International Journal of Middle East Studies* 30 (August 1998): 393.

51. Mary Kawar, "Transitions and Boundaries: Research into the Impact of Paid Work on Young Women's Lives in Jordan," *Gender and Development* 8 (July 2000): 56–58.

52. Keddie, *Women in the Middle East,* 135–36.

53. Amelie Le Renard, "Only for Women: Women, the State and Reform in Saudi Arabia," *Middle East Journal* 62 (Autumn 2008): 610–29.

54. Soraya Altorki, *Women in Saudi Arabia* (New York: Columbia University Press, 1998), 23.

55. Nora Alarifi Pharaon, "Saudi Women and the Muslim State in the Twenty-First Century," *Sex Roles* 51 (September 2004): 359–63.

56. Michael L. Ross, "Oil, Islam and Women." *American Political Science Association* 102 (February 2008): 107.

57. Pharaon, "Saudi Women and the Muslim State in the Twenty-First Century," 359.

58. Joshua Teitelbaum, "Dueling for *Da'wa:* State vs. Society on Saudi Internet," *Middle East Journal* 56 (Spring 2002): 234.

59. Le Renard, "Only for Women: Women, the State and Reform in Saudi Arabia," 612–16.

60. Kolleen Miller-Rosser, Ysanne Chapman and Karen Francis, "Historical, Cultural and Contemporary Influences on the Status of Women in Nursing in Saudi Arabia," *Online Journal of Issues in Nursing* (2006). Accessed October 10, 2008 from www.ebsco host.com.

61. Sifa Mtango, "A State of Oppression? Women's Rights in Saudi Arabia," *Asia-Pacific Journal on Human Rights and the Law* (2004), 66.

62. Pharaon, "Saudi Women and the Muslim State in the Twenty-First Century," 352–53.

63. Keddie, *Women in the Middle East,* 151.

64. Habeeb Salloum, "Women in the United Arab Emirates," *Contemporary Review* (August 2003): 101–2.

65. Sheila Carapico, "Women and Public Participation in Yemen," *Middle East Report* 173 (November/December 1991): 15.

66. Carapico, "Women and Public Participation in Yemen," 15.

67. Keddie, *Women in the Middle East,* 152.

68. Dawn Chatty, "Women Working in Oman: Individual Choice and Cultural Constraints," *International Journal of Middle East Studies* 32 (May 2000): 242–43.

69. Keddie, *Women in the Middle East,* 155.

70. Chatty, "Women Working in Oman: Individual Choice and Cultural Constraints," 252.

71. Gerard McElwee and Rahma Al-Riyami, "Women Entrepreneurs in Oman: Some Barriers to Success," *Career Development International* (2003): 339.

72. Chatty, "Women Working in Oman: Individual Choice and Cultural Constraints," 248.

73. Louay Bahry and Phebe Marr, "Qatari Women: A New Generation of Leaders?" Middle East Policy 12 (Summer 2005): 104–5.

74. Ali Al-Hail, "Why Women Use Email Disproportionately in Qatar: An Exploratory Study," *Journal of Website Promotion* 1 (2005): 100.

75. Bahry and Marr, "Qatari Women: A New Generation of Leaders?" 107.

76. Bahry and Marr, "Qatari Women: A New Generation of Leaders?" 108.

77. Malek Abisaab, "Unruly Factory Women in Lebanon: Contesting French Colonialism and the National State, 1940–1946," *Journal of Women's History* 16 (2004): 55–58.

78. Dima Jamali, Yusuf Sidani, and Assem Safiedinne. "Constraints Facing Working Women in Lebanon: An Insider View," *Women in Management Review* (2005): 584–85.

79. Cheryl Toman, "The Link Between Women's Studies Programs and Grassroots Organizations." *Arab Studies Quarterly* (Spring 2003): 55–59.

80. Randa Husseini, "Promoting Women Entrepreneurs in Lebanon: The Experience of UNIFEM," *Gender and Development* 5 (February 1997): 49.

81. Rola el-Husseini, "Women, Work and Political Participation in Lebanese Shi'a Contemporary Thought: the Writings of Ayatollahs Fadlallah and Shams al-din," *Comparative Studies of South Asia, Africa and the Middle East* 28 (2008): 276.

82. El-Husseini, "Women, Work and Political Participation in Lebanese Shi'a Contemporary Thought," 278–79.

SUGGESTED READING

Chatty, Dawn. "Women Working in Oman: Individual Choice and Cultural Constraints." *International Journal of Middle East Studies* 32 (May 2000): 241–54.

El-Husseini, Rola. "Women, Work and Political Participation in Lebanese Shia Contemporary Thought: the Writings of Ayatollahs Fadlallah and Shams al-din." *Comparative Studies of South Asia, Africa and the Middle East* 28 (2008): 273–82.

Gerber, Haim. Social and Economic Position of Women in an Ottoman City, Bursa, 1600–1700." *International Journal of Middle East Studies* 12 (November 1980): 231–44.

Keddie, Nikki R. *Women in the Middle East: Past and Present.* Princeton, NJ: Princeton University Press, 2007.

Kian, Azadeh. Women and Politics in Post-Islamist Iran: the Gender Conscious Drive to Change." *British Journal of Middle Eastern Studies* (1997): 75–96.

Moghadam, Valentine M. *Modernizing Women: Gender and Social Change in the Middle East,* 2nd ed. Boulder, CO: Lynne Reinner, 2003.

Nashat, Guity, and Judith Tucker. *Women in the Middle East and North Africa.* Bloomington: Indiana University Press, 2006.

Reilly, James. "Women in the Economic Life of Late-Ottoman Damascus." *Arabica* 4 (March 1995): 79–106.

2

⁓

Women and Family

Since the earliest recorded history, women have played a crucial role in Middle Eastern and North African families. Families are the primary culture-bearing unit of society, and in pre-industrial societies they are the primary economic component.[1] Most families in the Middle East and North Africa follow a patrilineal structure, dictating patrilocality, a system where women move to their husband's family after marriage. Women have obligations to their own nuclear family as wife and mother and also assume specific responsibilities when they move in with their husband's family. As such, a woman's relationship to others defines her role within that family structure. Throughout the region, a woman's status as wife, sister, daughter, and daughter-in-law have reflected her father's or husband's place in society.

The patriarchal structure in place prior to the rise of Islam led to traditions that subjugated women to men. The concept of endogamy, or marrying within one's own lineage in order to retain inheritance rights for men, also set the stage for women's oppression. A father exercised control over his wife and children, and when he died, the eldest son, or another male relative, such as his brother, would assume control of the family. Given the importance of marriage, a woman's marital status has always been the most crucial aspect of her identity in the Middle East and North Africa. Throughout the region's history, marriage has served as a union of two individuals as well as an alliance between families. In pre-Islamic nomadic society, marriage empowered women by making them the critical link between tribes. Marriage, specifically cousin marriage, served as a way to keep resources within the family. After marriage, a woman's productivity or worth was often associated with her fertility and, more specifically, her ability to produce male heirs. Societal preference for male children over female children was directly associated with the males' enhanced ability to support the family and assure the continuity of the family since descent in patriarchal societies is traced through male bloodlines. Islam emerged in this particular context, and through Islamic law attempted to ease some of the restrictions on women. Islam not only introduced important changes for women in the Middle East and North Africa, but also built upon existing practices.[2]

Since the seventh century and the advent of Islam, women's lives in the Middle East and North Africa have been shaped by religious affiliation and patriarchy. Under Islam, women initially gained access to a new set of rights and responsibilities associated with the practice of the faith. In the family, women were critical in raising their children according to Islamic values and practices. While most women generally remained subordinate to their male relatives, under Islam, they gained access to their own wealth and resources. However, as Islam spread outside of Arabia in the seventh and eighth centuries, women's roles were gradually limited to family life inside the home, where they focused primarily upon the domestic sphere while men dealt with all issues in the public sphere. Those who did not embrace Islam had various customs and traditions, resulting in distinct perceptions of gender relations and a woman's role in the family. In the ancient Levant, the lands bordering the eastern Mediterranean Sea including present day Israel, Jordan, Lebanon, Palestine, and Syria, people associated a woman's identity with her role as wife and mother. As such, women of the Levant had functions similar to those of Arabian women, although the influence of Christianity and Judaism had slightly different implications. In ancient times, most families in the Levant consisted of one husband and one wife. A few of the wealthier men had harems, but women could only have one partner at a time. In some cases, adultery was punishable by death. A key variation between Muslim and Christian families is that Christians emphasized men's role in raising and teaching children, whereas Islamic culture left child rearing to women. Furthermore, Biblical law had specific provisions for how children should treat their parents. Specifically, children were to have the utmost respect for both of their parents, especially their mothers who were responsible for her children's moral education. This respect for mothers, however, did not translate into an overall respect for women in society. Israelite women were often married without their consent. Much like women in Arabia, women in the Levant were clearly subordinate to men and subject to the control and authority of their male relatives. Evidence from the ancient Levant also reveals that widows and divorcées carried a stigma that often resulted in their marginalization in society. For example, women who were divorced or widowed were not appropriate marriage partners for high priests.[3]

While women in Middle Eastern and North African families might influence the male patriarch informally, as the Prophet Muhammad's wives did, women rarely held public positions of authority in early Middle Eastern history.[4] This changed somewhat as the Middle East transitioned from an agrarian, nomadic society to a more modern one where employment opportunities provided women alternatives to life inside of the home. State formation also offered women new responsibilities associated with citizenship along with benefits such as social welfare services designed to support the family. These changes shape modern day family formations and, in many ways, challenge traditional systems and perceptions of the family. For instance, in some more educated and urbanized societies, women marry later and subsequently have fewer children due to their access to contraception, employment opportunities, and education outside of the home.

EARLY ISLAM

Only four centuries after the advent of Islam in what is now Saudi Arabia, most of the Middle East converted to Islam. Because Islam's rise in the seventh century was such a pivotal event in the region, Muhammad's life offers crucial insights to family relationships. Ultimately, as people converted and Islam spread outside of Arabia, new communities embraced Islam and integrated their own cultural norms and traditions into the religion's practice. Muhammad had particularly interesting relationships with his female relatives. His views of women, shaped by pre-Islamic beliefs and his own experience, are tremendously important, given his role as Allah's messenger. Scholars suggest that his articulation of early Islamic principles improved the status of women. During his life, Muhammad often communicated a certain degree of sympathy toward women as well as a concern for their equal treatment, including full religious responsibility.[5] Muhammad came of age in a time and place where women had significant roles in society both in and out of the home. In Mecca, a center for trade and commerce associated with the presence of important religious sites, women participated in the economy. Muhammad's experience as an orphan informed his later view that the parentless, widowed, and unfortunate deserve fair treatment. Despite his status as an orphan, Muhammad's reputation for honest dealings preceded him. Eventually Khadija, a wealthy widow who was 15 years Muhammad's senior, took him into her trade caravan. While serving as his employer, Khadija broke with tradition and asked Muhammad to marry her. Their marriage produced four daughters who lived and two sons who did not survive infancy. Muhammad was monogamous in his marriage to Khadija and only practiced polygamy after her death. As his first wife and convert, Khadija was special for her role in encouraging Muhammad when he received the call to be Allah's prophet. She also defended Muhammad when he faced persecution for spreading his message. As an important partner in Muhammad's life, Khadija figures prominently in the lives of later converts. Many view Khadija as a role model for her steadfast efforts to encourage and support Muhammad as he delivered God's message.

The special relationship between Muhammad and Khadija reflects Muhammad's generally tolerant approach toward women in society. Although there are various accounts of Khadija's background, aspects of her life are illustrative of women's roles in Arabia at the time. For example, she was either a widow or divorcee who employed Muhammad, a very public role for a woman which was not a considered a disgrace at the time. She was also heavily involved in lucrative trade and was a member of the merchant aristocracy of Mecca. Due to her economic success, Khadija provided Muhammad with the luxury of time for spiritual contemplation. Scholars suggest that Khadija was the first person to accept Muhammad's prophetic call. Since Khadija had a favorable reaction to Gabriel's messages, she supported Muhammad in his subsequent efforts to serve as Allah's prophet. For these and other desirable attributes, Khadija serves as a role model for Muslim women. Because Muhammad depended on Khadija as he answered his prophetic call, she appears to hold a special place in Muhammad's private and public life. Many believe that she was his rock with whom he could share his burden. As such, Khadija represents not only wife and mother, but also a trusted partner on whom Muhammad relied for spiritual and emotional support.[6]

Several accounts emphasize Khadija's role as a source of encouragement for her husband. Some scholars contend that Muhammad would not have been a prophet without her support.[7] Even after Khadija died, a time particularly challenging for Muhammad, her role as a wife and confidante continued to influence Muhammad's leadership and faith.

Muhammad took multiple wives after Khadija's death in an effort to promote tribal and other alliances.[8] However, his devotion to Khadija persisted, as Muhammad periodically slaughtered a kid or sheep in her honor, making his favorite and youngest wife, Aisha, bitterly jealous. Unlike Khadija, who was perhaps 15 years Muhammad's elder, Aisha was only 9 years old when she went to live with him. Several accounts reveal Aisha's displeasure with the way that Muhammad spoke of his first wife.[9] Scholars believe that Muhammad's subsequent views of women and their role in society originated with the loss of Khadija. Coupled with domestic trouble within his harem, these facts shaped later hadiths, accounts of his words and deeds, which were generally unfavorable toward women.

Muhammad's wives continued to be an important part of his private and public life. In addition to raising his children, it has been noted that

Muhammad's wives counseled him in times of crisis. Umm Salamah, his sixth wife, offered Muhammad sound advice when his followers disobeyed his commands to shave their heads and slaughter sacrificial animals following a military victory over the Meccans. She told Muhammad to set the example by shaving his own head and sacrificing an animal. After Muhammad took Umm Salamah's advice, people followed his lead. On several other occasions, she offered wise counsel and a steady hand in military and political matters, indicating that Muhammad went to her for advice on the most critical of issues. Muhammad's widows even advised subsequent caliphs, Muhammad's successors, with Uthman going so far as to suggest that Muhammad's widows should have a say in choosing his successor. Both Aisha and Umm Salamah served as authorities on the life and sayings of Muhammad until their deaths. Therefore, while women in Muhammad's family certainly fulfilled traditional roles in the home, they also had key functions as advisors to the Prophet, contributing to the rise and spread of Islam.[10]

Despite the various roles that Muhammad's wives enjoyed, his attitude toward women changed later in life with his courtship of Umm Salamah and his marriage to Zainab bint Jahsh, the divorced wife of his adopted son Zaid. The latter union caused a great controversy, and hadiths from this period document a shift from Muhammad's generally accepting view of women to one that reflects his dealings with domestic problems in his own harem. Some believe that Muhammad's wives were a constant source of gossip circulating around Medina. People discussed the women's envy of one another and even called their public behavior into question. At one point, sources indicate that Muhammad threatened his wives with mass divorce. Even Muhammad's fathers-in-law advised him to take a stern stance with his harem. These men cautioned Muhammad against letting his harem become too independent. This particular string of events and other scandals led many to believe that Muhammad's efforts to safeguard his family's prestige led to the seclusion of women in Islam.[11] Alternate explanations of seclusion view the tradition as Muhammad's attempt to forbid his wives to remarry after his death or to physically keep people out of his private rooms. While seclusion and veiling do not appear mandatory for all women during the first Islamic century, the impact of these hadiths on women is significant.[12] Later interpretations led to seclusion for all women.

The evolution of women's role in the family reflects the patriarchal society in which Islam emerged despite Qu'ranic reforms that provided women with certain legal rights not found in Judaism and Christianity. In some respects, Islam corrected some perceived pre-Islamic Arabian societal injustices. For example, pre-Islamic Arabians practiced female infanticide, a practice that was banned after the rise of Islam. Under Islam, women also gained the right to receive their dowry after entering into a marriage contract. They could also retain wealth and inheritance, both privileges be-stowed upon women after the rise of Islam. However, despite these changes, women remained dependent upon male relatives who largely controlled important matters affecting "their" women's lives.[13] Under Islam, women received inheritances equal to about half of what their male counterparts received, yet only men were entitled to a free divorce. Polygamy, a practice the preceded Islam, actually expanded after Muhammad's lifetime as a way for women to produce more children, specifically more Muslims. In addi-tion, marriage between paternal cousins increased after the rise of Islam.[14] Because Islam emerged in the urban centers of Mecca and Medina, many pre-Islamic trends continued during Muhammad's life, such as the shift toward nuclear families as a way to protect wealth and resources.

Muhammad's message and influence initially improved the position of Arab women, ushering in legal reforms and limited participation in political and religious activities outside the home. In some circumstances, women even assumed limited leadership positions in the public sphere. Neverthe-less, women's most important role in society was within the context of the family. Muhammad quickly recognized the manner with which women could spread the religion through their influence in the family and commu-nity. Women's responsibility to educate the children in religion and culture uniquely positioned them to enhance the community by rearing good Mus-lim children. Muhammad's relationship with his family provided a crucial example for community expectations. As an orphan raised by his extended family, Muhammad advocated for marginalized groups who traditionally bore a social stigma. Sources indicate that Muhammad showed compassion and restraint with his own children. For example, he asked his daughters' permission before they were married and helped his wives with their do-mestic duties. Based on these aspects of his life, it appears that, early on, Muhammad had a generally tolerant attitude toward women.

FAMILY PATTERNS

As in pre-Islamic times, the family remained the most important social unit in early Islamic society. Marriages, mostly arranged by elder relatives or parents, served to empower women by making them the critical link between tribes and families. The union of man and wife cemented rela-tions between groups, which explains why marriages between first cousins remained the norm. Cousin marriage, specifically male children marrying a female paternal cousin, kept familial property intact. The modern ideas of love and companionship were not marriage's purpose, but rather a bonding of families and networks. Clearly, the network was more important than the couple's union. In cases of polygamy, older wives were often happy to share their household duties and responsibilities with other, often younger women. Although marriage contracts varied and were negotiated between the groom and bride's families, half the dowry was usually paid in advance. The other half typically remained in reserve and was only paid in the event of divorce. A man could easily obtain a divorce by simply repudiating his wife three times. Meanwhile, divorce was relatively impossible for women to secure. Nevertheless, divorce was rare because, after the rise of Islam, women were entitled to the other half of their dowry. Whereas pre-Islamic Arab customs allowed looser forms of marriage, Islam set forth religiously based rules to govern gender relations.[15]

Marriage marked an important rite of passage for women in early Islamic society. Once a woman left her parents, she deferred to her husband and his parents. In her marital home, a new bride was subject to the day-to-day authority of her mother-in-law, but in most families, the eldest male in the family retained overall decision-making authority over everyone in the home. The expectation of obedience between parent and child continued into adulthood, even between in-laws. Upon marriage, a woman went through a significant adjustment phase. New brides had to cope with the uncertainty associated with leaving their natal home to assume a new position in her husband's family as wife, daughter-in-law, and bearer of future generations. A newly married woman was in a precarious position in her husband's family until she successfully delivered a male heir. The birth of a son gave women a permanent position in the family. Generally, female children were a loss to the family upon marriage and were viewed as threat to the family honor, making them less desirable and somewhat burdensome. Muslim youths spent much of their free time with the family cementing kinship ties and, until marriage, a woman primarily associated with her relatives and a small group of close friends.

As Islam spread across the Middle East and beyond, people incorporated their own unique cultural norms into the practice of their new faith. As in pre-Islamic times, women's main roles in the family were as mothers, wives, and daughters, but now they were also responsible for inculcating Islamic values in their children. Under Islam, men assumed the responsibility of supporting their female family members financially. While polygamy continued, Islam added the requirement for men to deal justly with multiple wives. Although viewed in the West as a discriminatory practice to benefit men, polygamy helped some women in particular circumstances. The practice offered a way for society to cope with the consequences of warfare that left numerous widows and orphans in need of familial and financial support. Since paternity remained tremendously important, Islam prohibited polyandry and adultery. Generally, men could take concubines as long as paternity was clear, though the practice was discouraged. While there were Qu'ranic reservations about slavery, it continued throughout the Middle East and North Africa.

For newly converted Muslim families, the Qu'ran set forth guidelines for gender relations. For example, according to the Qu'ran, a godly Muslim family rests on the husband's authority over his wife and his economic responsibility for the family. Islamic women are to be obedient to their husbands. Furthermore, the Qu'ran set forth familial roles placing men in charge (*qiwamma*) in order to strengthen the family. Many argue that his idea of *qiwamma* extends to include the social and political preeminence of men in society. Religious mandates codified in law also shaped familial relations in the Middle East. Subsequent interpretations of religious and legal texts reflect the changing norms and traditions of the interpreters. As Muslim jurists and great Islamic thinkers developed Islamic law, they were influenced by both Islamic and non-Islamic ideas and traditions, specifically with regards to gender relations. Religious scholars continued to interpret Islamic texts to provide additional guidance for the Muslim community. After several iterations of religious and legal interpretations of the Qu'ran, the widely held belief emerged that a woman must primarily tend to her home and children. Although it is clear that the Qu'ran requires a man to support and protect his wife and for women to raise the children, the religious guidance does not specifically limit women's role outside the home.[16] Those who justify seclusion and veiling for all women often do so based on the guidance Muhammad set forth for his own harem. People still debate the applicability of Muhammad's admonitions for his wives to all Muslim women.

AGE OF THE RIGHTLY GUIDED CALIPHS AND BEYOND

As Islam spread to different lands and cultures after Muhammad's death in 632, it had significant consequences for women's role in the family. Initially Muhammad's female relatives had an important function in spreading his message by serving as experts and advisors on his words and deeds. While women were heavily involved in the family and raising good Muslim children, some women also had a role in spreading the faith to others outside of the family. Evidence suggests that shortly after Muhammad's death women continued to have an active role in the seventh century, enjoying the Qu'ranic mandated access to resources and other responsibilities. Nevertheless, women's roles shifted under the first four Rightly Guided Caliphs who succeeded Muhammad. Women continued to serve in traditional family roles as their functions in the public sector steadily diminished.

While Muhammad's first wife, Khadija, and her life experiences reflect pre-Islamic and early Islamic life for women, his subsequent wives' lives, such as those of Aisha and Fatima, provide a glimpse into women's role in society after the rise of Islam. For instance, Aisha and a select few of Muhammad's other female relatives were especially critical in recording his words and deeds. This afforded some women a special status due to their relationship and familiarity with the Prophet. Besides his widows, Muhammad's other female relatives enjoyed positions of honor due to their status as his surviving family members. For example, his daughter Fatima and granddaughter Zaynab served as role models and experts on his traditions and message, even assuming leadership roles at times. Extended family members, such as Zaynab's nieces, Fatima and Sukaynah, also achieved notoriety. Sukaynah, pursued by many but only known to associate with the distinguished men of her time, was known for her beauty, wit, and charm. Her experience indicates that she not only enjoyed the freedom to choose her mate, but she freely associated with men outside of her immediate family.[17] However, these few women's experiences were the exception. As Islam reached communities that largely retained pre-Islamic views of women's role in the family, women's activity was limited to that which could take place inside of the home. Later converts to Islam also adapted their pre-Islamic customs to fit their unique practices of the faith. These developments lead to further restrictions, limitations, and the segregation of women in many communities.

Soon women, even Muhammad's female relatives, experienced significant life changing events as Islam developed outside of Arabia under successive caliphs. The second caliph, Umar, enacted laws to restrict women's movement by prohibiting them from going to mosques. Later, as the state adopted the practices of conquered peoples, women faced more limitations and restrictions in their daily lives. When the third caliph, Uthman, was killed, sparking a civil war and subsequent split between Sunni and Shia Muslims, Aisha led efforts to avenge Uthman's murder. However, her efforts ultimately failed as her side lost the Battle of Camel, an event that many would later use to justify women's exclusion from politics and seclusion in the home. Later, society adopted increasingly hostile perceptions of women engaged in public activities. Elite family patterns also reflected the view that women should be restricted to the home. From the eighth century, the Umayyads, emulating pre-Islamic Persian kings of the Sasanians, acquired large harems of wives and slaves while secluding their women. In the ninth century, there was a renewed emphasis on the importance of patrilineal kin groups among the Arabs who sought to protect their wealth by maintaining control of women, and thus the purity of their bloodlines. The hadiths that emerged during the ninth century also reinforced an increasingly negative attitude toward women. Eventually, medieval Islamic society developed in a manner that was even more patriarchal and restrictive than early Islamic Mecca and Medina, where women had greater access to public roles in society outside of their traditional place in the home.[18]

Examples abound of new restrictions placed on women under subsequent caliphs who often accepted and perpetuated the inequitable practices of conquered peoples such as the Sasanians. Caliph Walid (705–715) secluded women in his home, and thus the trend was set in motion for his Arabian proponents. He did not allow his harem, composed of a significant portion of non-Arabian women, contact with the outside world. In one account, his wife, Umm al-Banin, hid a poet in her private chamber. After Walid caught her with the poet, she was forced to wear a veil. In addition, some 16 of Walid's 19 sons were born of non-Arabian women. His successor, Yazid III, was born of an enslaved Persian princess. Successive caliphs continued the reversion to pre-Islamic practices with respect to women's role in the family. Whereas elite women veiled and remained secluded under previous caliphs, under the Abbasids, these practices spread to all classes. Soon the primacy of women's roles in the family came at the expense of their roles in the public sphere. Initially, as Arabians moved to what is now present day Iraq, they found many of the same agrarian-urban cultural traditions that were predominant before the rise of Islam. As Arabians settled these new areas, they adopted local traditions. The implication of the reversion to pre-Islamic practices required women to focus on their role inside the home while simultaneously limiting their access to the outside world. When women ventured out in public, there was increasingly strict gender segregation. Women could only engage in activities deemed appropriate by men. Thus, the rise of separate spheres for men and women returned as Islam spread across the Middle East and North Africa.

The societal acceptance and assimilation of pre-Islamic practices in society took place from both the bottom up and from the top down. While scholars contend that elites accepted and perpetuated the practices and customs of conquered peoples, they also set up state and legal institutions to reflect these beliefs. Official policy ordered both poor and wealthy women to wear a veil and to remain secluded from men. By adopting and later codifying the practices of conquered peoples, Arabians, living as a ruling minority, perpetuated the local customs and traditions that led to women's diminished role outside of the home. Another factor in this reversion to pre-Islamic practices was connected with people's need for guidance beyond what was set forth in the Qu'ran and the hadith. Through the establishment of sharia law, Muslims gained a codified set of rules that prescribed appropriate behavior for different people spread throughout the region. Therefore, Islamic law reinforced a woman's role in society as the primary caretaker of the home and family, while limiting her access to the outside world.[19]

Urbanization and access to wealth among the middle and upper classes also shaped women's positions in the family. Families with domestic servants left women little reason to venture into public. Even infrastructure reflected the growing importance of gender segregation and seclusion. People built homes with inner and outer courtyards to prevent women from coming into contact with strangers. The wealthy, who could afford more elaborate homes, kept women and children secluded by high walls, courtyards, and corridors.[20] In some places, women could venture out to see friends, to bathe, and sometimes to shop in the bazaar. However, when in public, many women veiled, except slaves who were not required to cover themselves. To some, the veil marked social status. Muslim women were forbidden from being enslaved, so people imported slaves from distant lands. Physically attractive female slaves fetched a high price as their owners gained sexual rights. In addition, female slaves could secure their freedom upon becoming pregnant with their master's child. Slave women could achieve a higher status, similar to a wife, especially if they gave birth to a son who assumed an important leadership position. For example, Khayzuran, a slave, gave birth to the caliph Harun-al-Rashid near present-day Tehran, Iran. As urban practices of seclusion and separation spread to rural areas, there were fewer women with significant roles outside of the home. For these, and other reasons, some argue that women had greater sexual autonomy and levels of public participation before the rise of Islam.

Turks arrived in the Middle East in the ninth century without making drastic changes for most women in the region. Turks were primarily pastoral and spoke several Turkic languages. Much like the aforementioned Arabian tribes, Turkish women carried out a variety of tasks associated with moving large groups of animals and people from place to place in search of arable lands and pastures to graze herds. Initially, Turkish women's roles in the family were similar to those of women in pre-Islamic Arabia. As Turkish tribes arrived in the Middle East, they converted to Islam but retained many of their own cultural traditions. By the 11th century, Turkish tribes arrived in large numbers and, as a result, Turkish women assumed a variety of roles across different sectors of society. As other peoples arrived in the Middle East, they also changed their traditions to fit their new surroundings. The Mongols followed the Turks, and by 1258 the Abbasids fell to the Mongols. Evidence suggests that Turkish and Mongol women of the ruling class had authority over major decisions, perhaps reflecting more egalitarian and tolerant attitudes toward women. Nevertheless, Turkish and Mongol influence did little to change women's role in the family. Turks and Mongols arriving in the Middle East adopted the preexisting local practices and eventually assimilated to their new environment.

During the Ottoman period (1453–1924), women remained in the confines of their household and family. Family life provided women with protection, economic stability, and companionship. Therefore, marriage remained a woman's best option for a successful future. The state also incentivized marriage as a way to prevent social discord by providing married women with certain privileges and legal protections. Thus, marriage and family life remained women's most important rite of passage and served a greater societal function as it built networks and alliances within the community. This system marginalized those who did not marry and have children, as single women remained a threat to society. Ottoman women's experiences were also heavily dependent upon class. Poor families tried to marry their daughters to someone in a higher class. Female domestic servants and wage laborers frequently stopped working upon marriage, which brought them elevated status as wives. However, married women could not move about as they pleased and had to travel with a male relative and wear a veil in public. Scholars believe that married women of the artisan class identified with and preferred their role as wives and mothers in the home. Several women supplemented the family income by making textiles and embroidered goods while raising a family. Elite women, free of domestic duties, supervised servants and consumed luxury goods such as clothing and jewelry. They also frequented baths and supported schools with their wealth. Overall, across classes, marriage offered Ottoman women the opportunity to achieve a higher social status as a wife and mother. Upon the birth of a son, a woman's status in her marriage solidified, reducing the chances of divorce and marginalization.[21]

Parents spent considerable time and effort on their children's nuptials. Parents with a single daughter worked to find an appropriate husband and family with which to enter the marriage contract. The agreement to marry one's daughter was arranged between a woman's closest living male relative and the bridegroom, who had to pay the traditional, and often significant, dowry. Women received half of their dowry upon marriage and the other half remained for later, in the event of death or divorce. Cousin marriage, while fetching smaller dowries, allowed some women at least a modicum of familiarity with their husband-to-be if they grew up together in the same extended family. In many circumstances, new brides met their husband for the first time at their wedding. After marriage, the extended family maintained close contact with a newly married couple. After moving in with her in-laws, a newly married woman would often return to her father's home in the event of domestic conflict or other problems in the marital home. In times of significant domestic conflict, heading toward divorce, the married couple's families would step in to resolve the issue for the couple. Divorce was the least desirable outcome because it broke alliances and the economic and social investments associated with the union. A woman frequently rejoined her birth family when she divorced or when her spouse died. Her children, however, would often remain with her husband's family.

A woman's chastity before marriage and fidelity afterward were a direct reflection of her male relatives' honor. Even the perception of inappropriate behavior could have devastating consequences for a woman and her family. A woman's ability to threaten the social order was not uniform throughout all stages of life. Rather, small female children were not as repressed and scrutinized as young girls who reached puberty. At the onset of puberty, a girl's male relatives grew ever more vigilant about her whereabouts and contact with the opposite sex. Conversely, postmenopausal women enjoyed increased autonomy because they were no longer a threat to the family's honor. Efforts to maintain the social order and to ease the financial burden on families with young daughters meant that many women were betrothed while still children, even before the onset of menstruation. In this situation, prepubescent girls often did not have to consummate the union before the onset of their first menstrual cycle, even if the young bride moved into her husband's home immediately following the wedding. Because men had to pay a significant dowry upon marriage, men were often much older than their new brides, as it took some time to accumulate the wealth necessary to wed.

Society incentivized marriage as part of the rite of passage from daughter to a higher position as wife and mother. Mothers-in-law, in particular, garnered more power and influence in the family since they controlled their sons' wives in the home. While women remained subordinate to men, being a wife and mother freed women from the watchful eyes of their male relatives. However, marriage did not grant women complete freedom. Most new brides were at the mercy of their husband's mother, who could be excessively controlling and domineering. Women's only chance to achieve a slightly elevated status in the marital home was to have male heirs. Male children remained socially desirable, as they were the best insurance that parents would have someone to look after them. Female children were considered an asset since they helped with housework. Although boys were favored, girls also bore responsibility for their parents' welfare. If a woman with daughters lost her husband, her daughters had to look after her. While a widow had a good chance of remarrying, she commanded a smaller dowry. This made marrying a widow an attractive option for men with little means.

At the dawn of modern times, women faced persistent social pressure to focus on the family and remain secluded from male strangers. After World War I, some restrictions on women were lifted as they became an important part of the labor force in certain places like Turkey. Despite some new roles in society, most communities still viewed a family's honor as contingent upon the behavior of its female members. Women who chose to work outside the home could dishonor their family. As a result, in some places, women remained physically separated from men who were not blood relatives. Even as modern states formed and gave rise to urban areas, some women refrained from engaging in public activities, such as going to court, because it would put them in contact with male strangers. Hesitancy to engage in public places jeopardized women's religiously sanctioned rights to inheritance, which was most women's only source of income. While lower class women generally had more freedom of movement, wealthy women who did not have domestic responsibilities remained secluded in their homes. Servants, who could go out in public, enabled elite women to remain out of public view. Some wealthy women found ways to support charitable organizations like mosques, orphanages, or schools while remaining largely secluded. Many of these same cultural norms and practices continued into the 19th and 20th centuries, but the forces of globalization and its implications caused profound changes in many Middle Eastern families.

WORLD WAR I AND ITS AFTERMATH

In modern times, the family remains the most important social unit in the Middle East and women remain at the center of family life across the region. Familial relations dictate the manner with which people arrange themselves in relation to one another, whether they live in rural or urban environments. Most Middle Eastern states start with the assumption of a family characterized by a patriarchal structure with men fulfilling the role of the breadwinner and women serving as the homemaker and mother for the children. This structure, however, has been challenged by several factors, including women's role in the workforce. During crisis and conflict, the family is the only constant, especially when rulers lack the capacity to provide public goods. Family members provide one another with social, emotional, spiritual, financial, and even political support.

In general, each member of the modern Middle Eastern family has specific roles and responsibilities within the family unit. The early socialization of children in the Arab world falls entirely into the female domain. Mothers have almost sole responsibility for their care, education, and socialization. In Muslim families, the mother socializes the children and raises committed Muslims, while the father provides financial support for the family.[22] Most Middle Eastern boys and girls are socialized differently, reflecting society's beliefs about the role that each should play in the community as they mature. Although girls remain with their mothers, boys begin to separate after age five.[23] Upon the birth of a son and his circumcision, the family celebrates with a joyous event for which there is no commensurate celebration for the birth of a girl. Communities often take pity upon women who never have a son, and women who have sons receive the honorific title of Umm. Again, these social structures reflect societal pressure and incentives for women to focus on marriage and the family. Although family structures vary across different regions and socioeconomic classes, a few generalizations apply. In rural and village areas, girls as young as six or seven are required to do domestic chores such as cooking, cleaning, and caring for younger siblings. Girls are also usually required to obey their brothers, even younger ones, in preparation for married life. This applies in extended families as well.

For example, younger male cousins have authority over their elder female cousins. Many modern societies practice strict gender segregation both in and out of the home. Male guests in a home frequently socialize and eat with the men while women and girls dine in a separate room. Young boys remain with their fathers, and normally the least eligible woman serves the men. Boys receive fewer demands on their time, such as chores and house-work, while girls are expected to help their mothers. In rural areas boys work in agriculture, with animals, or learn a particular skill.

Societal culture and traditions have an important role in shaping individ-ual family members' relationships to one another. Boys and their mothers often have a very close relationship because she is one of the only women with whom they can show any affection. Mothers often favor their sons and indulge their desires.[24] This could be because fathers, husbands, and sons are responsible for protecting and supporting their daughters, wives, and mothers. This belief that male family members have the responsibility for women's welfare, inculcated in male children from a young age, ap-plies throughout the extended family. If a woman gets divorced, she usually returns to her father's or brother's home. However, more recently, these traditional arrangements have been changing. In the era of wage labor and increasing employment options, the number of female-headed households is growing. Currently, some upper class and professional women live on their own, without the supervision of a male relative. In addition, with grow-ing female employment, some men might take on more parental care than previously expected if other childcare options are not available. Another force of change associated with wage labor is that some men and women work far from home. When men work abroad, women assume responsibil-ity as head of the household. Whereas the extended family is prevalent in traditional economic settings, urbanization is more conducive to nuclear families due to space restrictions within increasingly crowded cities. This trend toward urbanization and shrinking families is evident throughout Middle Eastern history.

Although a patriarch is the sole authority in his private life, in the public sphere he must share this power with other patriarchs. While women might exert influence over their husbands or fathers through informal power, they almost never have real private or public authority.[25] Throughout the Middle East, the family is still the axis of society in political, economic, social, and religious terms. As such, families provide one another with access to mate-rial goods, institutions, jobs, and government services. Therefore, in the public sector, worker recruitment and discipline, wages, and benefits often reflect kinship ties. Several Arab states' national constitutions enshrine the privileged position of the family.[26] The following country studies will fur-ther explore women's roles in the family throughout the Middle East and North Africa in the modern era.

TURKEY

Women's experiences in Turkey, while similar to that of women across the Middle East, are also unique in many ways due to rapid change associated with government intervention into the lives of Turkish families. From early times, evidence suggests that women fulfilled significant roles in the public sphere in certain regions. Women in the Anatolian cities of Bursa and Kayseri during the 17th century did not appear to fit the stereotype of the Muslim women, relegated to the harem with a very small role in society. Some women actively participated in the economy, even investing in real estate. In addition, according to records of those who died listing family members, out of around 2,000 estates, only 20 men listed two or more wives.[27] However, in western Anatolia, prior to the 20th century, the household was the main unit of production and consumption with little or no intervention from the state. The patriarchal system was fully in place with the father as the dominant head of household and all women subservient to the males in the family. In 1917, a slight change emerged when the Young Turks enacted a family law that remained the policy until 1926 and gave women some rights in marriage. This law changed when Mustafa Ataturk, the founder of modern Turkey, adopted a more radical approach to gender equality in 1926. His policy was adapted from the Swiss Civil Code and granted women equal rights in divorce and child custody. Despite these secular reforms, people did not automatically embrace Ataturk's policies. In the rural sectors of Turkey, including both Turkish and Kurdish regions, people clung to their old traditions regarding gender. Some rejected a new law requiring civil marriages and in many places, practices such as underage marriage continued.[28] Resistance to change occurred in other places, but eventually more egalitarian laws, reforms, and protections gained some degree of public acceptance.

In Turkey, political, religious, and cultural factors shaped women's role in the family. Family patterns were affected by emigration and urbanization. Turkey's population has been historically diverse as home to Kurds, Greek Orthodox Christians, and Jews. These minorities often conform to their own family patterns, making Turkey an interesting place to examine women's roles in the family. The foundation of the Turkish Republic in 1923 and the subsequent establishment of a secular state had a profound impact on familial relations because it gave women unprecedented individual rights. The legal reforms allowed women to vote, outlawed polygamy, and took away men's right to unilateral divorce. In some cases, when a woman's husband dies, she will move in with her adult children or marry her husband's brother, often as a second wife. Turkey experienced rapid development and urbanization beginning in the 1950s, which also fostered new family patterns.

In Turkish families, women serve in traditional roles as mothers and wives. Although some Turkish extended families live together, historically there has always been a tendency in favor the nuclear family. This is due to urban migration placing people in areas that are not conducive to extended family cohabitation. However, even in bustling urban areas, kinship ties remain strong. Often, when people move to the city, they follow and depend upon the support of relatives, friends, and neighbors from the same rural village. Communities comprised of people with kinship ties find it especially important to protect women and their honor in urban settings. Nevertheless, despite efforts to supervise women living in cities closely, the availability of education and employment opportunities drastically altered women's role in the family.[29] As women gained access to employment and opportunities to socialize outside of the home, traditional expectations shifted. Women with more responsibility outside the home gained more power within the home. However, not all of these developments were positive or beneficial for women. During times of economic instability, women lost their jobs before men. Although the modern Turkish state brought compulsory education to all, men retained access to opportunities for advancement. For families dependent on a woman's income, the loss of a job destabilized the home. Despite rapid industrialization and urbanization, tribes and communal groups in eastern Turkey retained characteristics of classical patriarchy whereby tribal identity is based upon notions of common patrilineal descent. Therefore, in eastern Turkish tribes, property and women were controlled tightly through interrelated lineages. Close tribal bonds fostered unity, integration, and cooperation, leading many to believe that control over women is the key to maintaining control over property.

Turkish families provide individuals with social welfare, employment, protection, and other things that the government might not guarantee. As such families and kinship ties are people's main source of social protection, and this structure shapes family patterns. Since parents depend on their children for social welfare, they prefer their children marry someone with commensurate or higher social, educational, and economic status. Therefore, arranged marriages are prevalent. Recently, more couples have been marrying for love, although these cases are limited to the younger and more affluent communities in urban areas. In rural and poor urban communities, arranged marriages remain common. In Turkey, marriage is an agreement between two families or communities necessitating a third party or matchmaker to negotiate payment from the groom's family to the bride's family. The third party serves as a mechanism to protect both families' honor if negotiations break down. Interestingly, Turkey has had instances when the groom or his family "steals" the bride, often with the bride's consent. This marriage pattern occurs when negotiations are not progressing. Cousin

Kurdish girl eats as she is held by her grandmother in the Turkish Cukurca Township near the Iraqi border, 1991. (AP Photo/Burhan Ozbilici)

marriage is also widely accepted in Turkey and serves as a way to keep resources within the family.[30]

Once married, people expect women to have children, and their failure to conceive can result in divorce, as children are highly valued in the Turkish culture. Parental preference for male descendents is the norm in Turkey, as in most of the region. Sons remain in the family, carry on the family name, and have more opportunities for education and employment with which to care for aging parents. Because of the strong social pressure on women to marry and have children, few women have children out of wedlock. A study from 1998 suggested that only 1 percent of children were born to unmarried women. Despite these pressures on women to assume traditional roles in the family, fertility rates have fallen from 6.2 children per mother in the 1960s to 2.5 40 years later. Eastern and more rural areas have higher fertility rates than urban areas.[31]

Women in Turkey are responsible for the socialization of their children. Parents raise children to be obedient, loyal, and grateful.[32] Studies show that Turkish mothers, in particular, exhibit overprotective behavior when children are young, which transitions to more authoritative, controlling behavior during a child's adolescent years. Most Turkish children can freely express affection for their mothers while some fathers remain a distant authority figure in their children's lives. Mothers, who are closer to their children due to their day-to-day contact with them, often mediate when there is conflict between children and their fathers. In Turkey, power and authority in the family belongs to older men. However, as access to education and employment outside the home increases, women are participating more in familial decisions. Women also have more authority in families if the marriage was result of a romantic relationship, rather than an arranged agreement between two families. Similarly, when a woman works outside the home, she has more power to negotiate for how her income is spent. Despite women's increasing authority in family matters, elderly women are often completely dependent upon their offspring, which again, explains why male children remain desirable.[33]

Clearly, the Turkish economy, society, and culture are undergoing transitions that will continue to shape women's role in the family. While change is uneven throughout the state, some overall trends are worth mentioning. Women are having fewer children as families focus their attention on the quality of their offspring's upbringing, including education and employment opportunities at home and abroad. Today, more than 3 million Turks live abroad, impacting the family structure. Still, traditional expectations of women to marry and have children endure, along with an aversion to divorce, which is perceived as a separation of two communities, not just individuals.[34]

SAUDI ARABIA

As the birthplace of Muhammad and the location of two of Muslim's most holy sites, Islam is the defining factor for the nation of Saudi Arabia. What was once a land of impoverished Bedouins before the rise of Islam is now, with the advent of oil, a rich and modern state with many challenges and opportunities for women. In Saudi Arabia, retaining its Islamic identity is crucial, yet societal pressures are mounting to address women's issues.[35] In the Saudi Arabian family, a woman's status is contingent upon her ability to marry and reproduce. Saudi wives and mothers are primarily responsible for maintaining the family and providing the next generation with informal education. Like other states in the region, family honor is dependent upon a woman's actions and her public behavior. While traditional roles for women in the family endure, external pressures are changing Saudi family patterns. For example, after the Gulf War in 1991, with some prodding by the United States, a discussion ensued about the role of women in the Middle East. While international organizations are working to empower women through various initiatives and outreach programs, Islamist movements focus on ways to limit women's role in society to the family.

As in most Arab families, Saudi fathers are the dominant power figure and final decision-maker. Although women are entitled to certain rights and privileges under Islam, in Saudi Arabia, older men determine women's entitlements in the family.[36] While men provide economic support for the family, women are responsible for raising children and managing the household. Female children stay in their parental home until they are married. Saudi parents often arrange marriage as part of an agreement between the groom and the bride's father. Some Saudi women will not meet their husband prior to marriage. However, other women participate in their mate selection and in some circumstances, Saudi women can add specific terms to their marriage contract. Divorce occurs in the kingdom, but it carries a social stigma and women who divorce often lose their children in the process.[37]

While the extended family remains the norm in Saudi Arabia, with an increase in women's education and growing social mobility, nuclear families are becoming more common. In nuclear families, women who were traditionally subordinate to their mothers-in-law are enjoying the newfound independence associated with living in their own marital home and having access to wealth and resources. Additionally, much like other states across the region, women in the workforce are having fewer children and at a later age. Elite women, especially members of the royal family, employ several domestic servants in their homes and thus enjoy significant assistance in their role as the caretakers of home and family. Saudi women's specific role in the family largely depends on class and region. In urban settings, women have more options, whereas women who live in rural areas are restricted to their patriarchal family environments. Still, despite the location and social class in the kingdom, women's role in the family is primarily as a wife and mother. As is the case across the region, children belong to the husband's family and as a result, men normally win custody upon divorce. Even though men have the ultimate power in Saudi families, women maintain the family by producing, educating, and socializing the next generation.

Despite the fact that more women are entering the workforce in Saudi Arabia, historically, men control women's ability to work, travel, drive, and even obtain a government-issued identification card. Women cannot vote, must seek permission from a male to leave the country, and religious police enforce wearing of the veil. However, in February 2009 King Abdullah appointed a woman to a key governmental position overseeing female education. For many, this appointment signaled the king's support of working women, even if they are forbidden to drive or go out unveiled. While Saudi women live in a gender-segregated and unequal society, some conditions have improved. Now, women are allowed to study law, stay at hotels alone, and in some cases, obtain their own identification cards.[38] As women acquire new roles outside the home, some fear that the changes threaten the stability of the entire social system. Change is already taking place across the country as globalization creates new opportunities for women to assume more public roles. Access to significant wealth is also changing family patterns. Affluent extended families live separately as they have the means to do so. This precludes mothers-in-law from supervising their daughters-in-law and allows married couples more privacy.

External events have also had implications for the family. During the 1991 Gulf War, the Saudi government, realizing that it had an untapped labor pool, allowed women to serve as civil defense workers. As discussed in the chapter on women and work, studies show that female wage earners have fewer children and marry at a later age if they are educated and working in the public sector.[39] Despite the availability of new opportunities for women, few nongovernmental women's groups are active in Saudi Arabia. Only charitable groups focused on helping disabled or handicapped work openly in the kingdom.

Despite these restrictions on women's activities outside of the home, globalization and its implications are influencing women and shaping new roles in the family. With the influence of the Internet, women are enjoying access to information and communication with one another, and with the outside world. New forms of communication and information sharing challenge traditional social structures.[40] The Internet is certainly changing the way men and women communicate in Saudi Arabia. Traditionally, parents arrange meetings between men and women, but now the Internet provides an unsupervised space for online dating, networking, and communication. After marriage, women use the Internet and satellite television programming as an additional resource outside of the extended family network for advice and information. Women of all ages can experience new cultures and ideas without leaving home. This is an important change because women are no longer limited to their relatives for socialization and education. Although the Committee for Promotion of Virtue and Prevention of Vice (religious police) try to stop what they consider inappropriate online behavior, Saudi men and women are "virtually" communicating and "meeting" without their parents' consent. Increasing access to new technologies will continue to challenge the traditional structures that limit contact between men and women.

Urbanization, industrialization, and women's education have caused a conservative backlash in the form of Islamist movements.[41] Given the changes and development in the region, especially near bustling economic centers like Dubai and Bahrain, the Saudi royal family is pursuing efforts to make Saudi Arabia economically attractive for investment, travel, and even tourism. A recent effort to attract investment includes plans for multi-million dollar real estate projects with brochures showing women in shorts participating in leisure activities such as golf, something that goes against conservative traditions in Saudi Arabia. Nevertheless, the struggle to keep pace with development comes amidst ever-growing concern over Islamic extremism and an upsurge in unemployed young men who, like their female counterparts, would enjoy opportunities to prosper economically in this conservative state. Most arguments against development and more liberal policies toward women focus on the ramifications such changes will have on the family, widely considered to be the foundation of the social order.

The influence of globalization and the role of women is one of the most important issues for the ruling family to address in the future. King Abdullah recently stated that, in order to keep pace with modernization, "we will enlist the efforts of all sincere workers, men and women. All that will be done incrementally and moderately." Women will undoubtedly play a role in the future of Saudi Arabia, where unemployment reaches approximately 90 percent for women and where some 40 percent of the population is under the age of 15.[42] King Faisal, who ruled from 1964–1975, instituted revolutionary policies toward women, including opening the first government school for girls in 1964. This act enabled women's literacy to jump from 2 percent in 1964 to 70 percent by 1970. Currently, women's colleges are exposing Saudi women to English classes, the Internet, and to international films in a state where movies theaters were once banned. The education and employment of Saudi women will certainly influence the family unit, whether it manifests itself in lower birth rates, smaller families, or more informed wives and mothers. Furthermore, women have more opportunities to travel and exchange ideas; this interaction might shift family patterns and societal expectations of women.[43]

NORTH AFRICA

Upon independence from their French colonial rulers, the North African states emerged with different policies shaping women's role in the family as they went through the difficult transition from colonies to nation-states. Part of the transition consisted of incorporating various ethnic, tribal, religious, and linguistic identities into newly independent nations. In North Africa, as in other places in the Middle East region, kin groupings survived as the basic unit of society until independence. North African women were controlled and secluded from outsiders to keep them and their offspring within the kin group. Cousin marriage was prevalent, but when women married outside the kin group, the union served as way to establish key alliances with others. This method of maintaining community cohesion by controlling women changed after independence, when states set forth new legal parameters for gender relations.

As Morocco, Tunisia, and Algeria formed, women's roles in the family came under the influence of new laws governing gender relations and prevailing Islamic beliefs. Overall, women in North Africa were subordinate to men, who made many key decisions on their behalf. Much like other schools of Islamic law, Maleki law, followed in much of North Africa, privileged men by giving them the unilateral right to divorce and control over their marriages. A woman's legal guardian needed to approve her marriage. Morocco and Tunisia gained independence in 1956 and established codes of personal conduct that eventually altered women's role in the family. New requirements stipulated that a man needed two witnesses if he chose to repudiate and divorce his wife. Algeria struggled to codify family laws, and, as a result, internal political struggles between liberal and conservative lawmakers produced few changes. For some 22 years, Algeria lacked an overarching family law to guide gender relations. Finally, in 1984, a family law emerged that reconfirmed most of the Maleki laws with minor exceptions. If a man dies, children are automatically put under their mother's guardianship. Recently, the rise of Islamist extremists who target women in Algeria have put pressure on the state to deal with internal conflicts between liberal and conservative groups. Tunisia experienced the most radical changes to women's legal status compared to Algeria and Morocco, and these changes have had a profound impact upon women's role in the family. Overall, Tunisia's dramatic reforms weakened the patrilineal structure of society while empowering the conjugal unit. Women have gained more control of their lives, and this shapes their role in the family. In Tunisia, where pre-colonial structures are breaking down, progressive laws offer women more choices and opportunities than ever before.[44]

In rural Morocco, women's most important economic activities go on in her household.[45] Unlike urban women, those who live in remote villages focus on their household duties and raising children. As such, women depend on their fathers or husbands to deal with all matters outside of the home. Marriage is so prevalent that there are few single men living without women in their homes in rural Morocco. Often if a married woman dies, a female relative moves into the deceased's home to assume the household responsibilities. Alternatively, a widower might seek a speedy remarriage to fill the void in his home. Women between the age of puberty and menopause generally do not interact with men outside of their family in rural settings. If a male non-family member comes to the door of a home with only women present, he will wait outside until there is a man in the house. Women seldom venture out of the home, but when they do, they do not make eye contact with male strangers. In rural Morocco, looking a man in the eye, especially if a woman is of age to marry, can be taken as an open invitation to a sexual encounter. At most, some women might flirt with men by stealing a quick glance. As in most countries across the region, when non-kin males are invited to eat dinner in a friend's family home, women will eat in a separate room.[46]

Typically, relations between women and their mothers, sisters, and daughters are close since they work together to support the family, but tensions might arise from competition and conflict associated with living in such close proximity. Women have contact with other women outside of the home, usually seeing distant relatives and neighbors for special events or if someone is ill. Rural women in Morocco bear all of the responsibility of raising children and socializing them in the values and traditions of the family. When Moroccan women marry, they leave their homes and their families to live with their spouse, who is often a stranger. Newly married brides may find it difficult and lonely to embark upon life without their normal support network. Women are often closer to their children than to their husbands, especially early in marriage. Mothers-in-law are considered role models for new brides, treating new brides harshly, supervising their housework, and perhaps exacting retribution for how they themselves were treated. Daughters-in-law must endure criticism in an effort to prove their worth to the household. New brides usually only see their husbands in the evening and are often subject to marginalization from other women in the family. It is not until a woman has children, that she asserts herself in the family and, in time, proves herself to her husband's family. Eventually, a woman's relationship with her husband can become more egalitarian as she establishes her position as the woman of the house. As women go through menopause, they are no longer threats to the family's honor and therefore gain further security in their position in the family. Because of this, post-menopausal women can even interact with men outside of the home in certain circumstances.

A woman's status in rural Morocco is not necessarily fixed or tied to her husband's status in society. Even in the most rural parts of Morocco, a woman's status is dynamic. For instance, a woman's standing is shaped by her position in the lifecycle. While new brides are expected to be shy and quiet, post-menopausal women are allowed to interact with men and speak their minds. A woman who has a son has a higher status than a childless new bride. Women can also achieve prestige through personal achievement, such as having enviable character or morality or having excellent verbal skills. Women respect others who are thrifty with their household budget and those who keep their family's honor pure by never interacting with men outside of the home. Women also strive to keep family gossip and other personal affairs inside the home. Therefore, they can directly influence their status despite the assumption that their position is tied to their husband's wealth, employment, or position in the clergy. Maintaining the honor of young women in the family is of particular importance in the region and throughout the Middle East because a young woman can easily discredit and bring shame upon the whole family by becoming pregnant out of wedlock or by having an extramarital affair.[47]

Moroccans value males because only sons carry on the family name and assume responsibility for their parents. On the other hand, daughters leave the family after marriage and must support their own families. Furthermore, daughters can also easily damage the family honor; hence they are less desirable than male heirs. It follows then that male babies are preferred and celebrated more than female babies in Moroccan villages. Up until age two, males and females are treated similarly, remaining close to their mothers who supervise their toddlers and see to their needs. Boys and girls dress identically until early childhood when treatment and rearing diverges based on gender. At an early age, boys and girls are taught *hsim*, a concept meaning knowing or showing shame. Both boys and girls are expected to behave, but with girls, mothers emphasize patience and modesty, while boys do not have to exhibit bodily modesty.[48]

Recent changes to Morocco's family laws are changing women's traditional role in the family. Morocco's personal status code, which was pushed by a decade of pressure from progressive nongovernmental organizations, increased the legal marriage age for women from 15 to 18. Furthermore, polygamy was abolished. Now, women have equal rights to divorce and have certain custody rights to their children. Interestingly, these changes were based on religious principles, as the modernizing King Mohammed VI used Islamic jurisprudence to support these new Moroccan family laws. This is an example of the modern use of Islamic justifications for gender equality that will have ramifications in families and family life throughout the Middle East and North Africa.[49]

Algeria conforms to the traditional public/private sphere separating the sexes in society. Generally, men tend to affairs outside the home, while women maintain the family and focus on domestic matters. Crossing these boundaries has been problematic in some parts of the country, as Algerian women's efforts to break into the public sphere have met with resistance. For instance, Algerian women who choose to venture outside the home to go to school or to work in a factory are often perceived as intruders into masculine space. Those who disapprove of women assuming public roles in society proved willing to use violence against working women. In general, the victims of such attacks have been factory workers who tend to be young and unmarried due to the societal expectation that women will stop working upon marriage. Women in the workplace are often secluded, reflecting a societal preference for gender segregation. The Islamist movement, which grew during the 1980s and 1990s, supported women's subordination and took steps to limit women's access to the public sphere, something that the movement's leaders view as a threat to the social order.

Overall, the traditional view that women's activity should be limited to their role in the family endures in Algeria and opportunities for women to enter into the public sphere have been problematic. Some Islamist groups resort to violence when they perceive women's intrusion into the traditionally male public sphere. A group called Women Living under Muslim Laws opposes a harsh interpretation of sharia law in Algeria. This group provides information on international progressive Islamic systems for local activists who are fighting for greater freedoms.[50]

After gaining independence from France in 1956, Tunisia quickly transitioned from one that was primarily rural and agricultural to an urban industrial economy. With more than half the population living in the capital city, Tunis, women's roles in the family have been influenced by the larger changes occurring in Tunisia. Although Tunisia follows the traditional family structure of the region, economic opportunities and the adoption of a liberal personal status code grants women more rights and protections than their counterparts in most North African or Middle Eastern countries. Despite the socioeconomic development and liberal laws in Tunisia, women experience typical rites of passage associated with their role in the family. Many Tunisian women remain in their home until they marry and then move into their husband's home. Like in other states mentioned in this chapter, Tunisian women who marry a relative, though not necessarily a paternal cousin, command a lower dower price. If women work outside of the home after marriage, it is considered shameful and a sign that the husband cannot afford to seclude or support his women. While some single women live by themselves, it is still not socially acceptable. However, in urban centers like Tunis, the number of women living on their own is growing.

In Tunisia, and Tunis more specifically, women have an active and vibrant life outside their home among a network of family and friends. Women often visit one another to exchange gifts and news in order to maintain social ties and relationships. For Tunisian families, social networking provides insurance against economic and personal calamities as well as a venue for emotional and practical support, including access to jobs, goods, and information.[51] Therefore, while continuous visits to family and friends have a social function, networking in one's community actually provides families with future economic or emotional backing. While traditional family patterns endure, Tunisian women with access to economic and other opportunities will undoubtedly experience changes in the coming years.

LEBANON

In Lebanon, family is the basic unit of society. This is especially true in south Lebanon, an area that bears the brunt of the conflict with its neighbor, Israel. In times of stress and instability, the family replaces collapsed or inadequate governmental structures by providing key resources like food, work, and shelter. A mother's role in the family can extend beyond her immediate family into society, rendering women key figures in times of hardship. In some instances, civil war and deteriorating economic conditions allow women to evade patriarchal structures, granting them positions as agents of social change. This is due, in part, to the recognition of women's role in the socialization of children in Lebanon. As mothers, women in Lebanon produce and raise those who fight on behalf of the nation, thereby affording women a symbolic and nationalistic role in society. However, in their respective communities, women lack the commensurate position and status of men who retain both the symbolic and actual authority and decision-making power at all levels of society.[52] This phenomenon, though not unique to south Lebanon, exposes some of the challenges and opportunities for women and their role in the family amidst conditions of crisis and political instability.

Clearly, women's role in their families as wives and mothers is of the utmost importance in the South. Women provide resources and even social networks for the family and for the boys they raise. There is also a sense of duty in motherhood, and this idea extends beyond the home to the Muslim community worldwide. In this sense, motherhood goes beyond caring for the physical needs of the family and children by expanding into the spiritual and educational realm. One proverb clearly exemplifies this view and the role of women in society: "The woman who rocks the cradle with her right [hand] rocks the world with her left."[53]

Traditional family patterns endure in Lebanon, where men make major decisions on behalf of their female family members. As such, a woman's relationship with her father determines how she will live her life. Whether she has to wear a hijab (head scarf), study, or leave the home is largely her father's decision. The choice to marry is often a result of a negotiation between a woman's father and the groom's family. Morality and chastity are valued and expected of honorable women. Despite the availability of work outside the home and increasing levels of female participation in civic and political groups, society still values motherhood as the ultimate role of Lebanese women. While some women have achieved new levels of financial and other types of independence, nonconformist women risk marginalization for failing to adhere to certain societal expectations.

Some view the central role of the mother in Lebanese society as what differentiates them from the Western world. Women are seen as the bulwark against Westernizing trends for their central role in perpetuating traditions and moral values in the family. Families assume even more importance in times of crisis and volatility, when kinship provides people with access to key resources. The important role for women in Lebanese families is not limited to the Muslim community. Christian communities also value the

Syrian woman looks at mugs imprinted with pictures of Syrian President Bashar Assad and Hezbollah leader Sheik Hassan Nasrallah, at a gift shop in Damascus, 2009. (AP Photo/ Ola Rifai)

role that women play in families as wives and mothers, with special emphasis on the relationship between a mother and her son.[54]

In Lebanon, the Party of God, or Hizbullah, a Shia Islamist party, discusses its perception of women's role in family life and society. The organization states that women have complete freedom to work as a partner to a man, but they should not be on the front lines of the fight against enemies. Rather, women should be caretakers and in this role provide things such as medical and nutritional aid. This view characterizes the overarching "mothering" role assigned to women in Lebanon. Hizbullah even supports working women, as long as their employment does not interfere with familial duties. In some places, women whose dress symbolizes an affiliation with Hizbullah can walk the streets and interact with men without fear of being reprimanded.[55] Therefore, in some parts of Lebanon it is completely acceptable for women to be wage earners, with their primary loyalty to the home. As such, some women in Lebanon have complementary, yet different, roles in society and in the family.

KUWAIT

Much like other states in the Middle East, economic and social changes in Kuwait have had a dramatic influence on women's roles in the family.

In Kuwait, there is a significant disparity between rural Bedouin women who live in the desert and those who live in bustling urban areas like Kuwait City. As expected, urban families favor the nuclear formation over the traditional extended family formation and living arrangement. Despite this division, nuclear families behave like extended families, supporting one another even though they may not live under the same roof. Before the discovery of oil in Kuwait in the 1930s, some women raised their children and cared for their home on their own while their husbands worked abroad. Given Kuwait's geographic location, its main sources of employment used to entail harvesting pearls from the Gulf waters, shipbuilding, and other types of trade. However, the discovery of oil forged dramatic socioeconomic changes in what was once a very traditional society. After gaining independence in 1961 and the subsequent growth in the petroleum industry, Kuwait's economy skyrocketed. As a result, Kuwaiti women whose families reaped rewards from the petroleum industry's growth witnessed significant socioeconomic development and unprecedented access to the outside world in a short amount of time. Specifically, women gained access to educational opportunities. Kuwaiti women benefited from elementary through college level programs with the establishment of Kuwait University in 1966. Women also gained access to employment while simultaneously hiring domestic help.[56]

An influx of economic resources and development ushered in social change shaping women's role in the family. Kuwaiti women received an array of government benefits, including health, education, housing, and social services. As a result, women's role in the public sphere is also expanding. Kuwaiti women lead public and private organizations, taking advantage of opportunities to participate in activities outside the home. These factors are changing family patterns in Kuwaiti society. Prior to the infusion of oil wealth and infrastructure in Kuwait, fathers served as the heads of Kuwaiti households while women raised children and cared for the home. Currently, domestic servants, who typically come from South Asia, perform household chores in Kuwaiti homes. With domestic workers in their homes, Kuwaiti women regularly go out in public frequenting shopping malls and restaurants, especially in Kuwait City and other urban areas. At one point, the influx of immigrant workers outnumbered the Kuwaiti population. After the Gulf War, the Kuwaiti government worked to curb the inflow of foreign workers by providing economic incentives for women to have more children.[57]

Earlier in Kuwait's history, women followed traditional marriage and family patterns. Kuwaiti women typically married a member of their extended family, normally a parallel cousin. While Bedouin women mostly married within the same clan or tribe, urban women married men with commensurate socioeconomic status. In both cases, the potential spouse had to be thoroughly vetted by the male elders in the woman's family. However, these general guidelines are changing. Women are increasingly choosing their own marriage partners, although a woman's family retains authority in this area. In some cases, if two people are interested in one another, older women from the man's family will visit the woman and her family. If the older women approve of the bride-to-be, they will notify the male elders who serve as the final approval authority. While Kuwaiti women can weigh in on their mate selection, divorce rates are increasing. This is due, in part, to a lessening of the social stigma associated with divorce and women's ability to support themselves after a separation.[58] As is the case in other Islamic states, women experiencing divorce must remain in their husband's home for three months to encourage reconciliation and to ensure that she is not pregnant.

Kuwaiti women play an important role in the socialization of their children, and while some are employed, they remain the primary source of informal education for their families. Moreover, women transmit important cultural traditions to their sons and daughters. As they grow, children assume more responsibilities that correspond with their age and gender. Young male children are encouraged to serve as protectors of their siblings and help their father with his domestic and external duties. Young female children are encouraged to be the source of love and emotional support in the family while often assuming responsibility for certain household chores. Both men and women have opportunities to pursue education and employment outside of the home in Kuwait. Access to these resources will certainly influence family patterns in the future.

IRAN

Iranian women's marital and family status remain the most crucial aspects of their social identity, despite their increasing presence and success in the workforce and in institutions of higher learning. Families in Iran provide one another with a lifetime of emotional, financial, cultural, and religious support. As such, kin relationships are critical for individuals, especially on the male's side of the family. While families are shifting away from extended patterns to more nuclear formations, parents and children maintain strong emotional relationships and attachments to one another. This emphasis on the family means that a woman's role as wife and mother is of utmost importance, and it begins with her marriage and entry into her husband's family. In conservative regions, marriage is a woman's only option to fulfill her obligation to her own family. In Iranian society, remaining single is socially unacceptable and imposes economic hardship on a woman's family. Unmarried women bear a social stigma, and single women over the age of 20 are referred to as having "gone sour." While women are no longer having huge families, an infertile woman also suffers a stigma and may even be divorced for her inability to produce offspring. Marriage between relatives is acceptable and, in some places, encouraged in Iran.[59]

An Iranian woman's role in the family changes once she is married. After marriage, the responsibility for a woman's life transfers from her father to her husband. The husband then assumes authority for his new wife, as if she were property. With the transfer of responsibility often comes the shifting of any income the woman generates. Younger men within the family fulfill the role of custodians of the family's honor. Brothers of unmarried women constantly know where their sisters are and accompany them when they leave the house. Some women who earn wages from working outside of the home have to hand those earnings to their father or husband. While the custom of early marriage persists in Iran as an economic survival tool of the poor, it is declining. Advocacy groups concerned with early marriage believe that women who marry early may be coerced and abused. Some women who marry early have multiple pregnancies at a young age. Due to the coercive nature and health risks, there has been a worldwide effort to curb the practice of early marriage. The United Nations and other organizations associated with the human rights agenda for girls and women in the Middle East actively pursue measures to curb the practice. However, despite global efforts to raise awareness about women's issues including early marriage, there are lingering perceptions in Iranian society that too much education and too few children at an early age is detrimental to the community.

Iran has a slightly different set of family laws, norms, and traditions than other states in the Middle East. As a theocratic state that primarily follows Shia Islam, Iran allows women to marry at 13 years of age unless her guardian declares her ready at an earlier age. Obligation to family and kin group are the greatest determinant of the decision to marry in most parts of Iran. Resisting marriage, especially when it is pre-arranged between two families, is unacceptable for a betrothed Iranian girl. Women who fail to fulfill their marital obligation can bring great shame upon their family. It could even lead to bloodshed or a feud if one family promises nuptials. As mentioned in the chapter on law, unlike other states in the region, Iran allows couples to enter into temporary marriage. This form of marriage dates back centuries and was especially useful after the Iranian Revolution in 1979 as a way for men and unmarried women to be contractually married for a certain amount of time after the man pays the woman a sum of money. A temporary marriage agreement can last from 1 hour to 99 years and, once the contract is established, the couple can either stay together or part ways. The objective of temporary marriage is sexual enjoyment, while that of permanent marriage is procreation. If permanent marriage is like a sale, temporary marriage is like a lease whereby the temporary wife is simply a sexual partner and therefore precluded from the protection and social prestige of a permanent arrangement. However, children born of temporary marriage are supposed to have equal status with those born of permanent marriages. Temporary marriage can also be used for early marriage, as it gives couples the option to make their marriage permanent once they come of age. Iranians are allowed to remain temporarily married indefinitely. Some couples live together for years and never change their status to permanent marriage.[60]

Two revolutions in Iran shaped women's role in the family: the Constitutional Revolution of 1909 and the Islamic Revolution in 1979. By participating in the Constitutional Revolution, urban women assumed new public roles outside the home. Also, the Iranian state implemented programs to provide support for families in the form of social security, modern education, and new legal reforms. While these changes influenced the family, the Islamic Revolution significantly altered women's roles. Under the leadership of Ayatollah Khomeini, Islamic clerics encouraged early marriage by dropping the minimum age for girls to nine years old. In Iran, early marriages are not limited to rural or tribal areas. Some studies suggest that 53 percent of early marriages are among couples living in urban areas. Early marriage is also not indicative of a lack of education. In some parts of central Iran, where women have access to ample education opportunities, the practice of early marriage continues because patriarchal values are reinforced in conservative regions by Islamic values in the family.[61] The revolution caused other changes in the family. Polygamy was allowed, fathers retained the right to choose their daughter's husbands, unilateral divorce was permitted for men but not for women, and fathers had the sole right to custody after a divorce.[62]

Socioeconomic and religious movements in Iran have had a tremendous impact on women's role in the family. Some observers believe that education is the contributing factor increasing the age of marriage for women. Currently, around 18 percent of women are married before the age of 20.[63] Iran's growing population of unmarried youths concerns Islamic leaders who fear the moral corruption of society. As a result of this concern, some religious leaders have continued to encourage temporary marriage. However, some members of the middle class consider this practice a form of legal prostitution. While some Iranians still practice temporary marriage, it is done in secret. Despite these diverse marriage patterns, most couples in Iran are monogamous. Women's access to education, women's rights movements, and political participation all serve to limit the degree of polygamy practiced among Iranian men.

In certain regions of Iran, a dearth of economic opportunities is yet another factor shaping family patterns. Some young Iranian men without education or steady employment are postponing marriage, leaving young women to pursue their own formal education while also remaining single. This is a big problem for conservative communities in areas where woman's value is wrapped up in the concept of honor and is built around the idea of virginity and bearing children at a young age. Those opposed to an abundance of single women in a given community have linked this phenomenon to the idea of *fitna,* or moral and social disorder.[64] There has also been a backlash against women receiving higher levels of education, as some claim that it distracts women from focusing on family. Some studies document an increased incidence of violence against women by frustrated men who view unmarried women as a challenge or threat to their traditional authority. Such is the case in rural areas where women have to travel to school and are thus unsupervised during the day. Studies suggest that the backlash includes incidents of violence against women, increased suicide, and women running away from home.[65]

Looking ahead, some interesting trends emerge that will shape women's role in society and in the Iranian family. Women are waiting longer to marry and, once they do, more couples are getting divorced. In addition, women are increasingly free to choose their own spouse and to work outside of the home. These trends toward smaller, nontraditional family formations, combined with more opportunities for roles in the public sphere, will continue to influence Iranian society. Political participation is one area in which women have been particularly active. As such, women are making their voices heard among competing interest groups. In the past, and certainly in the present, family, religion, and politics form the central structures for social relationships in Iran. The interaction of these three institutions will persist to shape women's role in the family.

YEMEN

Yemen, once split between North and South, is large, poor, and experiencing few changes in women's roles in the family. In contrast to the more dynamic regions covered in this chapter, women in Yemen marry young, have more children, and have fewer rights than most other women in the region. Overall, Yemeni women are less educated, illiterate, and less likely to be employed outside of the home than most other Middle East or North African states. Women in Yemen are subject to a very conservative and patriarchal society that pressures them to conform to societal expectations. Yemeni girls marry at an early age, perhaps 13 in many places, and are denied involvement in the selection of their husband. Men can take up to four wives and have the unilateral right to divorce. However, this does not mean that women are merely pawns in a male dominated society. Yemeni women can and do take steps to affect their marriages, divorces, and family lives, however ultimate authority resides in religious courts, which usually favor men. Widows, divorcees, and girls without fathers sometimes have more freedoms when it comes to marital decisions.[66] While women have little say in their spouse selection, after marriage they can attain a slightly higher status by having sons and by using their social network to benefit the family. Women often communicate with one another to learn information about other families in their network, perhaps sharing this information to help men make decisions.

Northern Yemen, which is tribally organized, remains a place where women are mostly limited to familial roles defined by the rights and obligations of the kinship system. The public image of a woman is mostly a reflection of her place in the lifecycle and the status of her husband. Within this system men and women are strictly segregated into separate spheres, where women focus primarily on domestic duties and men focus on external affairs. While some women go to mosques, they have fairly limited access to other public places without the supervision of a male relative. Despite these limitations on their movement, women have opportunities to interact and network with female friends and family members on a regular basis. When women enjoy the company of others, it is primarily inside of someone's home. A residence is the only place where women can visit freely with other women, often while men are away from the house or at work. Women often gather to celebrate important rites of passage or just to spend the afternoon socializing. If women serve a meal, men eat first in a separate room and then women and children can eat. All women attend to household chores and care for children and animals. While women are closed off from the public sphere that men enjoy, they create their own social network. Within this network, some women can attain a certain degree of informal power by gaining access to influence over the decisions and perceptions of others in the community.

Yemeni women's limited access to the outside world is based on a long tradition of women's role in society that mandates a primary focus on family and home life. According to the Zaidi legal treatise, the main reference on all matters of Islamic law in Yemen written in the fifth century, the only stated duty of women is to allow sexual intercourse. A later amendment to the law states that women should not stay idle, but rather that they should work in the home.[67] While this view of women and their role in the family endures, recent scholarship highlights the importance of women's informal power in the family via networking and information sharing. What appears to be a simple cultural tradition of daily visits and information sharing among Yemeni women is actually the mechanism through which women gain power. They use information gleaned from social interactions to their advantage. As women share information about other members of the community, they can shape decision-making and public perceptions of these members. This important tradition of frequent visitation provides women a space independent from men's attitudes and evaluations. Hence, women have a network through which they can seek advice and feedback from other women who share the same lifestyle and responsibilities to their respective families.[68]

PALESTINIAN WOMEN IN THE WEST BANK

Several accounts of modern Palestinian women's role in the family focus on elites who fulfill roles similar to other elites in the Middle East. In many ways, it is more informative to examine women's roles in the West Bank family and in refugee camps where women must cope with significant socioeconomic challenges associated with raising a family in precarious environments of contested sovereignty. Palestinian women are in a unique situation because many lack the state support afforded to other women in the Middle East who live in independent and relatively stable, sovereign states. Therefore, many Palestinian women are completely dependent upon their families for the basic support necessary to survive. These circumstances shape family formations in the region. Due to the lack of economic opportunities, many Palestinian men leave home in search of work, fragmenting much of the traditional family structure. When men go abroad, women assume the responsibility for raising children in camps and villages, often completely dependent upon the extended family and remittances from husbands who live separate lives elsewhere. If men do not want to leave their families, some will move the family unit around the Middle East, often following work, and never fully enjoying the support associated with living near the extended family. Several observers point to the Palestinian experience in the West Bank as being one that did not improve the status of women. The argument follows that refugee camps have produced a new form of the patriarchal family that reversed improvements in the position and role of women in Palestinian communities.[69]

Family is the most important social institution in the West Bank villages and camps. There, women fulfill their traditional domestic roles as well as other positions outside the home, as needed. Palestinian society is characterized by patriarchy that gives men control over women's bodies and behaviors throughout their entire lives.[70] Families living in the West Bank, especially since the 1987 uprising against Israel, face deportations, imprisonment, injuries, death, and other hardships associated with the ongoing conflict. Due to a lack of employment opportunities in the territory, young Palestinian men often leave to work in the oil-rich Gulf States. From there, they send remittances to their families, typically to their fathers or older male relatives. If men who work abroad have families of their own, they will appoint a male guardian to look after the women and children. Women are often left with the difficult task of raising children on their own, without the

United Nations special coordinator for the Middle East, Robert H. Serry, center, visits Palestinian families a day after they were evicted from their house in the east Jerusalem neighborhood of Sheikh Jarrah, 2009. (AP Photo/Bernat Armangue)

support of a husband or steady income.[71] This is an extremely vulnerable position in a society that curtails a woman's freedom.

Conditions in the region reinforce the primacy of the family over individual wants and needs. Therefore, children learn from a very young age that the family's wellbeing and the community's perception of the family come before individual desires. Without an independent state, Palestinians depend on their families for all material and emotional support. Women fulfill an important role in the family by raising the children and seeing to the family's needs. Until age six, children are constantly with their mothers. As mothers, women transmit cultural and social norms as educators, caretakers, and role models for their daughters. Whether fathers are working abroad or not, men do not usually spend a lot of time with their children. When men return from work in the evening, many go out to socialize with friends.[72]

From a young age, Palestinian girls are subject to the authority of male family members. They learn their place in the family by observing their mother and other female relatives. Although infants receive roughly equal treatment, male children are preferred for their potential to support the family. Girls take on household responsibilities and learn from a young age that men dominate the family. Even male siblings have authority over their sisters. As young girls mature, they learn that their father or closest male relative controls every major decision in their lives. A father determines his whether his daughter will marry, work, or get an education, often leaving the daughter little to no opportunity to express her own desires. While a father officially chooses a wife for his sons, mothers participate in the selection based on their unique access to available women through social interaction with female friends. As in the case of a child's mate selection, women can informally influence marital decisions in the family. Mothers are particularly interested in their son's brides because, as mothers-in-law, women want a wife for their son who will be submissive, obedient, and, above all, physically able to have children.[73]

As children age, parents treat them differently according to their gender. By the time girls reach puberty, they are completely separated from boys. Puberty can be a particularly difficult time for girls. As their bodies change, their parents begin to restrict their movements and monitor their behavior, which can be quite oppressive. This is difficult for young women who must endure the stress of being repressed, treated differently, and scrutinized by the family. Marriage marks the most important rite of passage in the lives of Palestinian women. While Christian and Muslim marriage customs differ, most Palestinian women, regardless of religious affiliation, are expected to marry, move in with their husband or his family, and have children. Because marriage and family are viewed as the ideal states for women, divorce carries a social stigma such that many Palestinian women would rather suffer in silence than end their marriage. Despite the stigma, divorced women can remarry, but their status commands a lower dowry. Given the lack of employment in the West Bank, marrying a widow can help a man with little means find a wife.

Like puberty, marriage can also be a difficult transition for women who must assume new responsibilities and duties as required by in-laws and a new husband. Women often experience a rude awakening as their new mother-in-law piles on household duties such as cooking, cleaning, and caring for the entire family. Women often have to ask their husband or mother-in-law for permission to leave the house, money to support the household, and permission to work. Adding to the difficult transition is the dearth of knowledge most women have of their own bodies and of their expectation of sexual relations with their husbands. As if new wives were not already in the awkward position of having sex in their in-laws' home, they are also under immense pressure to have children. Failure to conceive within the first year of marriage could result in divorce.[74]

When Palestinian women have children, especially sons, their status is slightly elevated, but they remain under the control and in the service of their husband and his family. Women in rural areas come under pressure to continue to produce children. Since mothers spend most days with their children, they are their main source of affection. Meanwhile, fathers typically serve as the family disciplinarian, acting on feedback from their wives who use the threat of "telling father" as a way to keep children in line. While girls learn to be obedient to their male relatives, boys usually experience more leniency and freedom of action. As children grow older, parents continue to treat boys and girls according to their gender. In addition to caring for their own children, many women assume responsibilities for several members of her husband's family upon marriage. Women often have to care for their husband's aging or ailing family members and other people's children while their husbands are away at work. This holds true even if a woman's husband works abroad. Overall, the position of a new wife in an in-law's household leaves women in a very vulnerable position, one that women are expected to bear, without complaint, until they become mothers-in-law, assuming commensurate power and authority in the home. In Palestinian society, while joining a new household may be a difficult transition, especially in polygamous households, it is often better than the alternative of remaining single or being divorced.

IRAQ

Iraq is an interesting country study of a woman's role in the family because, while the country is patriarchal, tribal, and male-dominated like the rest of the Middle East, families in Iraq are also influenced by various state policies, warfare, and international sanctions. The consequences of these events have directly affected women and their role in the family. Historically, Iraqi families served as the basic unit of social organization and production. More recently, traditional familial structures are changing due to globalization, increased access to education and technology, and ongoing conflict in the region. Until the mid 20th century, the family supplied the necessary support for its individual members. With little state influence, Iraqi families provided basic goods for individuals, including religious education, training, socialization, job prospects, financial and emotional support, and defense. However, in the 1970s and 1980s, Iraq's economy shifted from an agricultural one to more industrial means of production, specifically with growth of the oil industry. Slowly, as the state employed more people, families lost control of the means of production and social institutions. Soon, women's traditional roles as wives and mothers were challenged because men and women left their paternal homes to find domestic and international employment. Economic opportunities and state policies eroded traditional family structures in the latter half of the 20th century.[75]

Classical Iraqi families are patriarchal and hierarchal with respect to gender and age. There is a clear distinction between men and women's spheres in Iraqi society, with men being dominant in both the public and private realms. Women are identified by their positions within the patriarchal structure, often as minors and subordinates. Things changed slightly in the 1970s as the state supported women's issues as a way to diminish tribal influence on society. Subsequent state policies with regard to women's rights, which were often uneven and contradictory, gave women some privileges that directly challenged the traditional patriarchal structure of Iraqi society. Despite state intervention, the extended family and its support of individual members endured, especially in times of crisis and instability.[76]

Like many of the aforementioned Middle Eastern states, Iraqi women face tremendous pressure to marry and have children. Marriage and fidelity are viewed as Iraqi women's main avenues for achieving recognition and acceptance in society. Furthermore, society judges a woman not on her individual educational or professional achievements, but on her husband's occupation and her roles as a wife and mother. Given these parameters, it is not surprising that single women are stigmatized for failing to fulfill their rightful role in the family. When choosing a marriage partner, families try to find a candidate of equal or higher socioeconomic or educational status. Men traditionally pay a dowry when marriage is accepted, with the first installment going to the bride or her guardian once the marriage certificate is signed. The second installment of the dowry is held in reserve and only paid if the husband files for divorce. After marriage, women identify themselves by their husband's income and socioeconomic status, regardless of their own professional achievements.

War, internal conflict, and sanctions have had a significant impact on the structure and organization of Iraqi families. In times of crisis, the Iraqi people have turned to their families for support, especially when the state failed to provide public goods or when armed conflict produced widows and orphans. For example, in the wake of the Iran-Iraq and later the Gulf War, one study estimated that some 20 percent of all Iraqi women lost their husbands. Women were then responsible for supporting their families in the absence of the traditional breadwinner. Subsequent international sanctions also challenged families' survival amidst a marked scarcity of goods and resources. State weakness only exacerbated social problems, leaving women with few support channels outside the extended family network. Nevertheless, even extended families proved unable to offer war-ravaged relatives support after the chaos of conflict and sanctions threatened the state and families' survival. Although the government provided certain programs, such as incentives for men to marry widows, Iraq's persistent involvement in international conflict has put incredible pressure on families.[77]

Given the social expectations of women to focus on the family, it stands to reason that those who fail to live up to these standards will suffer consequences. Divorcees carry such a social stigma that many Iraqi women would rather suffer an unhappy or abusive marriage than legally separate from their husbands. A divorced woman is viewed as a threat to her family's honor despite the fact that Iraqi law includes the right for a woman to seek a divorce. Some families will not let their female relatives associate with divorced women. Furthermore, it is difficult for divorced women to remarry because of the primacy Iraqi society places on virginity at marriage. Scholars argue that the stigma and vulnerability of divorced women was exacerbated when Iraq was under United Nations sanctions. Some men threatened their wives with divorce, knowing that such an act would leave the woman in an extremely vulnerable social and economic situation.

United Nations sanctions placed Iraqi families under a great deal of financial and emotional stress. Many women were already living in poverty prior to their application. Afterwards, women faced even more economic hardships as jobs and access to key resources dried up. Some Iraqi women who had aspirations to pursue outside employment and education soon found themselves forced to compromise their goals for financial security and social respectability by remaining at home. Even middle class families faced challenges associated with sanctions, and many resorted to selling their homes and moving to poorer neighborhoods. Amid the despair and insecurity during the period of sanctions, an increasingly negative attitude toward women emerged. Studies show that the economic stress on the system degraded Iraqis' ability to cope with the ramifications and resulted in increased hostility toward women.[78] The added pressure of the sanctions also undermined the support networks that families traditionally provided for one another. Some studies suggest that women who were dependent on one male breadwinner grew even more dependent and subordinate to male authority and exclusive control over resources.[79]

Despite the social, political, educational, and legal gains Iraqi women experienced in the latter half of the 20th century, war and sanctions undermined these advances. While women suffered considerably during the ongoing conflict and sanctions, those who had yet to marry also faced new challenges. The combination of war and sanctions made the difficult search for a suitable husband even more challenging for single women. In times of crisis, available men often chose to leave Iraq to find better opportunities elsewhere. A significant number of men who remained were mentally or physically disabled from years of warfare and violence. Still other men found it difficult to save up sufficient funds for a dowry. All of these circumstances led to a shift in traditional marriage and family patterns. For instance, rather than marrying someone who lived in physical proximity, many Iraqi women began to look for Iraqi husbands who lived and worked abroad as a way to escape the turmoil and financial hardships at home. Several communities reverted to more traditional practices and patriarchal views of women. The marked increase in polygamous households was due to the demographic shift in Iraqi society that left an excess of single women. Widowed and divorced women suffered social stigmas and, in some instances, discriminatory treatment.[80]

The most recent conflict in Iraq, starting with the 2003 U.S.-led invasion, also influenced familial relations and structures when foreign fighters associated with Al-Qaeda in Iraq (AQI) used marriage to form alliances, break down cultural barriers, and bond with the local Iraqi people. To acquire power and influence in Iraqi communities, key Al-Qaeda leaders started marrying into prominent Iraqi tribes. In Iraq, traditional marriage customs dictate that tribes marry their women to someone within the tribe, but in some circumstances women marry outside the tribe to cement a bond or resolve a grievance. It is rare to marry women to strangers or foreigners. Therefore, when AQI displayed open disregard for these important cultural traditions, conflict ensued. Al-Qaeda began killing sheikhs who refused to hand over their daughters in marriage, causing a revenge obligation leading to attacks on AQI. AQI's counter retaliation was intense and brutal, often resulting in the mass murder of the children of prominent sheikhs.[81] AQI's attempt to infiltrate and influence key families in Iraq pushed certain tribes to align with the U.S.-led coalition. Overall, Iraqi families have had to endure significant levels of ongoing violence, instability, and economic hardships. These challenges will certainly continue to impact Iraqi women's role in the family.

ISRAEL

Women have important roles in the Israeli family. Unlike other states in the region, Israeli women enjoy access to numerous opportunities to pursue education and employment outside of the home. However, despite generally tolerant views toward women, a woman's fertility and her functions as a wife and mother are particularly critical in Israeli society, as they are closely associated with religion, nationality, and public policy. In terms of religious beliefs, scripture tells Jews to "be fruitful and multiply," and in some sects this guidance is taken quite literally. For instance, some estimates show that, among followers of Haredi Judaism, an ultra religious group that makes up only 10 percent of the population, the average family has up to seven children.[82] Several other more traditional sub-communities in Israeli society do not practice family planning and subsequently have multiple children, an outcome perceived as natural and desirable. Despite their growing participation in the public sector, women in Israel are associated with their role in the private sphere, most specifically their responsibility for maintaining the home and family. As such, women are identified as wives and mothers despite their significant accomplishments outside the home. Still, Israel maintains egalitarian policies and societal views regarding women's opportunities to pursue education, employment, and leisure activities. Specific Israeli family dynamics range from the extremely traditional to very liberal customs and practices. Hence, a woman's experiences depend largely upon her community, religion, and family heritage in this ethnically and culturally diverse state.

Since Israel's founding in 1948, the country's population has increased six-fold. Much of this demographic change has been due to the immigration of people from all over the world. For this reason, Israeli families reflect the many cultures, traditions, and family patterns of peoples arriving from Muslim countries, North African states, the former Soviet Union, and the West. Arabs living in the state of Israel include different religious groups including Muslims, Christians, Druze, and others. Due to this diversity, a variety of family patterns and gender roles are present in Israeli families.[83]

Israel conforms to overarching trends in the greater Middle East, but is also dynamic and unique in many ways. Israel is a strong family- and child-centered society as indicated by high marriage rates, young age at marriage, high fertility, and low divorce rates. Like other countries in the Middle East, however, Israel is experiencing key changes in these realms for a variety of reasons. Israel is also a country grappling with the consequences of internal and external conflict that has shaped family patterns to some extent. The ongoing conflict and violence in the region makes the bearing and rearing of either Arab or Jewish children an important factor in the demographic makeup of the predominantly Jewish state, even though fertility rates overall have decreased over the last 25–30 years. For the Jewish population in Israel, traditional family culture is key to the survival of the nation. For many, the act of having and raising children and marrying within one's own faith group is part of a collective purpose "to ensure the continuance of the next generation of Jews."[84]

Israeli women have to cope not only with the many demands of modern life but also with the traditional expectations of women's role in the family. In Israel, family units have undergone significant change as women entered the workforce and institutions of higher learning. There is a new sense of openness to alternate family patterns, reflecting larger global trends. Like other states in the Middle East, Israel is experiencing an increase in single parent families, cohabitation, same-sex couples, and step and foster relationships that fundamentally alter women's roles in the family unit. Some 88 percent of single parent homes in Israel include single, divorced, separated, and widowed women. While these single parent households make up only 1.3 percent of the population, women leading single parent homes are educated, with over 85 percent having 12 years of schooling and being gainfully employed. Although the number of children born outside of marriage is growing, the increase is lower than rates in other Western democracies.[85] So, while family formations are changing, traditional patterns endure, as evidenced by the slower pace at which Israeli society is shifting to alternate household configurations.

Israeli families are heavily influenced by religion as it pertains to marriage and divorce. Religious courts control issues of personal status law. Although the majority of Israel's Jewish population is secular, the rabbinical courts decide most aspects of family status issues including marriage, divorce, and death. Christian and Muslims have their own courts to deal with family status issues. Rabbinical courts, however, are losing their control on family law due to an increase in non-traditional family patterns, even though the majority of young couples still participate in religious marriage. The state's support of families, motherhood, and children is evident in the ample resources allocated to incentivize growing families. For example, Israeli women who are struggling to conceive have access to significant support with fertility treatments, making Israel a leading state in fertility research and development. As a welfare state, public clinics in Israel support up to seven rounds of in vitro fertilization, a costly procedure. Israel's laws guarantee 12 weeks of paid maternity leave, child support, a prohibition on firing pregnant women, and a network of nurseries and childcare facilities smooth a woman's transition back into the workplace after childbirth. All of these initiatives and incentives ease the financial burden on growing families.[86]

While women's growing participation in the labor force has significantly changed family structures in Middle East, this phenomenon is especially evident in Israel. Israeli women have critical positions in the family, but they are also active members of the labor force. Women's expanding role in the workplace has caused dramatic shifts in the familial landscape of Israel, challenging women to strike a balance between home and work. Although Israeli society is more accepting of working women, it is not a conventional norm for Israeli women to forgo child bearing to have a career. Gainful employment makes women self-sufficient and affords them more decision making power in the family unit, yet in several conservative communities women who sacrifice family life for a career are viewed negatively. As a result, many women try to maintain active roles in both spheres. Consequently, the distinction between breadwinner and homemaker is blurring, especially in the younger and more educated communities.

In Israel, due to cultural beliefs, marriage is almost universal. However, in Islamic states in the region most single Jewish men and women have the opportunity to socialize without the supervision of an adult. Courtship often takes place in school or during compulsory military service, when men must serve 3 years and women serve 12–24 months after age 18. Although it is unacceptable to date in Arab communities, Israeli Jews are free to spend time together alone and in public. Some Jewish couples even live together before they are married. The exception to this form of courtship and mate selection is in ultraorthodox communities where dating is unacceptable, marriages are often arranged, and couples may only have chaperoned meetings before nuptials. Ultraorthodox communities also pressure couples to marry young because it is unacceptable to engage in sexual activity outside of marriage.[87]

Arab communities in Israel follow standard family patterns commonly observed in Islamic states. Women typically occupy a lower status than men, and wives are generally dependent upon their husbands to support them. Although there are fewer arranged marriages now than there were in the past, it is still socially unacceptable for unmarried men and women to go out together in public. With these restrictions in place, young couples usually meet through family members. Generally, Arab women in Israel need a male relative's consent before marriage. Once married, Arab women still have very little decision making power in the public sphere, but have some influence in the home, especially regarding children.

Despite the diverse population, most Israelis live with their nuclear family while maintaining close contact with their extended family. Once a family has children, society collectively assumes responsibility for the welfare of children. As mentioned, the state incentivizes reproduction by providing tax relief, certain allowances, healthcare, and other benefits for families with children. Due to high marriage and fertility rates and low divorce rates, most children grow up with both parents and siblings. The majority of married couples have children, leaving only about 10 percent of the population in the single parent category. The average family has 3.79 children, and most couples stay together, at a rate of about 75 percent. Muslims, ultraorthodox Jews, and Druze women have higher fertility rates than secular and highly educated Jewish and Christian-Arab women.[88]

Women also fulfill important roles in the public sphere since the state and extended family often support working mothers. Since the 1950s, the state has actively encouraged family-friendly policies such as maternity leave, subsidized childcare, and on-site day care facilities. Families themselves also have a key role in keeping women in the workplace. Consequently, it is common for grandparents to care for their grandchildren. However, the responsibility of caring for family members is not limited to children. Many Israelis find it shameful that some Western families place their elderly relatives in retirement homes. This perspective reflects the position of honor afforded to the elderly in both Jewish and Arab communities. Both groups emphasize maintaining close relationships with the elderly, who they see as a source of wisdom and strength for their extended families.[89]

Religious beliefs, community cultural norms, and family heritage shape Israeli parenting practices. While most mothers figure prominently in their children's socialization and development, parents socialize their children in many different ways. Most families raise and socialize their young on their own. Israel also has many kibbutzim, agricultural communities based on a socialist ideology where children are raised both by their parents and the community. Generally, Israeli children enjoy a special relationship with their mother, and this does not dissipate upon transition to adulthood. For many teenage Israelis, their relationship with their mother intensifies around the age of 18 when most Jewish men and women serve in the Israeli Defense Force. Furthermore, many children live with their parents after completing military service before finding employment or continuing their education.[90]

Israel's unique position in the Middle East as a Jewish state and its composition of diverse cultures and customs poses challenges and opportunities for women. As a country comprised of a large number of immigrants from some 70 different countries, many Israelis struggle to assimilate to the new culture upon arrival. Recently arrived families endure extremely stressful transitions to life in a new state. Parents, who normally lead and guide the family, may actually learn about their new culture and surroundings from children who serve as socializing agents in immigrant communities. Moreover, the ongoing violence associated with the Arab-Israeli conflict stress family life even further. Families have to cope with the instability, violence, and danger emanating from regional conflict, a situation that is taxing emotionally, financially, and, often, physically for people on both sides of the conflict. Women who have lost sons and husbands have had to acquire new roles in the family. This fact is especially acute in border communities where people suffer frequent attacks and chaos in their lives. Overall, families remain the key unit of socialization, support, and stability for individuals living in Israel.[91]

NOTES

1. Guity Nashat and Judith Tucker, *Women in the Middle East and North Africa* (Bloomington: Indiana University Press, 1999), xl.

2. Nashat and Tucker, *Women in the Middle East and North Africa*, xxx.

3. Mayer I. Gruber, "Women in the Ancient Levant," in *Women's Roles in Ancient Civilizations*, ed. Bella Vivante (Westport, CT: Greenwood Press, 1999), 144.

4. Charles Lindholm, *The Islamic Middle East, Traditions and Change* (Malden, MA: Blackwell Publishing, 2002), 235.

5. Jeri Altneu Sechzer, "Islam and Women, Where Tradition Meets Modernity," *Sex Roles*, 51 (2004): 263.

6. Nabia Abbott, "Women and the State in Early Islam," *Journal of Near Eastern Studies* 1 (1942): 121–22.

7. Abbott, "Women and the State in Early Islam," 123.

8. Nikki R. Keddie, *Women in the Middle East: Past and Present* (Princeton, NJ: Princeton University Press, 2007), 20.

9. Abbott, "Women and the State in Early Islam," 123.

10. Abbott, "Women and the State in Early Islam," 124.

11. Geraldine Brooks, *Nine Parts of Desire, The Hidden World of Islamic Women* (New York: Anchor Books, 1995), 83 and 86.

12. Nashat and Tucker, *Women in the Middle East and North Africa,* 45.

13. Valentine M. Moghadam, "Patriarchy in Transition: Women and the Changing Family in the Middle East," *Journal of Comparative Family Studies* 35 (2004): 142.

14. Keddie, *Women in the Middle East: Past and Present,* 18.

15. Arthur Goldschmidt, Jr., *A Concise History of the Middle East* (Boulder, CO: Westview Press, 2002), 108–9.

16. Nora Alarifi Pharaon, "Saudi Women and the Muslim State in the 21st Century," *Sex Roles* 51 (2004): 355.

17. Nashat and Tucker, *Women in the Middle East and North Africa,* 48.

18. Jane H. Bayes and Nayereh Tohidi, "Women Redefining Modernity and Religion in the Globalized Context," in *Globalization, Gender and Religion: The Politics of Women's Rights in Catholic and Muslim Contexts,* eds. Jane H. Bayes and Nayereh Tohidi (New York: Palgrave, 2001), 29.

19. Nashat and Tucker, *Women in the Middle East and North Africa,* 51.

20. Nashat and Tucker, *Women in the Middle East and North Africa,* 53.

21. Ian C. Dengler, "Turkish Women in the Ottoman Empire," in *Women in the Muslim World,* eds. Lois Beck and Nikki R. Keddie (Cambridge, MA: Harvard University Press, 1978), 236–38.

22. Moghadam, "Patriarchy in Transition: Women and the Changing Family in the Middle East," 138.

23. Sara Ashencaen Crabtree, "Culture, Gender and the Influence of Social Change Amongst Emirati Families in the United Arab Emirates," *Journal of Comparative Family Studies* 38, no. 4 (2007): 578.

24. Daniel Bates and Amal Rassam, *People and Cultures of the Middle East* (Englewood, NJ: Prentice Hall, 1983), 222.

25. Moghadam, "Patriarchy in Transition: Women and the Changing Family in the Middle East," 141.

26. Saud Joseph, "Gender and the Family" in *Arab Women Between Defiance and Restraint,* ed. Suha Sabbagh (Brooklyn, NY: Olive Branch Press, 1996), 195.

27. Haim Gerber, "Social and Economic Position of Women in an Ottoman City, Bursa, 1600–1700," *International Journal of Middle East Studies* 12, no. 3 (1980): 232.

28. Keddie, *Women in the Middle East: Past and Present,* 83.

29. Bernhard Nauck and Daniela Klaus, "Families in Turkey," in *The Handbook of World Families,* eds. Bert N. Adams and Jan Trost (Thousand Oaks, CA: Sage Publications, 2005), 379–80.

30. Nauck and Klaus, "Families in Turkey," 368.

31. Nauck and Klaus, "Families in Turkey," 370.

32. Cigem Kagitcibasi, "The Changing Value of Children in Turkey," in *Current Studies on the Value of Children* (Honolulu, HI: The East-West Center, 1982), 73.

33. Nauck and Klaus, "Families in Turkey, 374–76.

34. Nauck and Klaus, "Families in Turkey," 365.

35. Pharaon, "Saudi Women and the Muslim State in the 21st Century," 349–50.

36. Pharaon, "Saudi Women and the Muslim State in the 21st Century," 354.

37. Pharaon, "Saudi Women and the Muslim State in the 21st Century," 361.

38. "Step by Step for Middle East Women," *The Christian Science Monitor,* 101 (2009), 8.

39. Pharaon, "Saudi Women and the Muslim State in the 21st Century," 359.

40. Pharaon, "Saudi Women and the Muslim State in the 21st Century," 363.

41. Pharaon, "Saudi Women and the Muslim State in the 21st Century," 365.

42. Rachel Bronson and Isobel Coleman, "The Kingdom's Clock," *Foreign Policy* 156 (2006): 57.

43. Bronson and Coleman, "The Kingdom's Clock," 60–61.

44. Mounira Charrad, "State and Gender in the Maghrib," in *Arab Women Between Defiance and Restraint,* ed. Suha Sabbagh (Brooklyn, NY: Olive Branch Press, 1996), 222–23.

45. Susan S. Davis, *Patience and Power: Women's Lives in a Moroccan Village* (Cambridge, MA: Schenkman Publishing Company, 1983), 65.

46. Davis, *Patience and Power: Women's Lives in a Moroccan Village,* 127–28.

47. Davis, *Patience and Power: Women's Lives in a Moroccan Village,* 131–39.

48. Davis, *Patience and Power: Women's Lives in a Moroccan Village,* 23 and 156–57.

49. Isobel Coleman, "Women, Islam, and the New Iraq," *Foreign Affairs* 85, no. 1 (2006): 32.

50. Susan Slyomovics, "Hassiba Ben Bouali, If You Could See Our Algeria: Women and Public Space in Algeria," in *Arab Women Between Defiance and Restraint,* ed. Suha Sabbagh (Brooklyn, NY: Olive Branch Press, 1996), 213 and 216.

51. Paula Holmes-Eber, *Daughters of Tunis: Women, Family, and Networks in a Muslim City* (Boulder, CO: Westview Press, 2003), 44.

52. Shireen Hassim, "Family, Motherhood, and Zulu Nationalism: The Politics of the Inkatha Women's Brigade," *Feminist Review* 43 (1993): 20.

53. Zeina Zaatari, "The Culture of Motherhood: An Avenue for Women's Civil Participation in South Lebanon," *Journal of Middle East Women's Studies* 2 (2006): 33–34.

54. Saud Joseph, "My Son/Myself, My Mother/Myself: Paradoxical Relationalities of Patriarchal Connectivity," in *Intimate Selving in Arab Families: Gender, Self, and Identity,* ed. Suad Joseph (Syracuse: Syracuse University Press, 1999), 185.

55. Zaatari, "The Culture of Motherhood: An Avenue for Women's Civil Participation in South Lebanon," 56.

56. Taghreed Alqudsi-Ghabra, "Women in Kuwait," in *Arab Women Between Defiance and Restraint,* ed. Suha Sabbagh (Brooklyn, NY: Olive Branch Press, 1996), 229–30.

57. Fahad Al Naser, "Kuwait's Families," in *The Handbook of World Families,* eds. Bert N. Adams and Jan Trost (Thousand Oaks, CA: Sage Publications, 2005), 509 and 511.

58. Naser, "Kuwait's Families," 512–15.

59. Tremayne, "Modernity and Early Marriage in Iran: A View from Within," *Journal of Middle East Women's Studies* 2, no. 1 (2006): 84.

60. Tremayne, "Modernity and Early Marriage in Iran: A View from Within," 72–73.

61. Tremayne, "Modernity and Early Marriage in Iran: A View from Within," 75.

62. Coleman, "Women, Islam, and the New Iraq," 31.

63. Moghadam, "Patriarchy in Transition: Women and the Changing Family in the Middle East," 152.

64. Moghadam, "Patriarchy in Transition: Women and the Changing Family in the Middle East," 145.

65. Tremayne, "Modernity and Early Marriage in Iran: A View from Within," 81.

66. Tremayne, "Modernity and Early Marriage in Iran: A View from Within," 39.

67. Carla Makhlouf, *Changing Veils: Women and Modernization in North Yemen* (London: Croom Helm Publishers, 1979), 24–25.

68. Makhlouf, *Changing Veils: Women and Modernization in North Yemen*, 42.

69. Cheryl A. Rubenberg, *Palestinian Women Patriarchy and Resistance in the West Bank*, (Boulder, CO: Lynne Rienner Publishers, 2001), 13.

70. Rubenberg, "Palestinian Women Patriarchy and Resistance in the West Bank," 114.

71. Rubenberg, "Palestinian Women Patriarchy and Resistance in the West Bank," 73.

72. Rubenberg, "Palestinian Women Patriarchy and Resistance in the West Bank," 80 and 82.

73. Rubenberg, "Palestinian Women Patriarchy and Resistance in the West Bank," 83 and 94.

74. Rubenberg, "Palestinian Women Patriarchy and Resistance in the West Bank," 38, 84, and 98.

75. Yasmin Husein Al-Jawaheri, *Women in Iraq: The Gender Impact of International Sanctions* (Boulder, CO: Lynne Riener Publishers, 2008), 93–94.

76. Al-Jawaheri, *Women in Iraq: The Gender Impact of International Sanctions*, 94–95.

77. Al-Jawaheri, *Women in Iraq: The Gender Impact of International Sanctions*, 104–5.

78. Al-Jawaheri, *Women in Iraq: The Gender Impact of International Sanctions*, 121.

79. Al-Jawaheri, *Women in Iraq: The Gender Impact of International Sanctions*, 104–5.

80. Al-Jawaheri, *Women in Iraq: The Gender Impact of International Sanctions*, 98–100.

81. David Kilcullen, "Anatomy of a Tribal Revolt," *Small Wars Journal* http://smallwarsjournal.com/blog/2007/08/anatomy-of-a-tribal-revolt/.

82. Nina Toren, "Tradition and Transition: Family and Change in Israel," *Gender Issues* 21 (2003): 64.

83. Ruth Katz and Yoav Lavee, "Families in Israel," in *The Handbook of World Families*, eds. Bert N. Adams and Jan Trost (Thousand Oaks, CA: Sage Publications, 2005), 487.

84. Toren, "Tradition and Transition: Family and Change in Israel," 74.

85. Toren, "Tradition and Transition: Family and Change in Israel," 65.

86. Toren, "Tradition and Transition: Family and Change in Israel," 66–67.

87. Katz and Lavee, "Families in Israel," 487–88.

88. Katz and Lavee, "Families in Israel," 488.

89. Katz and Lavee, "Families in Israel," 499.

90. Katz and Lavee, "Families in Israel," 491.

91. Katz and Lavee, "Families in Israel," 502.

SUGGESTED READING

Abbott, Nabia. "Women and the State in Early Islam." *Journal of Near Eastern Studies* 1 (January 1942): 106–26.

Abbott, Nabia. "Women and the State on the Eve of Islam." *American Journal of Semitic Languages and Literatures* 58 (July 1941): 259–84.

Al-Jawaheri, Yasmin Husein. *Women in Iraq: The Gender Impact of International Sanctions.* Boulder, CO: Lynne Riener Publishers, 2008.

Adams, Bert N. and Jan Trost, eds. *The Handbook of World Families.* Thousand Oaks, CA: Sage Publications, 2005.

Joseph, Saud, ed. *Intimate Selving in Arab Families: Gender, Self, and Identity.* Syracuse: Syracuse University Press, 1999.

Moghadam, Valentine M. "Patriarchy in Transition: Women and the Changing Family in the Middle East." *Journal of Comparative Family Studies* (Spring 2004): 137–62.

Smith, W. Robertson. *Kinship and Marriage in Early Arabia.* London: Adam and Charles Black, 1903.

Toren, Nina. "Tradition and Transition: Family and Change in Israel." *Gender Issues* 21 (Spring 2003): 61–76.

Tremayne, Sonraya. "Modernity and Early Marriage in Iran: A View from Within." *Journal of Middle East Women's Studies* 2 (Winter 2006): 65–94.

Zaatari, Zeina. "The Culture of Motherhood: An Avenue for Women's Civil Participation in South Lebanon." *Journal of Middle East Women's Studies* 2, no. 1 (Winter 2006): 33–64.

3

---∞∞∞---

Women and Religion

The Middle East is the birthplace of the world's three major monotheist religions: Judaism, Islam, and Christianity. It is also home to several other smaller, more localized religions such as Zoroastrianism (mainly in Iran) and Yezidi in Kurdish Northern Iraq, among others. Because the overwhelming majority of the Middle East is Muslim, this chapter will concentrate on Islam, but will also assesses the impact of Judaism and Christianity on the roles that women play with regards to religion in those particular communities.

Women's role in religion is indicative of their place in society throughout history. In ancient times, several communities across the Middle East worshipped female deities associated with women's unique roles in different aspects of life ranging from fertility to creation and agriculture. In Biblical times, women served as sages, priestesses, and prophetesses and often as intercessors with divinity. Across several different religious groups, women also worked in the service of religious institutions. For instance, women worked as caretakers in local temples or as religious advisors to political leaders. In the early years of Islam, women filled important roles spreading the faith both in and out of the home. After Muhammad's death in 632, his female relatives served as experts in his traditions for successive caliphs and other religious leaders. Some of Muhammad's female family members helped record the Qu'ran and the hadith, a collection of his words and deeds. Later, as Islam spread outside of Arabia in the seventh and eighth centuries, women's role religious practices diminished as men assumed the most important leadership positions in the Muslim community during the Age of the Rightly Guided Caliphs.

Women's diminished role in orthodox religious practices was not limited to Islam. The masculinization of the major monotheistic religions limited women's religious role in Judaism and Christianity as well. For example, Jesus appointed men as his apostles and women were excluded from the priesthood and other positions of authority in the church. Women could not even approach the altar in Eastern Orthodox churches.[1] In the Judaic law and oral traditions, women were often excluded from the centers of holiness, precluding them from performing or even participating in the liturgy.[2] In every major religion, women were excluded from leadership roles in orthodox worship. Since adherents of the three major monotheistic religions venerated a single, male god, positive attributes were associated with the masculine.

Although women historically have had limited leadership roles in the major monotheistic faiths, religious beliefs and practices remain crucial aspects of women's identity because they provide answers to questions of ultimate meaning while also providing direction for everyday life. In the Middle East, religion has multiple components, ranging from commitment or identification with certain principles, acceptance of religious practices, and adherence, to religious norms.[3] Women's role in the family makes them uniquely positioned to transmit religious beliefs and practices to future generations. However, women's role in religion has not been limited to the private sphere. Throughout Middle East history, a few women have also had important roles as religious leaders in the public realm. Although some female religious leaders dealt exclusively with other women and children, there are a few notable women who served in prominent positions within their respective religious communities. Some women, known for their authority in religious matters, advised leading male political and spiritual leaders of their day. In tribal nomadic communities, women exerted religious influence and authority through their intercession with the supernatural. Even today, in places like Morocco, people believe that certain women have the gift of magic and an ability to engage with the divine. In several places, women were also associated with the occult and dark spirits. Evidence suggest that some women prepared spells and served as fortune tellers who used their religious authority to produce sons, guard them, and keep their husband faithful.[4]

In many ways, religion served as a source of power, comfort, and opportunity for women in the Middle East. Through the centuries, non-orthodox religious spheres provided a forum for female power.[5] As such, some female religious leaders served their respective communities as leaders and authority figures based on their unique understanding and relationship with divinity. Conversely, different groups have mobilized religion and religious ideas to subordinate or to exclude women from different roles in society. In certain places, women's spiritual power and ability to communicate with the divine threatened the male-dominated order. Thus, religion has been a source of liberation and limitation, of oppression and of opportunity for Middle Eastern and North African women.

Despite historical limitations on women's role in religion, in the contemporary Middle East and North Africa, a few female religious leaders and educators ascended to positions of increased authority in religious institutions. A look at the historical evolution of women's role in religion will highlights aspects of this fascinating and tremendously important part of their lives in the region.

PERCEPTIONS OF WOMEN IN RELIGIOUS TEXTS AND PRACTICES

Most pre-Islamic religions, polytheistic sects, and the scriptural religions of Judaism, Zoroastrianism, and Christianity support male-dominated attitudes and practices. Judaism and Christianity, in particular, viewed women in the form of Eve, as introducing evil into the world.[6] The Qu'ran, however, tells a very different story of Adam and Eve. In the Qu'ran, both Adam and Eve sin by eating the forbidden fruit. Some believe that this version of the story absolves women of the sole blame for mankind's sinful ways in Islam. In the Bible, Eve gives the fruit to Adam and in doing so, commits original sin. Some argue that women in Christianity were subsequently associated with Eve's weakness leading to expulsion from the Garden of Eden and the ensuing hardships that followed. Despite the more gender-neutral version of the story in Islam, later hadiths also blame Eve for Adam's downfall. Perhaps these different versions of the story reflect the fact that Islam came under the influence of highly feudalized societies of Byzantine and Persia, which ultimately disadvantaged women.[7] According to some interpretations, Eve was forced to bleed once a month and to give birth against her will as a punishment for her sinful ways.[8]

Evidence suggests that other religious sects also limit women's participation in religious worship and rituals based upon their natural bodily functions like menstruation and childbirth. In the Sunni tradition of Islam, women who are menstruating are considered impure for the purposes of touching or reading the Qu'ran. Hence, menstruating women are exempt from prayer, from making the pilgrimage, and from fasting during Ramadan, the ninth month of the Islamic calendar. This practice implies a societal perception that women's prayers are less important to god.[9] Zoroastrians, an ancient religious group started in 1000 B.C.E. in Eastern Iran, also restricted women's religious activities, as they believed that impurity flowed from the discharge of women's blood during menstruation and childbirth. While Zoroastrian women could worship, they could not become priests, as their natural bodily functions rendered them impure.[10] Overall, the three major monotheistic religious communities supported patriarchal systems leading to the subordination of women. These attitudes shaped what would later constitute both prescribed and the proscribed behavior for women in the Middle East and North Africa. Pre-Islamic religions and practices also influenced gender attitudes of Islam, both in its doctrinal and legal evolution.[11]

WOMEN'S ROLES IN RELIGION DURING THE RISE OF ISLAM

Islam is not a monolithic religion. After it spread out of Arabia in the seventh and eighth centuries, its followers brought their own languages, customs, legal systems, and previous religious beliefs to their unique practice of the faith. As such, Islam evolved with an assortment of customary laws that, as long as they did not conflict with sharia, Islamic law based on the Qu'ran, sunna and hadiths, varied greatly from place to place. Islam also encompasses a highly complex set of ideas, beliefs, doctrines, assumptions, and behavior patterns.[12] In many ways, Islam can be evoked either to liberalize opportunities for women or to levy new restrictions on them.[13] Today, more than 300 different ethnic groups consider themselves Muslims and, as such, women serve in various roles in their respective religious communities. A historical look at women's role in early Islam will further illustrate their roles in religious activities in different parts of the Middle East.

Given Muhammad's role as Islam's greatest prophet, his wives' and daughters' roles in the religion provide a good foundation upon which to base an examination of women's functions in the community of the faithful, also known as *umma*. Women who lived with Muhammad had a special role in spreading the faith and, later, in relaying his words and deeds. Also of note is the place from which Islam emerged. Before the rise of Islam, people traveled to Mecca, in what is now Saudi Arabia, to worship in the large sanctuary that housed a shrine containing images of pre-Islamic gods and goddesses, including Christian and Jewish relics. As a center for trade and commerce, people profited from those who made pilgrimages to Mecca's holy shrines, some of which were devoted to three pre-Islamic goddesses.[14] Muhammad's own tribe, the Bani Hashem, provided the pilgrims with water. People also came to Mecca to worship at the Ka'ba, which is a black piece of a meteorite of unknown antiquity that housed as many as 360 idols.[15] Some believe that Adam built the temple and that Abraham dedicated it to God.[16] Others believe that Abraham built it.[17] While in Mecca, people frequented the busy market and took advantage of the thriving trade industry that grew in this economic and religious city. Muhammad, supported by his wife first wife Khadija, and his daughters, received his message to be Allah's prophet and eventually claimed the Ka'ba for Islam.

Muhammad's female relatives retained special roles in the faith from the time he received his calling to be Allah's prophet until after his death, especially when his succession was in question. His first wife, Khadija, was tremendously supportive during the critical time when Muhammad first received his calling from the Archangel Gabriel. Khadija's lucrative trade business allowed Muhammad time for spiritual contemplation in a cave near the mountain Hira, where he first underwent a profound religious experience that lead him to believe that he was called to become God's messenger, charged with revealing the truth to humanity.[18] As a show of faith in her husband, and in his calling to serve as Allah's prophet, Khadija was Muhammad's first convert to Islam. She was also a steadfast believer in Muhammad and his message when everyone else shunned him. Muhammad's pursuit of his calling caused his family great adversity and later, after Khadija died, he reflected on the significance of her devotion to his prophecy. Khadija also took responsibility for her children's spiritual education, a role shared by many Muslim women even today. Other early converts included his daughters, his cousin, and son-in-law Ali, who persevered in the face of adversity. Early on, local Meccan elites felt threatened by Muhammad's monotheistic message. Business leaders profited handsomely from pilgrims visiting Mecca's religious sites, and his message went directly against their business interests. In time, Muhammad's activities evoked such concern that the local community boycotted his tribe by refusing to do business or to intermarry with them. When it grew too dangerous to stay in Mecca, Muhammad moved his family and 70 of his followers to Medina, some 200 miles to the northeast. However, Muhammad later returned to claim the holy sites in Mecca for Islam.

While Khadija and her life experiences reflect pre-Islamic and early Islamic life for women, Muhammad's other wives and their experiences offer a glimpse into women's role in the religious community after the move to Medina. Unlike Mecca, with its flourishing trade and tourism-fueled economy, Medina was more rural and populated by feuding tribes, for which Muhammad was invited to broker peace. While there, Muhammad married several women in an effort to cement alliances among warring factions. Through intermarriage, women served as a conduit for peaceful relations among feuding tribes. As Muhammad mediated amongst different factions, he took wives who were not originally Muslim. Early on, a woman was free to accept or reject Islam regardless of what the men in her family decided to do. There are cases where women acted independently and exercised religious freedom in this early time. Two of Muhammad's wives, Safiyah, who converted to Islam, and Raihanah, who did not, were Jewish. He also had a relationship with a Coptic Christian woman, Mary, who sources indicate was likely Muhammad's concubine.[19] Copts are an ancient, pre-Islamic Christian community that survives today, mostly in Egypt, and constitute the largest Christian community in the Middle East. Through his relationships with local tribeswomen, Muhammad brokered peace amongst warring factions and consolidated religious and political power. This helped him to establish a state, based on Islam, where people were protected in their identity as Muslims. All the while, women participated in communal religious activities, passing their beliefs onto their children who would become the next generation of Muslims. Women were also critical in transmitting hadiths and in collecting the Qu'ran, often by memorization.

Muhammad's wives and daughters were not the only women with important roles in early Muslim communities. Other women also participated in a many religious practices during the rise of Islam. Women, who helped build the first mosque in Medina, were allowed to worship in public. By praying in a mosque and engaging in this outward and public display of piety, women also taught their children how to be good Muslims through personal example. Women contributed to religious festivals and listened to Muhammad's teachings. During funerals, women prayed over the dead.[20] Unlike successive caliphs who prohibited women from going into mosques and later segregated them, Muhammad allowed men and women to pray together.[21] Evidence suggests that Muhammad took his granddaughter to the mosque to pray. He let her sit on his shoulders and put her down when it was time to prostrate. Women were not only faithful practitioners of Islam, but also held leadership roles during Muhammad's lifetime. Evidence suggests that women led ritual prayers and made the call to prayer for both men and women. Muhammad himself trained one woman, Umm Waraqa bint Abdallah, to lead prayers.[22] However, there is very little evidence of other women leading prayers from this time period. Perhaps women's most permanent role in early Islam was in the recording the Qu'ran and the hadith. Men and women recited the Qu'ran and the hadith, working from memory. Muhammad's female relatives were special contributors to both works based on their relationships with prophet and their intimate knowledge of his ways. As such, these women hold important positions as the first Muslim women to inhabit the region.[23] Women's role in recording the Qu'ran and hadith is also significant because both texts still figure prominently in the lives of millions of Muslims today. After consolidating political and religious power in Medina, Muhammad and his followers fought their way back to Mecca, where they destroyed the idols in the sanctuary except the Ka'ba. Later, the hajj, or the pilgrimage to Mecca, was established as one of the five pillars of Islam.

After Muhammad died in 632, his female relatives remained key members of the Muslim community with crucial roles in spreading Islam beyond

Arabia. For instance, Aisha and Muhammad's other widows remained important recorders of the hadith. This afforded his female relatives a special status in Islam for their knowledge of his words and deeds. Aisha, the second wife, unable to conceive a child, was only 19 when Muhammad died, leaving her with a rather bleak future as a widow without male heirs. Nevertheless, due to her relationship with Muhammad, she became a religious authority and author of some 2,210 hadiths. In the ninth century, religious scholars threw out all but 174 of her contributions, perhaps because of her gender. For years after Muhammad's death, Aisha lived in the room where he was buried and profited from believers who paid to spend time there. Aisha also retained status when her father, Abu Bakr, was chosen as Muhammad's successor.[24] However, Abu Bakr's selection was not unanimously accepted, with some questioning the legitimacy of the manner with which he was chosen. Following tribal custom, Muhammad's closest associates gathered and chose among themselves. Fatima, Muhammad's daughter by Khadija, strongly opposed Abu Bakr's selection as Muhammad's successor. She believed that her husband, and Muhammad's cousin, Ali, should be the second caliph. This schism reflects the importance of women's role in the early Muslim community during the struggle for succession. According to some scholars, Aisha favored her father, Abu Bakr, because of an ongoing feud with Muhammad's daughter by Khadija, Fatima, who naturally favored her husband Ali. Also, being Muhammad's widow and the daughter of the second caliph afforded Aisha an elevated position in the Muslim community.[25] Fatima, convinced that Muhammad's preference was for her husband, Ali, to be the second caliph, gave rise to the Shiites, also known as the Partisans of Ali or the Shi'at Ali. Those who supported Abu Bakr are known as Sunnis. The schism reflects a tension between the two competing principles of political and religious legitimacy in Islam. Sunnis believed that legitimacy resided in the will of the community, while Shiites held that legitimacy was conferred upon Muhammad's descendents.[26]

Women have a particularly important role in Shiism because of Muhammad's granddaughter Zaynab's role in defending her brother, Husain, and his son, Ali, the lone surviving male member of her family who would go on to become the fourth Shia imam. Zaynab gained notoriety at the battle of Karbala in 680, a defining moment in Shiism, when soldiers of the second Umayyad caliph Yazid I massacred Ali's son, Husain, and 72 of his companions and family members. During the battle, Zaynab lost two sons and witnessed the slaughter of her closest family members, who were denied access to water for one week. When Yazid's men tried to kill her nephew, Ali, she shielded him with her body. After the battle, Zaynab accompanied her brother's head back to Damascus and also saved his son's life. More importantly, Zaynab lived to tell the story of Husain's heroism, to the extent that some scholars believe that Shiism owes its existence to her.[27] Today, Shias still commemorate the Battle of Karbala, mourning the loss of Husain, an important martyr in Shiism. Like Muhammad's daughter Fatima, Zaynab also served as a role model and expert in his traditions and messages that continue in Shia communities today. Indeed, Shia clergy told women that they were obligated to participate in the historic elections in Iraq in 2005 by invoking the memory of Zaynab's courage in the Battle of Karbala to motivate Iraqi women to boldly exercise their right to vote.[28] Men, and especially women, frequent a mosque where Zaynab's house once sat in Cairo, as well as her shrine in Damascus, where she is buried.[29] Zaynab's nieces, Fatima and Sukaynah, also achieved notoriety, as did other women in Muhammad's family.[30] However, despite this handful of women with significant roles in Islam, subsequent caliphs limited women's role in the religion as it spread across the Middle East and North Africa. This is largely because Islam reached communities that retained pre-Islamic views of women, curtailing their role in the public sphere. Rather than change their cultural beliefs and practices to mirror those of the Prophet, many newcomers to Islam adapted their pre-Islamic traditions to fit their unique practice of the faith.

Women also took an active role in efforts to disrupt the spread of Islam in Arabia by starting new religions upon Muhammad's death. In celebration of his passing, some women painted their hands with henna, a tradition associated with weddings, believing that they no longer had to adhere to Islam. Salma bint Malik served as the leader of an armed rebellion against Islam. Upon learning of these celebrations and revolts, the caliph Abu Bakr had the women's hands severed at the wrist. While the reasons for the women's celebrations are unclear, scholars believe that some women perceived Islam as repressive and feared further subjugation if the faith spread.[31] Other women used Muhammad's death as an opportunity to start new religions before Islam took hold in Arabia and elsewhere. A woman, Sajah bint 'Aws, was one of a few "false prophets" to emerge during the time of the first caliph. Revolts erupted in Yemen where six women led the charge against the spread of Islam. In defiance of Islam, this group in Yemen also tried to bolster support for new religions.[32] Other new groups formed elsewhere, such as the Kharijis of Oman. The Kharijis had different ideas about women's issues than those espoused by Islam. Kharijis rejected concubinage and child marriage. They thought that God gave Muhammad privileges that should not be afforded to other men and they also permitted women participate in warfare, specifically in holy war.[33] Nevertheless, several Muslim women put themselves in great danger to defend Islam. In fact, the first Muslim martyr, Sumayyah bint Khubbat, was a newly converted Muslim and slave who faced severe persecution and later died for her beliefs.[34]

THE AGE OF THE RIGHTLY GUIDED
CALIPHS AND BEYOND

Although women's role in Islam diminished after Muhammad's death, a few women fulfilled important positions as the religion spread under the Rightly Guided Caliphs. During this period, women experienced more restrictions on their ability to fulfill their religiously mandated obligations. For example, Caliph Umar tried to keep women out of mosques, but when that failed, he ordered separate prayer leaders for men and women. He also prohibited women from going on the hajj, a prohibition lifted only in the last year of his life. Then, when Uthman, the third caliph, was murdered by a rebellious faction, Ali came to power. Aisha, who some argue always resented Ali, led an armed rebellion against him. Scholars argue that Aisha's leadership of this particular rebellion forever altered the balance of power between Muslim men and women, mostly because she was unsuccessful. Aisha led troops in battle against Ali atop a camel, assuming a very public role as both a religious and military leader. Nevertheless, she was soon defeated and, as hundreds of her followers died, she was largely blamed for the conflict in which Muslims killed fellow Muslims. Thereafter, people subscribed to the idea that women were unfit to lead political, religious, or military organizations. After Aisha's defeat, she stayed out of politics but remained a religious authority.[35] Her detractors used her military defeat to preclude women from leadership roles in society. In fact, the hadith stating that, "those who entrust power to a woman will never enjoy prosperity," is what would-be reformers of the 17th century Ottoman Empire had in mind when they deplored the interference of palace women in imperial affairs from the time of Murad IV (1574–1595).[36]

Muhammad's other widows and female relatives also advised caliphs Umar and Uthman. Uthman went so far as to suggest that Muhammad's widows should have a say in choosing his successor. Both Aisha, even after her devastating military campaign, and Umm Salamah served as authorities on the life and sayings of Muhammad until their deaths in 678 and 680, respectively. Furthermore, Muhammad's other female relatives enjoyed positions of honor due to their status as family members of the Prophet. As mentioned, his daughter Fatima and granddaughter Zaynab served as role models and experts in his traditions and message, even assuming leadership roles. Even Zaynab's nieces, Fatima and Sukaynah, achieved notoriety. Sukaynah, in particular, was known for her physical attractiveness and wit, affording her some degree of choice in partners.[37] However, not all women enjoyed Sukaynah's liberties. Women's role in society and religion changed under subsequent caliphs as Islam spread across the Middle East and North Africa. Gradually, women were excluded from key religious positions, as they were no longer allowed to enter mosques. Scholars suggest that the few women who had significant roles in their religious communities, such as Mary and Fatima, only enjoyed those positions because of their relationships with men who were the real religious authorities.[38]

At the beginning of the 11th century, Islam divided into three religious streams: Sunni, Shia, and Isma'ili. The divisions had much to do with the Muslim community's divergent views of the identity of the true and rightful successors of the prophet. Of these groups, the Shia Muslims recognize the succession of 12 Imams, ending with Muhammad ibn Hasan al-'Askar who they believe, rather than dying, went into occultation or hiding. As such, Shiite Muslims believe that the 12th imam will return one day to establish true justice in the world. Those who believe in this succession are often referred to as "twelvers." The Isma'ili Muslims, a different branch of Shiite Muslims, agree with the Shiites on the first five imams, but believe the sixth imam to be Isma'il and the seventh to be his son, Muhammad ibn Isma'il. The Isma'ilis first appeared in southern Iraq and later established themselves in Yemen and North Africa, where the Isma'ili branch of Islam became the religious doctrine of the Fatimid state, whose capital was established in Cairo.[39]

The Fatimids got their name from Fatima, Muhammad's daughter, the wife of Ali, and the mother of Husain and Hasan. As someone who spent considerable time with Islam's prophet, Fatima was known for her devotion and piety. Several accounts describe the manner with which she

Egyptian Muslim women perform Eid al-Adha prayers, or the Feast of Sacrifice in Cairo, 2009. (AP Photo/Mohamad Al Sehety, File)

worshipped, fasted, and devoted herself to spreading the faith. As such, her name is associated with the dynasty that spread across North Africa, Egypt, and Syria in the 10th century. The Fatimids emerged from an alliance between charismatic leaders and tribesmen in Algeria. As the Fatimid Empire spread, its leaders practiced religious tolerance and used administrators who were Sunni, Jewish, and Coptic Christians. In part, this tolerance may be due to the Isma'ilis' belief that humans are ranked according to their degree of spiritual enlightenment. Although the Fatimid Empire eventually split and fell to the Saladin in 1171, the Druze, a splinter group of Isma'ilis formed.[40] After a brief stronghold in Persia, the Mongols destroyed the Isma'ilis. Today, Isma'ilis are found in India, Syria, the Persian Gulf, East Africa, and beyond. One Isma'ili group in particular, the Nizaris, pay special homage to the Agha Khan, a descendent of the seventh Imam.[41] Currently, the Agha Khan retains a robust foundation that is active in Muslim communities all over the world and employs women and supports development projects that directly benefit women worldwide.[42]

It is important to highlight that, within a given country, Muslims might follow different religious leaders based on their sect. The various religious establishments hold a variety of views on women. For example, some Sunnis follow a Saudi Arabian clergy (Najd) with beliefs and practices emphasizing female segregation. Other Sunnis abide by the views of an Egyptian clergy (Alazhar) that supports female integration in society. Shias might follow the Iraqi (Najaf) school that retains traditional views toward women or the Iranian (Qom) clergy who support women's political rights as guaranteed by the post-revolution constitution.[43]

The Druze, a group originating in the 11th century, broke with the Isma'ilis when their Persian leader, al-Darazi, started preaching among a mountain-dwelling rural population in southern Lebanon and parts of Syria. Although women do not have equal status with men in Druze communities, Druze perceptions of women are noteworthy for their divergence with other Islamic religious groups. As a religion that espoused equality and freedom, the Druze forbid slavery and polygamy, both of which were widely practiced in the 11th century. They also granted women complete legal equality. As such, Druze women had the same marriage and divorce rights as men. Consequently, daughters and sons had equal rights to their parents' inheritance. Though women were not in key leadership positions, their overall position in society reflects a more egalitarian view of the sexes. In practice, despite the egalitarian ideals of the Druze community, women lacked true equality because the larger society favored men. Consequently, Druze men had better access to education, employment, and opportunities.[44]

Like Muslim women, Jewish women's role in their religion was also diminished, especially among the most orthodox communities, during the

Egyptian Muslim women study Islamic lessons at al Azhar mosque, the highest Islamic Sunni institution, 2009. (AP Photo/Amr Nabil)

Age of the Rightly Guided Caliphs. One study of Jewish women in Cairo during the 10th through 13th centuries indicates that women were excluded from the studying of scripture and without religious education, women were disqualified from leadership roles in society. As Jewish communities grew increasingly urbanized, Jewish women in Iran and Iraq were secluded just as Muslim women were. However, it appears that Jewish women could go to the synagogues at a time when Muslim women could not enter mosques. Sources indicate that a few Jewish women were able to accompany their husbands on trips to shrines and to Jerusalem.[45] Therefore, Jewish women were at least participants in certain religious observances, even if they did not hold leadership positions in their communities.

When Turks entered the Middle East in the ninth century, Muslim women's role in religion was primarily limited to relating the hadith and engaging in activities associated mystical Islam, or Sufism. Women with active roles in mystic Sufi orders believed in a direct union with Allah, regardless of gender. While elite women supported madrassas (Islamic schools) financially, they did not attend them. Women received religious education, but it was informal and often took place in the home. Elite women continued to support various philanthropic activities such as education by managing endowments into the Ottoman period.[46] Throughout the centuries, elite women engaged in philanthropic work as a way to achieve positions in society and in their respective religious communities. However, this outlet was only a viable option for elite women with the means to help others. Perhaps women's most enduring role in religion was their contribution to raising good Muslim, Christian, or Jewish children. After all, women raised most male religious leaders.

Islam's tolerance of "People of the Book" continued into the Ottoman period. In early Islam, non-Muslims were free to practice their own religions, but they had to pay a special poll tax and were excluded from military service. Some were encouraged to convert as a result of discriminatory treatment, but overall, Islamic states had much more religious tolerance than pre-modern Christianity.[47] Therefore, Jews, Christians, and other religious minorities could maintain their religious customs and traditions for a price. Subsequent authorities maintained policies of religious tolerance. The Ottoman Empire was classified according to a system of ethnic and religious groups called millets. Under this system, various millets or different groups were separately recognized such as the Jews, Armenians, and the Greeks; however, Muslims were considered one millet and included Turks, Arabs, and Kurds.[48]

Religious texts are important to examine women's role in religion. The differences between the sexes are clear in the Qu'ran and the hadith, but much is left to interpretation and the interests of the reader. Some scholars stress the manner with which the Qu'ran improved women's position in society and in religion. In fact, the Qu'ran contains several revelations that include identical moral admonitions addressed to men and women. It also imparts certain religious obligations and responsibilities to both men and women. The hadith and interpretation of words and deeds of the prophet is problematic. Hadiths were written in the ninth century. Before then, they were memorized and passed down orally. Some believe the hadiths are the root of male supremacy in Islam.[49] Furthermore, both texts were subject to the interpretation of religious scholars. Negative views of women were reflected in theological and legal interpretations of the Qu'ran, hadiths, and other works.[50] Since these texts were written over time and subsequently interpreted by different people, it is difficult to discern whether or not women are accorded equality in Islam. In a well-known verse of the Qu'ran, men are clearly described as having natural authority over women. It suggests that men control women because God has given preference to them. Therefore, to be considered righteous, women must be obedient.[51] Some scholars argue that, despite women's deficiencies, they are guaranteed certain rights reflecting the compassionate nature of Islam. Since men provide for them, women are liberated from the concern of their economic well-being.[52] As such, men and women in Islam are not duplicates of one another; rather they are complements with biological differences that lead to the natural separation of sphere and occupation. Some believe that this division of labor reflects that the shortcomings of one sex are compensated for by the strengths of the other.

A key question that arises in debates among Islamic scholars is whether Islam fosters women's rights or quashes them. There are several schools of thought regarding the role of women in Islamic society. One strand offers a modernist interpretation of Islam, which finds the Qu'ran egalitarian, yet argues that the less reliable hadith have become more misogynistic and rigid over the centuries. Islamic modernists argue that the true interpretation of Islam is compatible with modernization, but has been distorted by folk traditions and un-Islamic interpretations. Exploring some of the changes that the Qu'ran brought in the context of the times, Islam appears to have improved many aspects of women's lives, including making specific rules for inheritance and property rights. Although inheritance laws provide that women receive half that of their male relatives, men are required to provide for women and pay a bride price directly to them. Women, on the other hand, are not obligated to provide for men. Modernists also argue that many of the customs that have become associated with Islam actually stem from pre-Islamic roots. Islam set limits on issues such as plural marriage and clearly spelled out the rights and obligations of both men and women. Some verses in the Qu'ran reflect the kind and just view that Islam has toward women. For example, when discussing the issue of divorce, the Qu'ran declares that a woman must be "retained in honor or released in kindness."[53]

WOMEN'S ROLE IN SUFISM

Sufism, or Islamic mysticism, is a branch of Islam that many claim favors the "feminine" aspects of religion, such as emotional intuition, ecstatic experience, hidden knowledge, magical practices, and immersion in the encompassing womb of God's love.[54] As such, Sufis emphasize mysticism and one's personal relationship with God. Sufism began as a movement of people who sought to achieve a direct experience of "ultimate reality" through personal contact with God. Unlike the legalistic demands of the sharia, Sufism allows individuals to seek his or her own spiritual path. While the origins of the word "Sufi" are unclear, it appears to come from the rough, wool *suf* worn by mystics in Baghdad in the early eighth century as they went from town to town preaching spiritual discipline and asceticism.[55] Women have also had prominent roles in Sufism as mystics and religious leaders. In their role as Sufi mystics, women extend and amplify the teachings of the Qu'ran in the spirit of universal love, most famously through their devotional musicians, dancing Zhikrs, singing Qawwalis, and poets. Sufi women have a number of beliefs, cultural rituals and even types of sisterhoods within which they advance their relationship with God.

Sufi practices vary from place to place, often reflecting diverse cultural practices and traditions. Sufism is also associated with asceticism and stresses personal piety and emotional catharsis. The path to reaching truth or knowledge proceeds in stages guided by a teacher-master Sufi also called a sheikh, or *pirs.* Once a person has made it through all stages of learning, he or she reaches a new level of consciousness. Thus, Sufi masters transmit their experience and knowledge to those who are new to the religion and its practices. A Sufi order normally consists of a few masters or true mystics who devote their lives to Sufism and several laypersons who, after initiation, gain association with the order but live otherwise normal lives. Sufis express their sentiments through poetry, dance, stories, fables, and folk tales.[56] Some claim that the first Sufis were Muhammad's female relatives, starting with Khadija, his first wife. Her role has been thoroughly explained in other parts of this chapter, but in terms of her role as a Sufi, Khadija's devotion and support of Muhammad in the face of adversity and her embrace of his message contributes to her high status in Islam. Fatima, Muhammad's daughter with Khadija, is also known for her deep mystical understanding of Islam. Many Sufis consider Fatima to be the first Muslim mystic.[57]

Women established Sufi orders parallel with men's by the late Abbasid period[58] and, by the thirteenth century, Sufism developed into a mass movement.[59] To this day, Sufis retain different orders that are named for their founders, who are regarded as saints. Among women's orders, masters lead study and perform spiritual exercises in a lodge or *zawiya.* Some *zawiyas* are sanctuaries where saints are buried. Some Sufi lodges associate with one another in loose forms of hierarchy with the order becoming a network for its members and some lodges serving as hostels for pilgrims and travelers. Other orders have schools for children and community centers. Some Sufi women, especially Muhammad's relatives, are known for their *baraka* or holiness. Others can acquire *baraka* if they live with extreme piety and divine grace. Some Sufis claim to perform miracles and possess the ability to heal the sick. Sufi saints are usually recognized in their lifetime, unlike Christian saints who are canonized post-mortem. Perhaps the most important female Sufi mystic was a freed slave from Iraq, Rabi'a Al' Adawiya. She taught that love should replace fear as the motive for religious devotion.[60] She was also the first saint to clearly articulate the Sufis personal relationship with god. Rabi'a claimed that she did not worship God for fear of hell or for want of heaven, but out of love for God. Over the years, women continued their activity in Sufi orders, and although many women were not publicly active in Sufism, they were participants in the privacy of their own homes. Some Sufi women participated in rituals and ceremonies alongside Sufi men, while others, such as Rabi'a, worshipped in solitude.[61]

The Bektashi order of Sufism permits integrated ceremonies. Perhaps one of the most important roles of Sufi women has been their service as spiritual leaders of men. Examples abound of great male Islamic mystics and metaphysicians who credit their knowledge and relationship with the divine as a result of women's tutelage. Two male Sufi masters, Ibn 'Arabi and Bayazid Bestami, describe their masters as elderly women from whom they received spiritual guidance. Another Egyptian Sufi master, Dhu an-Nun al-Misri, described the highest among all Sufis as a woman in Mecca, Fatemah Nishapuri, whom he regarded as a saint. Female Sufi mystics were known for their profound understanding of the Qu'ran and for their prophetic dreams. In worship, some sang and rejoiced while others wept, like Persian mystic Sha'wana who drew a crowd as she celebrated her relationship with God. Women also composed songs, poems, and other expressions of their faith. Often these compositions were transmitted orally, but some Sufis wrote their artistic expressions of faith and made collections, or *divan*, of their personal Sufi experiences.[62]

Today, Sufi women have an important role in passing their traditions and practices to future generations. Many write about their religious experiences and rituals, while others teach and share their experiences with men and women in their respective orders. Women have continued to practice Sufism in their homes, even when the state banned Sufi orders. The home served as a place of safety where women could experience spirituality. Such was the case in the 1920s when Ataturk's government drove Sufi orders into private homes in Turkey and also in Libya during the Italian colonial period when Sufi Senussi lodges kept Islamic learning alive as a way to resist the occupation.[63] In 1881, Egyptian authorities prohibited Sufis from using musical instruments in women's presence during rituals. Authorities also insisted upon segregation when Sufis visited cemeteries. Evidence suggests that states found Sufi orders, and more specifically women's roles in Sufi orders, troublesome.[64] However, it appears that Sufi practices persisted because they could go on inside the home, out of public view.

There are several explanations for women's active role in Sufism, but the real reasons for their participation are unclear. The fact that Sufis see both men and women as equally able to forge an individual relationship with God might, at least partially, explain the appeal.[65] Another reason why Sufism endures among women can be attributed to the manner with which its practices adapt across a wide variety of people and places. Unlike orthodox religions, Sufism changes and is responsive to the moods and exigencies of the moment.[66] Finally, women's role in Sufism and mysticism might also be related to the location where it is practiced. Unlike Christianity, Islam and Judaism are practiced in the home. The home is where rituals marking religious holidays take place and where women tend to pray. Hence, women, whose realm is often limited to the home, might have a tendency to favor practices that can go on in the comfort and privacy of their own residences.[67] Sufism also offers women who can go out in public a venue to worship. Today, more women than men seek out *baraka,* or holiness, at major Sufi shrines and saints' tombs. In places where women are barred from participating in formal mosque prayers, women find special meaning in their relationships with saints and therefore seek out opportunities to visit holy sites.[68] Visiting shrines also provides women with opportunities to socialize, commiserate, and to share with other women.

Women also had roles in other types of marginalized rituals and practices and operated on the fringes of orthodox religions. Such women served as healers, midwives, and mediums claiming to possess divine qualities. These women were often viewed with skepticism by certain mainstream religious establishments in the Middle East because women's rituals are often marginalized or devalued in relation to orthodoxy.[69] For example, all three monotheistic religions refer to witches who have divine, and often evil, powers. Scholars suggest that women with the power to heal the sick and to cast spells are viewed in a negative light because their supernatural power threatens the male-dominated social order. As such, women who exercised divine power were perceived as dangerous outsiders.[70] In the late 1800s in Ottoman controlled Damascus, some women performed magic and sorcery. Although this activity was not sanctioned by the religious establishment, women established their own popular religious beliefs which required the use of amulets and fortunetellers.[71]

In parts of North Africa, several older women were and are still perceived as having divine powers. In Morocco, some women serve as fortunetellers, seers, sorceresses, magicians, and midwives, positions inherited from their mothers. However, a woman's activities can enhance or detract from her association with divinity. Fortunetellers and seers use tarot-like cards to tell fortunes, discover the cause of illnesses, and to find the whereabouts of missing persons. Often these women are paid for their services. Sorceresses often prepare potions and spells to address people's concerns. For instance, a sorceress might use a potion to help a woman's husband find her more sexually attractive. In the case of midwives, they not only deliver children, but also perform activities to ward off evil spirits during birth. Moroccan men view all of these women with apprehension.[72] Much like other places in the Muslim world, Moroccan women invoke the name of Fatima, Muhammad's daughter, to ward off the evil eye from newborn babies. Many believe that Fatima's hands are a symbol of protection and, as such, symbols of hands appear on doorknockers, vehicles, bracelets, and necklaces to protect the wearer from evil.[73]

Women also serve as unorthodox ritual leaders for other women within the framework of orthodox communities. For example, some Kurdish-Jewish women, who were excluded from the synagogue and formal prayers, established their own rituals, symbols, and prayers as a way to experience spiritual life within an orthodox establishment that inhibits women from full participation in religious rites.[74] By personalizing their own religious rituals and traditions, women found comfort and satisfaction in spiritual communication despite their exclusion from leadership positions in orthodox religious groups. Again, these traditions gave women a venue to share their spirituality with other women in their local community.

WOMEN'S OUTWARD SIGNS OF PIETY

Islam is an important source of shared meaning for people in Middle Eastern and North African society, therefore one of a woman's most important religious roles in her family is protect its honor. In many communities, a man's reputation is contingent upon the behavior of his female relatives. For women, some of the most visible signs of conformity and acceptance of this role come in the form of veiling, seclusion, and adherence to gender segregation norms. The oft-discussed issue of veiling has been associated with traditions already present in the Middle East prior to the advent of Islam. Although the exact reasons why veiling emerged are still unknown, several theories shed light on potential reasons. In the early years of Islam, veiling was associated with upper class women and provided a sign for others that the veiled women came from a particular socioeconomic class and thereby should be unmolested. An Assyrian legal text of the 13th century B.C.E. allowed for respectable women to veil and prohibited prostitutes from doing so. Crucial for Islamic society is the purity of the male line, and although the Qu'ran mentions modest dress for both men and women, it does not specifically mandate that women cover their bodies from head to toe. The social custom of complete veiling and seclusion reflects folk traditions of particular economic groups. For rural women, their inability to work in the fields veiled made it more likely that they would adhere less rigidly to the custom of veiling. Elite women remained in seclusion and were veiled more often than less well off women. The Qu'ran discusses the hijab not as a veil, but as a partition for the wives of the Prophet when they spoke with men who were not members of their family. As such, it appears that veiling came from pre-Islamic practices and seeped into Islam as a way to protect women and symbolize that they were not available to men other than their husbands.[75]

The veil symbolizes many things to a variety of people. For some in the West, the veil screams of misogyny and the persecution of women, but for

Egyptian Muslim woman wearing a niqab veil in the sea at a beach in the Mediterranean city of Alexandria, 2009, next to a girl in more casual dress. (AP Photo/Amr Nabil)

others in the Muslim world, the veil reflects a rebellion against the imposed secularism of the Western world, as in Turkey or in Iran during the period of the Shah. The perception that the veil always reflects a form of female subjugation might not be the perception for some who don the hijab. For other women, the veil illustrates a commitment to their faith and traditional values and reiterates that they should be respected. Some women argue that wearing the veil gives them access to the public realm. This is in line with the modernist's interpretation of women's seclusion in the harem, as it affords particular rights and benefits for women who remain out of the public eye. Similar to arguments propagating single-sex education, seclusion allows women freedom among women. Some proponents of the veil contend that, without it, men are vulnerable and will fall victim to unregulated sexual access. Women are thus responsible for maintaining the family honor by containing the lustful desires of men.[76] Many Muslims emphasize that veiling is Qu'ranic and point to the passage that urges women "not to display their beauty and adornments, but to draw their head cover over their bosoms and not display their adornment."

Clearly, veiling reflects a very complex reality shaped by social, cultural, and political factors that should be viewed within the historical context. Veiling and seclusion stem from the ethos in the Qu'ran of sexual modesty and the concept of honor that goes along with it. Depending upon the social or economic status of women, the level of veiling or seclusion has been interpreted widely. These concepts are closely connected with the concepts of honor and shame in the Muslim and Arab world where communal perceptions define a person's worth. A woman who dishonors her family by going out unaccompanied by a male relative or who is seen with a man who is not an appropriate family member brings shame upon her family. The parents are then blamed for not bringing her up properly or for being unable to control someone for whom they are responsible. According to Islam, women should be under the authority of their fathers, brothers or husbands.[77] The seclusion that followed from the veil led to several detrimental ramifications for women. Many women were unable to go out and get an education or find suitable employment. Their lack of education then made it difficult for them to know what rights were actually afforded to them by Islam; this fact put them squarely under the control of their male relatives.[78] Recently, the veil has taken on a symbolic importance. For women in the Middle East, the veil and the hijab are emblems of piousness, submission, and for some, repression. For some Muslim women in the West, the veil serves as an assertion of identity or even solidarity with their counterparts in the Middle East.

As evidence of the significance of these social norms, many of the worst curses in the Middle East and North Africa have to do with sexual promiscuity of one's mother or sister. Hence, the ideas of honor and shame have come to be socially and religiously mandated expectations of women. In many places, women internalize these norms and use them to gauge their own self worth. In powerful families, a woman's behavior is also tied to the political and social status of the family. Hence, when a woman violates the norms of expected behavior, her actions can damage her entire family's prestige, influence, or reputation. Again, this is often the case because a man's worth is predicated upon his ability to control and protect the women of his household. For example, women of the Saudi ruling elite are closely watched for potential violations of certain gender norms. They are also forbidden from marrying outside of the family.[79]

Overall, the importance of veiling varies across the Middle East. In some places, like Saudi Arabia, the veil is viewed as an indisputable religious obligation and as a symbol of the depth of religious conviction and solidarity with other Muslim women.[80] In other states, like the United Arab Emirates, the veil is not mandatory, but is still common in some places such as mosques. Some view the hijab as a way to allow men and women to interact outside of the home by protecting a woman from the gaze of men while she is out in public.[81] Some states have several rules associated with the veil that are crucial for women to maintain. Saudi Arabia has some of the most stringent rules on women's dress. There, a woman's clothing must not attract attention; as such, many of the coverings are black. Additionally, the hijab must be loose-fitting, made of sturdy material, and must not resemble men's clothing or those of nonbelievers.[82]

Given these limitations on women's roles in Saudi Arabia, one might expect that they have little role in religion in the land of the Prophet's birth. In contrast to Sufis and other religious sects that perform various rituals, dances, and votive offerings, Wahhabism, the puritanical reformist state religion of Saudi Arabia that has been the dominant for the past two centuries,[83] strictly forbids techniques of personal and spiritual empowerment that are

During a protest in Cairo, an Egyptian holds a poster showing 32-year-old pregnant Egyptian woman, Marwa el-Sherbini, with the words "the veil martyr." In 2009, she was stabbed by a German man in a courtroom. The woman was to testify against the man in court after he allegedly called her an Islamist and a terrorist in 2008. German prosecutors say the 28-year-old man was driven by a deep hatred of foreigners. (AP Photo/Mohammed Ahmed)

contrary to orthodox standards. In many ways, this limits women's role in the faith because unorthodox traditions are often a woman's only outlet for spirituality. Furthermore, women cannot attend a mosque, the most important emblem of a community living according to God's laws.[84] Wahhabis focus instead on religious education through reciting and sometimes reading the Qu'ran and the hadith. Some argue that women gained access to religious education through Wahhabism and its emphasis on the study of the Qu'ran and the hadith. Evidence suggests that, in the early 20th century, some Saudi girls received religious education in private homes. Rather than learn to read the Qu'ran, most students memorized verses. Girls were secluded after puberty so those without the help of a relative or tutor had their religious education curtailed at an early age.[85] Early on, there were only a few religious schools for girls in other parts of the Middle East. For instance, in 1914 the Ottoman government created a school in Basra where girls learned the Qu'ran, hadith, and needlework. During this same time period, another school in Bahrain taught girls to memorize the Qu'ran.[86]

Wahhabis were particularly concerned with women's role in religion, as they were often the group most likely to stray from orthodox practices and traditions. By being excluded from worship in local mosques, women tended to seek intercession through votive offerings at shrines, caves, and special trees. In the Wahhabis' view, women were emotionally weak and susceptible to challenge God's judgment. Wahhabis also took issue with women who followed witchcraft, told fortunes, and practiced healing rituals, all activities viewed as forms of polytheism. These unorthodox practices troubled Wahhabis who believed that some women were assuming power that belonged only to God.[87] Subsequent religious scholars reinforced these assumptions about women, stating that they should practice religious rituals in the home and should not compete intellectually with men. Overall, women were viewed as emotionally weak, sexually provocative, dependent on men, and unable to fully understand the complexities of Islam.[88] However, women did have outlets for spiritual development within the confines of their own homes by gathering in small ritual support groups that sometimes ventured out to visit shrines and cemeteries against the wishes of the religious establishment.

In the early 20th century, women who could read were able to fulfill leadership roles in certain religious communities. For example, in Bahrain, literate women served as imams for other women. Literate women also read during religious ceremonies, and as healers could recite holy words for the infirm. Some women even earned money by reading the Qu'ran for paying customers. Despite these avenues for religious participation, literate women were viewed with skepticism and suspicion. Men worried that literate women would use their skills to communicate with men who were not relatives.[89] Across the Gulf States, women had few opportunities to pursue religious education, and men consistently had access to better schools than their female counterparts. While Wahhabis theoretically endorsed women's access to religious education, in practice, they directed their efforts toward men, yet the Wahhabi movement's emphasis on education provided some women with new levels of religious education, even if most of it occurred in the home. The disparity in educational and religious opportunities reflects gender hierarchies in society as a whole. Thus, the secular and state-sponsored education that followed also targeted male students, giving women fewer opportunities to assume leadership roles in society and religious communities.[90]

RELIGIOUS COMMUNITIES

Across the Middle East and North Africa, women hold a variety of religious roles in society. Some countries have allowed women more opportunities to lead religious activities, while others have constrained a woman's participation in the religious realm. The next section explores several communities' approaches and perspectives on women's roles in religion.

Israel

During the Ottoman period, the Holy Land experienced a huge wave of immigration. Jewish women who arrived in Palestine experienced new roles in religious life, especially those living in Jerusalem. Several laws and regulations established women as inherently impure. Such legal restrictions prohibited women from access to Jewish learning and prohibited them from participation in religious activities in the synagogue or in the study hall. However, early female immigrants enjoyed the opportunity to visit holy sites and subsequently to participate actively in religious observances. In Jerusalem, women fortified their religious experience by caring for the stones of the Western Wall, whitewashing tombs, and supporting husbands who devoted themselves to Torah study. Jewish women also opened up soup kitchens for new immigrants and the poor to enable them to devote their time and effort to Torah learning.[91] Other women in the region used philanthropy as a way to achieve a role in their religious communities.

Active participation in Judaism was not limited to women with means. Poor women often begged for money at the Western Wall, while other women cleaned the area, taking special care of worshippers by offering water, fruit, and spices.[92] Jewish women were not alone in their religious activities in Jerusalem. Other faithful women also came to Palestine in the second half of the 19th century. Christian women all over the world traveled to the Holy Land to follow in the footsteps of Jesus. There was also a marked influx of elderly Jewish widows from the Balkans and Europe who immigrated to Jerusalem and stayed, perhaps to prepare intensively for the world that awaited them after death. These women played an active role in the community, marking special holidays and contributing to the diverse landscape of Jerusalem.[93]

Like other women in the region, Jewish women visited and spent time in spiritual contemplation at holy sites. In the 19th century, most women's favorite pilgrimage site was to the matriarch Rachel's tomb in Jerusalem. Rachel, Jacob's favorite wife, continues to serve as an inspiration to Jewish women. Her tragic story unfolds in the Old Testament when, after meeting and deciding to marry Jacob, her father decides instead to let Leah, Rachel's sister, marry him. Later, Rachel also marries Jacob, but she proved unable to have children for a number of years. In the Bible, Rachel's tears had supernatural powers to bring on the redemption of the nation. In a society that valued fertility and children, Rachel's struggle to conceive is an issue that many women face. Finally, though she had been barren, she conceived two sons, but she faced an early death while on the road to Ephrath. In her role as the "mother of the nation" Rachel's tomb remains an important place for women seeking a spiritual connection with this female saint who also personifies the Jewish Diaspora for her role in weeping for her children's exile and the joys of redemption.[94]

Of late, Israeli women have pushed for new positions of religious leadership. Since the 1980s, women have been able to learn the top level Torah, the first five books of the Bible, in religious institutions. This is significant because top level Torah learning and education was traditionally an all-male activity. Women are also organizing efforts to support their increased presence in the political and religious life of Israeli society. International and national political caucuses of religious women have drawn thousands to their conferences, signaling a growing place for women in positions of religious and political leadership. Women are also writing Torah scholarship, a new phenomenon in the history of Orthodox Judaism.[95] These religious activities are not limited to adult women. Some young girls teach Jewish culture in non-religious schools as a way to educate future generations. Once exempt, some religious women are now obligated to serve in the Israeli Defense Forces.[96] A special program, originally only for men, allows women to continue their Torah study while serving in the military. As such, women are accepting new roles in Israel's spiritual and public realm.

Maronites in Lebanon

In general, while women's roles in orthodox religious communities diminished, women had active roles in unorthodox communities. Examples abound of women in leadership roles among the religious minorities in the Middle East. One such group is the Maronite Christian community in Lebanon, the largest of the Uniate churches in the Middle East. The Uniate churches form a group that abandoned Eastern Orthodox traditions and rites in the 12th century, assumed Latin traditions, and recognized the authority of the Pope. They follow Saint John Maroun, and, as Uniates, cut themselves off theologically from the dominant intellectual traditions of the Christian East. Originally, Maronites were mostly found in northern Syria, but later they resided in the mountains of Lebanon where they enjoyed near autonomy throughout the Ottoman period. In 1750, Hindiyya Ujaymi founded her own holy order, the Sisters of the Sacred Heart of Jesus, the first exclusively women's order in the Maronite Church. Her leadership role was based on the claim that she had experienced a mystical union with Christ while she was in her 20s. She established a convent where she spoke about her relationship with divinity. In time, her open proclamations became controversial and her order was abolished. The Vatican later proscribed her writings.[97] Later, scholars discovered similarities between her writings to both Jewish and Muslim mysticism, particularly in the ways that she assimilated Western and Eastern traditions. After her order was abolished, she lived a quiet and secluded life until she died in 1798.

NOTES

1. Eleanor Abdella Doumato, *Getting God's Ear, Women, Islam, and Healing* (New York: Columbia University Press, 2000), 35.

2. Denise L. Carmody, "Judaism," in *Women in World Religions,* ed. Arvind Sharma (Albany: State University Press of New York, 1987), 195.

3. Michael O. Emerson, "Through Tinted Glasses; Religion, World view, and Abortion Attitudes," *Journal for the Scientific Study of Religion* 35 (1996): 43.

4. Charles Lindholm, *The Islamic Middle East, Traditions and Change* (Malden, MA: Blackwell Publishing, 2002), 242–43.

5. Nikki R. Keddie, *Women in the Middle East: Past and Present* (Princeton, NJ: Princeton University Press, 2007), 212.

6. Keddie, *Women in the Middle East: Past and Present,* 14.

7. Nora Alarifi Pharaon, "Saudi Women and the Muslim State in the 21st Century," *Sex Roles* 51 (2004): 356.

8. Keddie, *Women in the Middle East: Past and Present,* 34.

9. Doumato, *Getting God's Ear, Women, Islam, and Healing,* 105.

10. Jamsheed K. Choksy, "Women During the Transition from Sasanian to Early Islamic Times," in *Women in Iran from the Rise of Islam until 1800,* ed. Guity Nashat and Lois Beck (Urbana: University of Illinois Press, 2003), 52.

11. Keddie, *Women in the Middle East: Past and Present,* 14–15.

12. Samuel P. Huntington, *The Third Wave: Democratization in the late Twentieth Century* (Norman: University of Oklahoma Press, 1991), 310.

13. Pharaon, "Saudi Women and the Muslim State in the 21st Century," 362.

14. Keddie, *Women in the Middle East: Past and Present,* 20.

15. Arthur Goldschmidt Jr., *A Concise History of the Middle East* (Cambridge, MA: Westview Press, 2002), 26.

16. Daniel Bates and Amal Rassam, *People and Cultures of the Middle East* (Englewood, NJ: Prentice Hall, 1983), 34.

17. John Bunzl, *Islam, Judaism, and the Political Role of Religions in the Middle East* (Gainesville: University of Florida Press, 2004), 7.

18. Bates and Rassam, *People and Cultures of the Middle East*, 36.

19. Geraldine Brooks, *Nine Parts of Desire, The Hidden World of Islamic Women* (New York: Anchor Books, 1995), 86.

20. Guity Nashat and Judith Tucker, *Women in the Middle East and North Africa* (Bloomington: Indiana University Press, 1999), 44.

21. Bates and Rassam, *People and Cultures of the Middle East*, 46.

22. Nashat and Tucker, *Women in the Middle East and North Africa*, 44.

23. Camille Adams Helminski, *Women of Sufism, A Hidden Treasure* (Boston, MA: Shambhala Publications, 2003), 3.

24. Brooks, *Nine Parts of Desire, The Hidden World of Islamic Women*, 87.

25. Brooks, *Nine Parts of Desire, The Hidden World of Islamic Women*, 81.

26. Bates and Rassam, *People and Cultures of the Middle East*, 41.

27. Vali Nasr, *The Shi'a Revival* (New York: W.W. Norton, 2007), 41.

28. Nasr, *The Shi'a Revival*, 189.

29. Nasr, *The Shi'a Revival*, 42.

30. Nashat and Tucker, *Women in the Middle East and North Africa*, 48.

31. Brooks, *Nine Parts of Desire, The Hidden World of Islamic Women*, 88.

32. Keddie, *Women in the Middle East: Past and Present*, 24.

33. Keddie, *Women in the Middle East: Past and Present*, 28.

34. Nashat and Tucker, *Women in the Middle East and North Africa*, 39.

35. Brooks, *Nine Parts of Desire, The Hidden World of Islamic Women*, 89.

36. Gavin R. G. Hambly, *Women in the Medieval Islamic World* (New York: St. Martin's Press, 1998), 9.

37. Nashat and Tucker, *Women in the Middle East and North Africa*, 48.

38. Doumato, *Getting God's Ear, Women, Islam, and Healing*, 35.

39. Kais M. Firro, *A History of the Druzes* (Leiden, The Netherlands: E. J. Brill, 1992), 4–5.

40. Bates and Rassam, *People and Cultures of the Middle East*, 67.

41. Bates and Rassam, *People and Cultures of the Middle East*, 68.

42. For more information about the Agha Khan Foundation, see http://www.akdn.org/akf_issues.asp.

43. Katherine Meyer, Helen Rizzo, and Yousef Ali, "Islam and the Extension of Citizenship Rights to Women in Kuwait," *Journal for the Scientific Study of Religion* 37 (1998): 133.

44. Firro, *A History of the Druzes*, 24–25.

45. Keddie, *Women in the Middle East: Past and Present*, 46–47.

46. Keddie, *Women in the Middle East: Past and Present*, 52.

47. Keddie, *Women in the Middle East: Past and Present*, 27.

48. Ayse Saktanber, *Living Islam* (New York: I. B. Tautis, 2002), 128–29.

49. Keddie, *Women in the Middle East: Past and Present*, 19.

50. Keddie, *Women in the Middle East: Past and Present*, 30.

51. Quoted in Jane I. Smith, "Women in Islam: Equity, Equality, and the Search for the Natural Order," *Journal of the American Academy of Religion* 47, no. 4 (1979): 518.

52. Smith, "Women in Islam: Equity, Equality, and the Search for the Natural Order," 518.

53. Qu'ran, as quoted in Beverly Milton-Edwards, *Islam and Politics in the Contemporary World* (Cambridge, UK: Polity Press, 2004), 124.

54. Lindholm, *The Islamic Middle East, Traditions and Change,* 230.

55. Bates and Rassam, *People and Cultures of the Middle East,* 70.

56. Bates and Rassam, *People and Cultures of the Middle East,* 69–70.

57. Helminski, *Women of Sufism, A Hidden Treasure,* xx.

58. Keddie, *Women in the Middle East: Past and Present,* 44.

59. Bates and Rassam, *People and Cultures of the Middle East,* 72.

60. Bates and Rassam, *People and Cultures of the Middle East,* 71–73.

61. Helminski, *Women of Sufism, A Hidden Treasure,* xx.

62. Helminski, *Women of Sufism, A Hidden Treasure,* xxii.

63. Shemeem Burney Abbas, *The Female Voice in Sufi Ritual* (Austin: University of Texas Press, 2002), xiv.

64. Nashat and Tucker, *Women in the Middle East and North Africa,* 96.

65. Helminski, *Women of Sufism, A Hidden Treasure,* xxv.

66. Bates and Rassam, *People and Cultures of the Middle East,* 69.

67. Abbas, *The Female Voice in Sufi Ritual,* xiii.

68. Fatima Mernissi, "Women, Saints, and Sanctuaries," in *Women and National Development: The Complexities of Change,* ed. Wellesley Editorial Committee (Chicago: University of Chicago Press, 1977), 101–12.

69. Doumato, *Getting God's Ear, Women, Islam, and Healing,* 39.

70. Doumato, *Getting God's Ear, Women, Islam, and Healing,* 36.

71. James A. Reilly, "Women in the Economic Life of Late-Ottoman Damascus," *Arabica* 4 (1995): 97–98.

72. Susan S. Davis, *Patience and Power: Women's Lives in a Moroccan Village* (Cambridge, MA: Schenkman Publishing Company, 1983), 78–79.

73. Davis, *Patience and Power: Women's Lives in a Moroccan Village,* 123.

74. Doumato, *Getting God's Ear, Women, Islam, and Healing,* 38.

75. Smith, "Women in Islam: Equity, Equality, and the Search for the Natural Order," 521.

76. Quoted in Jen'nan Ghazal Read and John P. Bartkowski, "To Veil or Not to Veil?: A Case Study of Identity Negotiation," *Gender and Society* 14, no. 3 (2000): 399.

77. Bates and Rassam, *People and Cultures of the Middle East,* 215.

78. Smith, "Women in Islam: Equity, Equality, and the Search for the Natural Order," 521.

79. Bates and Rassam, *People and Cultures of the Middle East,* 219.

80. Pharaon, "Saudi Women and the Muslim State in the 21st Century," 360.

81. Pharaon, "Saudi Women and the Muslim State in the 21st Century," 360.

82. M. Khan, *Islam Rediscovered: Discovering Islam from its Original Sources* (New Delhi: Goodword Books, 2001), 226.

83. Bates and Rassam, *People and Cultures of the Middle East,* 76.

84. Doumato, *Getting God's Ear, Women, Islam, and Healing,* 40.

85. Doumato, *Getting God's Ear, Women, Islam, and Healing,* 84–85.

86. Doumato, *Getting God's Ear, Women, Islam, and Healing,* 86.

87. Doumato, *Getting God's Ear, Women, Islam, and Healing,* 222.

88. Doumato, *Getting God's Ear, Women, Islam, and Healing,* 225.

89. Doumato, *Getting God's Ear, Women, Islam, and Healing,* 90.

90. Doumato, *Getting God's Ear, Women, Islam, and Healing,* 92–93.

91. Margalit Shilo, *Princess or Prisoner? Jewish Women in Jerusalem 1840–1914* (Lebanon: Brandeis University Press, 2005), 224–25.

92. Shilo, *Princess or Prisoner? Jewish Women in Jerusalem 1840–1914,* 23.

93. Shilo, *Princess or Prisoner? Jewish Women in Jerusalem 1840–1914,* 10.

94. Shilo, *Princess or Prisoner? Jewish Women in Jerusalem 1840–1914,* 31.

95. Leah Shakdiel, "An Army of Women Learning Torah," in *Gender, Religion, and Change in the Middle East,* eds. Inger Marie Okkenhaug and Ingvild Flaskerud (Oxford, UK: Berg, 2005), 160.

96. Shakdiel, "An Army of Women Learning Torah," 123.

97. Bruce Masters, *Christians and Jews in the Ottoman Arab World* (Cambridge: Cambridge University Press, 2001), 113–14.

SUGGESTED READINGS

Abbas, Shemeem Burney. *The Female Voice in Sufi Ritual.* Austin: University of Texas Press, 2002.

Bayes, Jane H. and Nayereh Tohidi eds. *Globalization, Gender and Religion: The Politics of Women's Rights in Catholic and Muslim Contexts.* New York: Palgrave, 2001.

Beck, Lois and Nikki R. Keddie eds. *Women in the Muslim World.* Cambridge, MA: Harvard University Press, 1978.

Bunzl, John. *Islam, Judaism, and the Political Role of Religions in the Middle East.* Gainesville: University of Florida Press, 2004.

Carmody, Denise L. "Judaism." in *Women in World Religions,* ed. Arvind Sharma. Albany: State University Press of New York, 1987.

Doumato, Eleanor Abdella. *Getting God's Ear, Women, Islam, and Healing.* New York: Columbia University Press, 2000.

Helminski, Camille Adams. *Women of Sufism, A Hidden Treasure.* Boston, MA: Shambhala Publications, 2003.

Okkenhaug, Inger Marie and Ingvild Flaskerud eds. *Gender, Religion, and Change in the Middle East.* Oxford, UK: Berg, 2005.

Sechzer, Jeri Altneu. "Islam and Women, Where Tradition Meets Modernity." *Sex Roles* 51 (2004): 263–272.

4

⟨⟨⟨⟩⟩⟩

Women and the Law

Women in the Middle East and North Africa have been viewed as inferior to men, especially with regards to the law. Although literacy rates across the Middle East and North Africa have improved, for long stretches of history, many women were illiterate and depended upon men to speak for them. As such, they did not understand their legal rights or were severely constrained by the patriarchic structure of society. Some argue that, prior to Islam, customary laws were even more restrictive for women than Islamic law. The advent of Islam brought with it legal changes regarding marriage, divorce, property ownership, and inheritance rights. As time progressed, some legal interpretations became more restrictive, while others allowed women greater freedom in the areas mentioned. With increased education, women have become more vocal with regards to their legal rights. Consequently, in many Middle Eastern and North African countries today, women can initiate divorce, own property, and inherit equally with men. Despite legal rulings favoring women, actual practice has not always reflected the laws' intent as traditional values seep into decision-making.

This chapter discusses Islamic law relating to women including marriage, divorce, property ownership, and inheritance and explores specific countries' personal status laws.

ISLAM

Islam underscored the role of the family to lessen the power of the tribe. With an emphasis on the family unit, the importance of men and women's rights within that social unit intensified. Several laws stand out with regards to both family and women. The Qu'ran prohibits female infanticide, a practice that was quite common in pre-Islamic Arabia. The Qu'ran incorporated inheritance rights for women, which was a change from what existed prior to Islam. Additionally, men were limited to four wives, as opposed to the occasional unbounded polygyny that existed prior, and the Qu'ran discourages, although permits, divorce. Modernists argue that Islam sets limits on issues such as plural marriage and clearly spelled out women's and men's rights and obligations. During Muhammad's time, women enjoyed religious freedom, and they were allowed to convert to Islam or refuse conversion without the permission of a male relative. In Muhammad's family, some women opted to convert while their husbands did not.[1]

After Islamic law was codified, pre-Islamic ideals regarding women seeped into Muslim thought. The emergence of a class of male legal scholars or *ulema*, coupled with the expansion of Islamic scholars outside of Arabia, led to strict interpretations of the Qu'ran that have continued to the present day. These scholars hold particular views of the ideal Muslim woman. One writer describes her as follows:

> She never leaves the house, even to see neighbors or her acquaintance[s]. She has no women friends, confides in nobody, and relies only on her husband. She accepts nothing from anyone, excepting her husband and her parents. If she sees relatives, she does not meddle in their affairs. She is not treacherous, and has no faults to hide, nor wrong reasons to proffer.[2]

One oft-cited phrase in the Qu'ran discusses a husband's authority over his wife and his responsibility to provide for her and the children of that union. "Woman's righteousness is realized when she accepts her place and obligations in this divinely legislated system."[3] Yet in the Qu'ran, both women and men originated from the same being and share equal status. One reason for the seemingly contradictory nature of Islamic law is that interpretations of women's status differ significantly between conservative and more modernist views. In the Qu'ran, several passages point to equality of the sexes. One refers to a woman's right to own property, emphasizing that neither a father nor a husband can interfere with that privilege. Even if the wife is rich, the husband is still required to support her and their children. After the prophet Muhammad died, the religious scholars developed a body of law made up of the Qu'ran and the sayings (hadith) and actions (sunna) of Muhammad. The sharia, however, could not cover every issue that arose and therefore scholars needed to explore the problems and apply *ijtihad*, or independent reasoning. By the 11th century, Sunni scholars had consolidated the legal rulings into several schools of law and no longer permitted independent reasoning. To understand the Islamic view on personal status issues and the law, it is important to explore the areas of marriage, divorce, inheritance, and property ownership.

MARRIAGE

In Islam, men can marry up to four wives, but the Qu'ran contains apparently conflicting statements about polygyny, the marriage of a man to more than one wife. In one verse, it is written that men can marry up to four wives only if they are able to treat them equally. Another verse in the Qu'ran states, "no matter how you try you will never be able to treat your wives equally." Some modernists interpret this as meaning that Islam is actually recommending monogamy. The law also allows men to have concubines.[4] Muslim women are forbidden from marrying non-Muslims, but men can marry women who are from accepted religions such as Judaism or Christianity, known in Islam as "people of the Book." Any children of the union will be Muslim.

In marriage, women have the right to dictate aspects of the marriage contract, yet in reality the father or male guardians usually make the key decisions. Bridegrooms must give women a *mahr*, loosely translated as a dowry, but families determine the amount of that gift. A woman may receive her dowry directly, as opposed to the payment going to the woman's family, but again, this is not always the case. Cultural factors influence women's rights with regards to marriage despite the laws that are written in the Qu'ran. For example, a woman's mother-in-law has extraordinary control over a new wife and, in many situations, this relationship can be a challenging one for the new bride. The marriage age varies according to country, but in the early period of Islam, girls could be married off as early as age eight. According to Islam, marriage should occur after puberty, but the interpretation of when puberty occurs is debated in legal opinions.[5] Along with marriage comes the anxiety of producing a male for the family, given the strong patriarchal nature of Islamic society. This puts a tremendous amount of pressure on a new wife.

In Shia Islam, a type of marriage called mut'a is permitted. This type of marriage is temporary and the union can be as short as one day. When the contract expires, the marriage is dissolved, but if children result from the union, then the father must follow the normal rules of marriage and family support. Temporary marriage is rejected by most Sunnis, who view it as a form of prostitution and, since divorce is discouraged in Islam, something against the rules.[6]

Another aspect of marriage discussed in the Qu'ran is adultery, which prescribes 100 lashes as punishment for both the man and woman involved. The punishment of adulterers by stoning is discussed in a hadith and made its way into Islamic law from Jewish law. To make proving adultery difficult, thereby avoiding harsh punishment, the Qu'ran requires four witnesses to the act and any accuser who cannot produce four witnesses is subject to lashing. In early Islam, stoning was rarely invoked, but what did occur and continues today are honor killings to protect the dignity of the tribe and family. In some cases, a woman who was suspected of misconduct was killed by one of her male relatives for bringing shame to the family.

DIVORCE

Marriage is important in Islam, and as such the Qu'ran discourages divorce. However, because divorce is permitted, Islam is very clear about the conditions under which one can divorce. The belief is that other avenues of reconciliation should be attempted before one divorces. In the Qu'ran, Muhammad stated his disdain for divorce, "Of all the things that Islam has permitted, divorce is the most hated by Allah."[7] Some verses in the Qu'ran reflect the kind and just view that Islam has toward women. For example, when discussing the issue of divorce, the Qu'ran declares that a woman must be "retained in honor or released in kindness." For the most part, men have the right to divorce unilaterally by making a pronouncement three times that the marriage is over, yet this issue of repudiation is more complicated than just uttering the words "I divorce you" three times. The idea behind this action is that a man must say these words and then refrain from sexual relations with his wife for three months. During this period, he can revoke his proclamation of divorce. If the words are uttered quickly in succession, there is no opportunity for reconciliation.[8] Again, this law was implemented to offer the possibility of settlement since Islam discourages divorce. If a divorce occurs, the husband is required to provide for the woman if she is pregnant and support any children who live with her.

The concept of why the male has the unilateral right to divorce needs to be seen within the Islamic context. The male shoulders the financial obligations that are a consequence of divorce, and therefore it is believed that he has the right to make the decision about whether a divorce should occur. According to Islamic law, women can initiate and obtain a divorce if the husband has delegated her that right in a marriage contract; however, he still has the right to divorce his wife when he wants. A woman can also give up all or part of her dowry to obtain a divorce from her husband. Further, a woman's right to divorce is determined by the particular legal school that is followed in her region. There are four main legal schools of thought in Islam: Maliki, Shafii, Hanbali, and Hanafi. The Hanafi school is the most conservative and allows women to divorce only if a husband is unable to consummate the marriage or has gone missing. The other schools have a variety of reasons under which they allow divorce.[9]

In Islam, a couple can write a marriage contract and incorporate any stipulation, including ones that would be conditions for divorce. If a person breaches that contract, that the breach could be a reason for divorce. Conditions are not necessarily helpful to women, as exemplified by the stipulation that, if the husband takes a second wife, the first wife is automatically divorced. If a man divorces his wife, she does not have to return gifts to him that she has received over the course of their marriage, and he is required to provide for her material rights. If a woman divorces a husband, she has to pay him part of her dowry or whatever payment was agreed upon in the marriage contract. In reality, in many countries in the Middle East and North Africa, men divorce their wives arbitrarily, while wives have difficulty divorcing their husbands. Over time, however, it has become more difficult for men in most countries to divorce their wives by simple repudiation. In other cases, women can appeal to a judge to rule that the husband must grant her a divorce.

One important part of divorce concerns the custody of any children resulting from the union, and Islamic law favors the husband in custody issues. According to Islamic law, a man or his family will gain custody of the children, yet depending upon the school of law followed, women can raise minor children until a certain age. In a particularly famous case memorialized in the 1987 book *Not Without My Daughter,* when an American woman married to an Iranian man divorced, he took their daughter and moved to Iran. The story documents the woman's difficulty in getting back her child. In Bahrain, family law is not codified, leaving judges to make arbitrary rulings, usually not in favor of the women. There are several cases pending in Bahrain where women who have accused men of abuse are being sued for slander. Few shelters exist for women, and police are reluctant to take statements from women and follow through with their accusations.[10]

INHERITANCE AND PROPERTY RIGHTS

Prior to Islam, women had no rights of inheritance, but the Qu'ran gave women the right to inherit half of what a man receives. Although the inequity of this law on the surface is quite clear, modernists argue that the law made sense in Islamic societies because men had the obligation to provide for women, while women were free of any financial responsibilities to the household. Islamic feminists argue that since women work today, the law should be adapted. Other more conservative theorists interpret the Qu'ranic stipulation that daughters should receive half the inheritance that their brothers do as evidence that women are inferior to men, yet this interpretation is flawed since inheritance laws revealed during Muhammad's lifetime need to be interpreted within the context of those times, when gender roles differed significantly. Since a man was deemed responsible for full support of his wife and children, it made sense that men should receive more inheritance. Women, on the other hand, were allowed to keep their money to do with as they pleased. Theory and reality, however, did not always coincide, and many instances occurred where women did not receive their fair share of an inheritance. In other cases, men used what belonged to their wives.

Concerning property rights, in Islam women have the right to own land. Since women were allowed to own land in Ottoman Damascus, they had recourse in the sharia courts to defend their property rights. In many cases, the disputes were over inheritance rights. In several cases, women of lower status represented themselves in court, reflecting the women's belief that the court was a useful place in which to pursue their demands.[11]

WORLD WAR I AND AFTERWARD

The personal status laws of many countries in the Middle East and North Africa differ significantly. Some countries, such as Turkey, have instituted secular codes and place very few restrictions on women, at least according to the law. Other countries, such as Saudi Arabia, rule according to a conservative interpretation of Islamic law and therefore have much more stringent rules regarding women's roles under the law. This section explores the personal status law of several countries in the region beginning with the period after World War I to illustrate the range of interpretations across the Middle East.

IRAN

Iran passed the Marriage Reform Law in 1931, a law that was touted by some as the most progressive legislation in an Eastern nation. The Shah's aim in passing this law was to create a modern, Western judicial system and, although family law was still influenced by Shia legal concepts, new procedures for marriage and divorce lessened the clerics' power in these areas. Although the clerics' authority decreased in regards to most personal status issues, it was not until the Shah passed the Family Protection Law (FPL) in 1967 that real reforms occurred by giving women and men equal rights in divorce and custody and by curtailing polygamy. Many Iranians viewed this law as just another program by the despotic Pahlavi regime, and, as such, it lacked the legitimacy that women's groups hoped it would have.[12] In 1975, the Shah attempted to strengthen the FPL by raising the minimum marriage age for women to 18 and 20 for men. After the Iranian revolution in 1979, which ushered in a conservative and theocratic regime, the highest religious leader, Ayatollah Khomeini, denounced the FPL. Although the law was not abrogated, judges were no longer secular, but were religious clerics who used sharia as their guide. Iran returned to unilateral divorce for men and a much more limited scope of when women were entitled to divorce. The Ayatollah decreased the age of marriage for women to nine, and in custody issues, men or their families usually gained custody of the children after a certain age. Additionally, birth control was banned and day care and family planning centers were closed. When the constitution was rewritten by the new regime, an emphasis was placed on motherhood and domestic life for women, while all laws were to be based on "Islamic precepts."[13] This factor had important implications for marriage, divorce, custody, and inheritance rights.

In this conservative atmosphere, women, along with some men, countered the changes. Eventually, gradual modifications to the law were enacted, and children whose fathers had been killed in war were allowed to remain with their mothers rather than being sent to their paternal relatives. Other, more positive, changes occurred with regards to divorce. Women were entitled to better economic compensation after male-initiated divorce and the rules governing polygyny and divorce were changed to limit some of men's privileges.

When the Ayatollah died in 1989, Ali Akbar Hashemi Rafsanjani became president and began to improve women's status by rationalizing any changes with Islamic concepts. One of the greatest challenges that Rafsanjani faced was the growing Iranian population. To address this issue, the government instituted family planning options while still banning abortions. Additionally, the minimum age for marriage for girls was raised to 15. In the 1990s post-revolutionary period, debates that had been quelled regarding women's rights under the law reemerged. Women began to play a larger role in politics and in proposing legislation concerning the personal status code.[14] In 1992, the Iranian parliament, or *Majlis*, introduced changes to divorce law that would let women who were unfairly divorced by their husbands get financial support from them. Although the bill was rejected twice by the Guardian Council—a group that can nullify any bill passed through the *Majlis*—it was eventually passed. The government appointed female advisors, and, in January 1996, women were permitted to act as judicial counselors in cases of divorce. This move was important in two ways. First, in divorce cases, the female advisors explored women's rights more thoroughly than male counselors. Second, the appointment of female advisors was a step in the direction of reinstating women as judges.[15] When the reformist President Mohammad Khatemi was elected in 1997 on a platform of increasing democracy, human rights, and gender rights, hopes were high that he would be able to implement significant changes for women.

TURKEY

From 1908–1918, the Young Turks were in power in Turkey. The Young Turk movement espoused centralization and secular reform for Turkey. A 1916 law recognized adultery and taking a second wife as grounds for divorce, and by 1917 the Family Law code incorporated these key reforms into one legal code. A major change for women came during World War I when women were needed to assist the war effort. During the Turkish War of Independence, from 1918–1923, women became politically mobilized and this impacted their rights after independence. When Mustafa Ataturk, the founder of modern Turkey, attained power in 1923, he subordinated Islam to secular law. Although he recognized and permitted people to raise their children as Muslims, school was mandatory until the age of 16 for both genders. Ataturk perceived women and their incorporation into all aspects of society as an important component for raising Turkey's status in the international community. In 1926 he remarked, "If henceforward the women do not share in the social life of the nation, we shall never attain to our full development. We shall remain irremediably backward, incapable of treading on equal terms with the civilizations of the West."[16]

In 1926, when the secular Turkish Civil Code—based on the Swiss model—was enacted, it was the first time that Islamic law was not used to interpret family law. The civil code provided some key challenges to Islamic law by outlawing polygamy, allowing women the same rights to divorce as men, and permitting Muslim women to marry non-Muslim men. Despite these changes, women in rural Turkey remained subservient to men and bound by Islamic law. Additionally, due to the difficult nature of the agricultural work and women's large contribution and time commitment in that realm, many rural women were unfamiliar with the new laws, yet sweeping changes in the Turkish political structure led to a dissemination of ideas even in the rural sector. When the Civil Code was enacted in 1926, elite women mobilized to publicize information about women's new rights. When the two party system emerged in Turkey after Ataturk's death in 1938, politicians began to visit rural areas to mobilize the population. Each of the parties had a women's wing to address women's issues, and the national government passed information down to the village headmen who circulated the information about civil marriages and the ways to acquire licenses.

Ataturk not only changed Turkey's legal system, his drive for modernization also led to significant social changes and a structural transformation of the family. In the rural areas, where subsistence farming was prevalent, the move to agricultural production for market sales impacted the family structure. When controversies arose, many people, including many women, turned to the new legal system for support, indicating their trust in the legal system. A small study of the Bodrum district in Western Anatolia from 1950 to 1965 revealed that the number of divorces initiated by women doubled, reflecting the faith and use of the courts by women to obtain their divorces. Prior to Ataturk's reforms, women had very little recourse with regards to divorce. Court documents from the 1960s also reflect a shifting attitude toward the patriarchal, extended family structure. In divorce cases, judges began to recognize that one reason for divorce was the failure of husbands to set up a separate household for their wives so that they did not have to live with his parents.[17] These cases reflect the fact that some rural Muslim women were using the secular court system to make their cases for divorce and broach other grievances. Despite these changes, judges could still rule against divorce in cases of domestic violence. One particular case in the 1980s propelled the Turkish feminist movement into action. A woman who was pregnant with her fourth child and frequently beaten by her husband was denied a divorce. The judge explained his decision as follows, "one should not leave a woman's back without a stick, her womb without a donkey."[18] Feminist groups united to protest and, eventually, though not without key challenges, set up shelters for battered women with the support of the federal government.

When the Justice and Development Party (AKP) came to power in 2002, it changed Article 10 of the Turkish constitution to increase gender equality. The article stated that the "state became the guarantor of gender equality" and by doing this, Turkey made the Convention on the Elimination of All Forms of Discrimination Against Women (CEDAW) a part of Turkish law. The implication here is that women's issues were getting more attention. The party advanced a program to address women's issues, including women's education and violence against women. The government established Turkish courts dealing with family law and increased paid maternity leave to 16 weeks. The AKP also abolished a particularly egregious law that pardoned a rapist if he married his victim. Shelters for abused women and children were established in areas with populations of more than 50,000 people.[19]

Although the AKP professes its adherence to the secular nature of the Turkish state, its Islamist leanings have concerned some Turks who believe that it could have a negative impact on women's rights. In 2004, some AKP members wanted to pass a law that criminalized adultery, as it had been prior to 1926. Many in the AKP believe that family is the center of Turkish values and should be preserved. After pressure from the European Union and women's groups, who believed that the law would work against women, the legislation was withdrawn.[20]

EGYPT

Until the 19th century, sharia law governed all aspects of life in Egypt, and the judicial system consisted of only Islamic courts. Egypt's legal system became secular at the end of the 19th century and, due to French influence in Egypt, the French civil, commercial, and legal codes were adopted. Personal status law, however, remained within the realm of Islam and followed the conservative Hanafi legal school. Although a decree in 1923 set the marriage age for girls at 16 and boys at 18, these rules were not always followed. New provisions were put into effect under the Personal Status Law of 1929.[21] The Personal Status Law of 1929 contained certain key provisions that improved women's rights with regards to divorce, although judges could still force a wife who left home without permission to return to her husband. A woman could seek a divorce if a husband deserted her, disappeared or was incarcerated, maltreated her, had a contagious disease, or failed to provide for her. The 1929 law also superseded the Islamic divorce law, which allowed a man to state three times that he wanted to divorce his wife. According to Islamic law, if a man stated his desire to divorce three times, the divorce was irrevocable. One interesting change in the 1929 law was that it allowed judges to select their interpretation of sharia law from the four major Sunni schools of law. So, although the Hanafi School was the most prevalent school of jurisprudence in Egypt, lawmakers could select from the other three, which, in some cases, provided more liberal views with the potential to support more gender equality.

The Personal Status Law of 1929 allowed for polygyny, which remained unregulated by the authorities. An important modification to this law only occurred in 1985 when a man was required in a marriage contract to inform the woman of his current marital status. Additionally, he needed to divulge the names of his other wives so that an official letter could be sent to their homes informing them of the new marriage. The wives were then allowed to request a divorce by illustrating that the new marriage caused them financial or other harm, although the wife's right to request a divorce expired after one year.[22]

When Gamal Abdel Nasser came to power in 1952, he worked toward gender equality, as encapsulated in the 1956 constitution, which included equality before the law and in employment. Nasser did not address the issue of family and religious law which guided personal status issues, therefore, despite Nasser's attempts to integrate women into the economy and political life, he steered clear of controversial family issues.

When Anwar Sadat first assumed power after Nasser's death in 1970, he allied himself with Islamist groups and, in 1971, actually agreed to modify the constitution. Whereas the earlier constitution called for gender equality, under the new wording, gender equality applied as long as it was not in contradiction with sharia law. President Sadat's wife, Jihan Sadat, was a great advocate for women's rights and pushed for legal avenues to ameliorate conditions for women. Clearly, Jihan Sadat influenced her husband on gender issues, and in the latter part of the 1970s, Sadat reformed Egypt's family law. The new law permitted first wives to leave a husband who took a second wife. If a wife left the home to protest polygyny, the authorities could no longer force her to return home, as they could previously, and she was allowed to divorce. The law also provided for alimony and other financial support if a woman had custody of the children.

After Sadat's assassination by a militant Islamic group in 1981, Hosni Mubarak succeeded him as president. After some protests against Sadat's reforms, in 1985, the High Constitutional Court of Egypt struck down the 1979 law, although eventually certain provisions were reinstated. According to the 1985 law, wives could no longer obtain an automatic divorce if a man took a second wife, and the burden was on the wife to prove that the polygamous marriage was harmful to her.[23] A woman who left home without her husband's approval could be considered disobedient and could lose her right to her husband's financial support. Although there is no basis for this concept of obedience in the Qu'ran, Islamic jurisprudence discusses it. The Egyptian court system was reorganized in the 1990s after significant pressure from women's groups. The reorganization was enacted to facilitate court procedures in family law. In 2000, a new law was passed giving a woman the right to divorce even without her husband's consent if she paid back her dowry. This law was hotly debated in parliament and the Egyptian press, although it eventually passed. Those who opposed the law argued that, by making the procedures for divorce easier, the Egyptian family would be destroyed. Despite changes in the law, a two-tiered system exists in Egypt with regards to personal status that discriminates against women relegating them to the status of minors. In effect, Egypt has two separate legal systems, one for men and another for women. In some cases, men can still divorce their wives by saying three times "you are divorced" and then have it registered with a religious notary. Women, however, must use the court system, which is often slow and inefficient. Women are also required to have a mediator since women are not viewed as rational enough to make important life choices.[24]

MOROCCO

In North Africa, as in most other places in the Middle East, women became a symbol of anti-colonial resistance, an untouchable realm where sharia law guided family status issues.[25] The varying political circumstances of the North African countries led to very different family codes, especially during the period following independence. Morocco achieved independence from France in 1956 and was ruled by King Muhammad Hassan II from 1961–1999. A family code, or *Mudawwana,* was adopted in 1957 and continued to support polygyny and a male guardian's need to grant permission for a woman to work, travel, or marry. The code included several reforms, such as setting the minimum age for marriage at 15 and ending forced marriage. For the most part, decisions regarding family law and personal status were left to local authorities. Many Moroccan women were extremely disappointed with the *Mudawwana,* which was based on an interpretation of Islam, while other laws, such as the penal code implemented after independence, were based on civil law or the French code. Additionally, the constitution promulgated in 1962 contained contradictory text with regards to gender equality. By the 1980s, Morocco was joining the rest of the region in a resurgence of Islamist thought, which espoused veiling and stricter rules on women moving freely without male approval.

Along with the growth of the Islamist movement, the feminist movement in Morocco also continued to blossom, so that by the 1990s centers on gender and women's studies had emerged in several universities.[26] Women continued to oppose the *Mudawwana* and, in 1992, they began a large campaign to gain millions of signatures supporting changes to the law. King Hassan responded to the protesters by creating a commission of religious leaders to review the proposals. In 1993, some significant modifications to the family code were enacted, including lessening the power of a guardian and giving a woman over the age of 21 the right to sign a marriage contract without a guardian. Polygamy remained, but judges would have to rule as to whether a man could take another wife. The reforms also dictated that mothers could get custody of their children in cases of divorce, yet if the mother remarried, the father and not the maternal grandmother would get custody. For many women, and especially feminists, this law did not go far enough in giving women key rights over their children.

When King Hassan died in 1999, his son, Mohammed VI, took the reins and voiced his support for gender equality. He bolstered his verbal encouragement with high-level appointments in the government. The government advanced a "Plan for Women's Integration" in 2000 with 215 measures addressing health, labor, and education. Fourteen of those measures dealt with personal status issues. Although some key opposition existed to substantial revisions in the *Mudawwana,* as evidenced by large protests in 2000, the king was determined to advance the cause of women. In October 2003, King Mohammad proposed to the Moroccan parliament a more liberal law with regards to women's rights. It called for increasing the age of marriage to 18, allowing women the right to divorce, making polygamy permissible with the consent of the first wife and a judge's ruling, allowing judges to decide whether or not a divorce is valid, and giving women the right to inherit family assets. By 2004, the new *Mudawwana* was accepted even by many of the Islamist groups because the king cloaked his reforms in Islamic concepts that were palatable to the more conservative religious groups.

An estimated 500,000 fundamentalists demonstrate in Casablanca, Morocco, over a government plan to reform women's status, 2000. The
plan would fully replace the practice of repudiation with court divorce and would also support
a literacy program for rural women. (AP Photo/
Abdeljalil Bounhar)

TUNISIA

Tunisia has been one of the most progressive states with regards to family
law and women's rights in the Middle East and North Africa. In the 1920s,
as in Morocco, the women's movement linked its aspirations to those of
the nation. The major battle during this period was not women's rights,
but throwing off foreign domination. Once independence was achieved,
women's rights were a concern of the government. In 1956, when Tunisia
gained its independence from France, it adopted a Code of Personal Status
(CPS) as part of a larger movement to create a modern state. Although
Tunisia is a patriarchal society, the state stepped in to legislate rights for
women that improved their legal status, although initially women were excluded from voting for the body that would write the new constitution.

President Habib Bourguiba took his cue from Kemal Ataturk, the founder of modern Turkey, whom he admired and emulated with regards to centralizing and modernizing his country. Contrary to Ataturk, however, Bourguiba attempted reform within an Islamic context called *ijtihad.* As previously mentioned, *ijtihad* refers to the ability of legal scholars to interpret Islamic law in a flexible manner to respond to the needs of a changing society. Bourguiba was influenced by certain Islamic reformers, such as Jamal al-Din al-Afghani, who believed that modernity and Islam were not in opposition to one another. The Tunisian government abolished religious courts while maintaining control over other aspects of the religious establishment.[27] Since President Bourguiba based his interpretations of laws on Islam and because Tunisia's constitution declares Islam as the state religion, advances in women's rights were acceptable to a wide segment of the population, both secular and religious.

The CPS of 1956 abolished polygamy and stipulated that men who engaged in this practice were subject to a one-year prison term or a fine. Tunisia was one of the only countries in the region to completely abolish the practice of polygamy. Bourguiba's rationale for banning polygamy was framed in Islamic concepts. He argued that men could not possibly treat all of their wives equally, as stipulated by the Qu'ran, and that polygamy needs to be understood in its historical context. Since polygamy is not an obligation in Islam, although permitted, governments have the right to limit or ban it.[28] A woman also needed to consent to marry and could not be forced to marry against her will. The CPS set the minimum age for marriage for women at 17 and for men at 20. In exceptional cases, a judge could rule that people could wed at a younger age. This law raising the marriage age supported Bourguiba's quest to create a modern state, as delaying marriage reduces population growth and allows women the opportunity to pursue an education. The 1956 CPS also protected a woman's assets by allowing her to separate her holdings from those of her husband's and granting her complete control over those assets. The CPS also stipulated that women have the right to an abortion, as long as the procedure is done in a hospital. Furthermore, a woman could pass her nationality to her children if her husband consents.[29] Although the law does not give a woman total control with regards to her children, the law is much more liberal than some other Middle Eastern countries. For example, in Saudi Arabia, a woman cannot pass on her nationality at all. If a Saudi woman marries a foreigner, the child does not receive Saudi citizenship.

Like Morocco, in the 1980s and 1990s, Tunisia faced a growing internal Islamist opposition. Some Islamist parties agreed to the CPS, but others vowed to repudiate it when given the opportunity. Under President Zine El Abidine Ben Ali, who assumed power in 1989, reforms continued, prompting the World Bank to declare Tunisia the leading country with regards to gender equity in the region. Women in Tunisia comprised over 50 percent of university students and the education gap between men and women began to narrow. In 1993, the state strengthened rights for women in an attempt to curry their favor in the face of growing Islamic resistance by dropping the rule that women needed to obey their husbands. Additionally, women gained greater custody rights along with better laws assuring that women and their children receive alimony. The new laws also made domestic violence a crime and were tougher on men accused of honor killings.[30] Although these laws on are the books, tradition hampers their implementation. When the law in 1993 repealed the duty of the wife to "obey" her husband, elements of the patriarchal structure remained. A man is still considered head of the household who provides for the needs of the family, although women are allowed to work without asking a husband's permission.

Although the care of the children is entrusted to both the mother and the father during a marriage, the father retains sole guardianship over the children. If a husband dies, however, the wife automatically becomes the guardian for her children. This differs significantly from other countries in the Middle East and North Africa, where the patrilineal nature of society determines that a relative from the husband's family will become the children's guardian. In the event of divorce, a judge can decide to place the child with either parent. With the law in 1993, the legal status of a mother vis-à-vis her children was transformed. The law gave a woman the right to approve her child's marriage as a minor, a right that only fathers retained prior.

In August 2006, Tunisia changed the minimum age for marriage of both sexes to 18. To marry, partners are required to get a medical certificate guaranteeing against any type of sexually transmitted disease that could affect the physical and mental health of the partner.[31] Divorce cannot be extra-judicial; it must be decided upon in court and not by unilateral repudiation. Either party can bring a request for divorce to court and, after obligatory attempts to reconcile, the court will render a judgment. In Tunisia, if there is mutual agreement for the divorce, then it will be granted. Other grounds for divorce include harm, infidelity, and a husband's failure to provide for his wife.

IRAQ

In the early 20th century, although the Iraqi leadership began to encourage more rights for women, specifically in the field of education, prior to 1959, Iraq had no civil law dealing with personal status issues. In the 1940s, female activists were concerned with key issues such as polygamy, child marriage, divorce, and dowry rights. Women, and especially peasant women, were treated as a commodity and were traded at a young age for livestock or other women. In many cases, peasant women who could no longer work were divorced arbitrarily by their husbands. Women, under the threat of arbitrary divorce, endured beatings and humiliations to prevent being kicked out of their homes. With regards to child custody, Sunni and Shia laws differed. According to the Sunni Hanafi school, mothers had custody of daughters until age nine and sons until age seven. Shia law, however, allowed mothers custody of daughters until age seven and sons until age two.[32] Since women were not key players in the legislative process in the early years of Iraq's independence, many issues pertaining to women were ignored. When the Iraqi Women's League was founded in 1952 to champion the rights of women and children, personal status issues gained more attention. By 1959, the organization boasted 25,000 members.[33] During the same time period, Iraqi Kurdish women were heavily involved in the Kurdish independence movement, and the two groups together were instrumental in promoting women's rights on all levels.[34]

In 1959, under the leadership of Abd al Karim Qasim, the government enacted a personal status law that gave women some of the most extensive legal rights in the Middle East. Whereas the Islamic clergy of both the Shia and Sunnis controlled personal status issues prior to 1959, the new law allowed any trained judge to rule on personal status matters. Under the new laws, the marriage age for men and women was 18, men and women received equal inheritances, and arbitrary divorce was forbidden. The law also discussed a woman's right to a dowry and gave women preferential treatment in custody issues. However, loopholes in the law made it difficult for divorced mothers to keep their children after age seven without a court ruling to extend the period of custody. With regards to marriage, if a marriage were going to take place prior to the age of consent, a judge would need to rule on the case. Additionally, polygamy was restricted by regulations requiring a man who wanted to take a second wife to get a legal ruling from a judge proving that he could treat both wives equally.[35] Although Iraq appeared to be very progressive relative to other Middle Eastern states, the main changes occurred more in Baghdad's urban setting than in the more rural areas that adhered tenaciously to their patriarchal structure. Forced and early marriages continued despite the new personal status law.

During General Qasim's rule, he appointed a female government minister, Nasiha al Dulaimi, who was the president of the Iraqi Women's League. Dulaimi continued to push for changes in personal status laws. Qasim also selected a female judge, a move contested by some more conservative members of society since Islamic law explicitly denies women this role. When, in 1963, Abd al Salam Arif ousted General Qasim in a coup, Arif diluted Qasim's personal status law after an appeal by traditional religious leaders. Arif reverted back to allowing sharia law to dictate key women's issues, most notably inheritance. The Ba'ath party assumed power in 1968, and by 1970 had passed the Iraqi Provisional Constitution, which championed women's equality. The government also ratified the International Covenants on Civil and Political Rights (ICCPR) and Economic, Social and Cultural Rights (ICESCR) in 1971, which provided for protection under international law.

Despite the fact that the Ba'athist regime was brutal, women under it made significant advances in employment and education. In 1978, an amendment to the personal status law was introduced with rules more favorable to women. To deter polygamy, the 1978 amendment required men to register their marriages with the court and, by doing this, allow judges to rule on whether or not a man could take a second wife. Men who married outside the court could get a three to five year prison sentence. In custody issues, maternal custody was granted until age 10, which could then be extended by judicial ruling. By the time Saddam Hussein's harsh rule began in 1979, women enjoyed more civil and social rights than women in other Middle Eastern countries.

Hussein manipulated the personal status laws as rewards or punishments for following his rules. For example, during the 1980s and 1990s, when Iraq was at war with Iran and later invaded Kuwait, women were encouraged to divorce husbands who had deserted the military or committed treason. Men who divorced women of Iranian origin qualified for government grants.[36] During the early part of his rule, Hussein wanted to achieve rapid economic growth by implementing literacy programs, which benefited both males and females, thus, by the 1990s, Iraq boasted one of the highest literacy rates in the Middle East for women. There was, however significant dissent from more traditional elements of Iraqi society, many in the Shia population, who disagreed with the personal status code and the new more public role of women. After Hussein invaded Kuwait in August 1990 and the international community imposed sanctions on his country, the economy went into a tailspin. In order to appease groups that were hard hit by the economic crisis due to the Iran-Iraq war, Hussein's invasion of Kuwait, and the United Nations' sanctions on Iraq, Saddam began to court Islamic and tribal groups; this fact had a significant impact on laws pertaining to women. Sentences for men who committed honor killings were reduced from eight years to six months, setting the stage for increased killings of women in Iraq. Although the Kurdistan Regional Government in the north repealed the law in 2000, honor killings continued, due, in part, to the lenient sentences meted out by the judicial system.[37] In 1993, Hussein decreed that men could marry more than one wife without consulting with the first wife. By the year 2000, women needed to be accompanied by a man to travel abroad, a significant change from prior rules. Rape was also a favored tool of Saddam's government to force information from opposition groups. Men carrying a card whose job was the "violation of women's honor" were tasked with raping women and sending videotapes of the act to their family members in order to extract information.[38]

After Hussein was overthrown by a U.S.-led coalition, the Iraqi Governing Council (IGC), the U.S.-appointed interim government in Iraq, voted for Resolution 137 in December 2003, which replaced the existing family law with sharia law. This fact concerned Iraqi women around the country. Interestingly, only three women were appointed to the ICG in July 2003, and of 25 ministries, only one was headed by a woman. As for Resolution 137, women's groups swiftly mobilized to counter the disturbingly nebulous resolution, which failed to detail which Islamic law would replace the earlier legislation. Under United Nations Resolution 1438, the Coalition Provisional Authority (CPA) was created to temporarily administer Iraq until the time was right to transfer power to an Iraqi government. After meeting with women's groups, the CPA, which held the real power at that time in Iraq, vetoed the resolution. In response to the veto, conservative Shia leaders made their intentions to impose Islamic law on a variety of areas apparent.

During the writing of Iraq's new constitution, the role of Islam in the new document was highly debated. Moderate Shiite leader Grand Ayatollah Ali al-Sistani claimed that the Shias were not interested in a theocratic government, but wanted Islam to be incorporated in the new document. The drafting committee was composed of 55 members, 8 of whom were women, although secular women were marginalized in the process. The key question for the committee was whether or not Islam was going to be the source of legislation or just a source. Despite some strong opposition from secular Sunni groups and Kurds, eventually the new constitution incorporated provisions that would strengthen Islamic influence. Article 2 of the constitution makes Islam the official religion of Iraq, a key source of legislation, and holds that no law can contradict its "undisputed rulings."[39] The Supreme Court reserved the right to interpret whether other laws contradicted Islamic laws.

Another issue that worried secular groups and women during Iraq's transition period after the overthrow of Hussein was Article 39, dealing with personal status law. The article states that Iraqis are "free in their personal status according to their religions, sects, beliefs, or choices." Some women's groups believed that the legislation could prove benign if people were truly going to be judged by their standards, but if a conservative government dictates that the interpretation of sharia law that will be used to judge, then women might not fare well under the new system. What is clear to many women, whether secular or religious, is that, since Islam is afforded a key role in Iraq's constitution, women's rights will have to emerge within some type of Islamic framework.[40]

YEMEN

Yemen's fiercely patriarchal tribal structure has influenced the role of women in that country for decades. With the demise of the Ottoman Empire, North Yemen gained its independence, while South Yemen became part of a British Federation of Saudi Arabia until 1967. The 1969 Marxist takeover in South Yemen led to the passage of a new family law in 1974 that made some far-reaching changes and differentiated South Yemen completely from North Yemen in its treatment of women. The new law stated that marriage required the consent of both parties, and imposed a minimum age of marriage for girls at 16. Men and women were given equal rights in divorce, and custody laws were modified to grant women the opportunity to raise their children. Although the laws were sweeping, they were difficult to enforce in traditional Yemeni society. Universal suffrage was granted in 1970, and women were permitted to run for office. Women's groups were formed too, such as the General Union of Yemeni Women, to address women's issues including education and literacy. By 1983, women graduated from the University of Aden at rates equal to men.[41]

Prior to 1990, when North and South Yemen united, the two countries had vastly different laws regarding women. In the northern Yemen Arab Republic (YAR), sharia law was prevalent and there was no separate family law until 1979. Due to local interpretations of Islamic law and tribal practices, there was no uniform way of dealing with family law in the YAR. In 1970, after the end of a civil war between the North and South, the North promulgated a constitution based on Islamic law. Although it called for equal rights for men and women, in areas where the law was vague, Islamic law would prevail. In the YAR, marriage to a minor was legal, although there were laws preventing its consummation until after puberty. The YAR permitted polygyny, although men were supposed to treat each wife equally and divorce was available to men through simple repudiation, while women had to sue for divorce.[42]

In the South, also known as the People's Democratic Republic of Yemen (PDRY), although Islam was recognized as the state religion, under the Marxist regime the people held power and legitimacy. With regards to women, the constitution made all people equal before the law and it strived to ensure that women had state support to work and care for families.[43] Women held a variety of jobs, even that of judge, a position that Islamic law prohibited women to hold. In family law, the legal age for marriage was 16 for men and 18 for women. Marriage was defined as consensual, and partners were granted equal responsibilities, including economic ones such as maintaining the household. Divorce had to go through the courts whether initiated by the husband or the wife. Men could only take another wife if the court allowed it. Women could retain custody of the children and, at times, a woman was even allowed to keep the marital home.[44]

When North and South Yemen unified in 1990, the secular laws of the South were discarded in favor of the more religiously based laws of the North. Despite some resistance from Southern women and socialist leaders, Northern law prevailed in the new Personal Status Law of 1992. When the North and South first united, each territory maintained its law until a new constitution could be written. During this period, some men took advantage of the confusion and divorced their southern wives while in the YAR, where divorce was unrestricted, or married another wife since polygyny was permitted. The new constitution was founded on a previous version that had been drawn up with the input of both states in 1981. Islam was declared the state religion, and Islamic law was the main source of legislation. There was, however, some key dissent by more conservative groups in the North that favored Islamic law as the only source of legislation. Although the constitution called for equal rights for men and women, it discarded many of the declarations of state sponsorship to help women enter the labor force and manage their family lives.

The 1992 Personal Status Law offered the state very little control over family issues. The new family law provided fewer benefits for women than did the PDRY family law of 1974, although in reality, many of those southern laws had been ignored by the more traditional elements of Yemeni society. As such, the new family law of the united Yemen reflected a more realistic view of what was actually occurring in society. Additionally, with the collapse of the Soviet Union and a decline in supporters of socialist ideology, the Yemeni Socialist Party lost confidence in some of its policies and was willing to accept the YAR's changes to the constitution. In contrast to family law in the South, the 1992 Family Law in the united Yemen permitted a man to marry up to four wives, but gave a woman the right to divorce a man if she did not believe her husband treated her equally. However, the concept of "equal" was open to the court's interpretation, and in many cases the wife did not have any recourse. A woman could gain custody of her children in divorce, but could not work outside the home unless someone was there to care for her children. The concept of a wife's "obedience" to her husband was reiterated. Furthermore, the marriage age for girls was lowered to age 15, although the law did not stipulate any punishment if this aspect of the law was violated.

In many instances, what was written in the law did not match reality. For example, the new law called for post-marital maintenance if a man divorced a woman through simple repudiation and where the divorce would impoverish her. Since the new law did not require court involvement in divorce—a man could divorce his wife unilaterally—women were required to file for a separate court appearance to gain financial support; they almost never filed for the support.[45] After the 1994 civil war between North and South Yemen, the Yemeni Socialist Party was completely defeated. As such, the path was open to amend the 1992 Family Law and remove any restrictions that had been placed on men with regards to polygyny, divorce, and marriage age. When the amendments were passed in 1998, women lost any vestiges of the rights they had retained. The minimum age for marriage was abolished, polygamy was unrestricted, and women did not have the right to compensation after unilateral divorce.[46]

Although there was not much reaction to the change in the family law by Northerners, the Organization for the Defense of Democratic Rights and Freedoms, a group opposed to reversals in the PDRY law, protested what it perceived as a step back for both women and men. The press in the South carried discussions about the new law. Despite the protests, the law was passed and affected the status of women, especially at the household level.

PALESTINE

The legal status of Palestinian women was laid out in the Palestinian legal code enacted by the Ottoman government between 1876 and 1877. Prior to 1948, when the state of Israel was born, the 1917 Ottoman Law of Family Rights prevailed in the Palestinian territories. Women's status was also influenced by Islamic law and custom. Both of these factors, coupled with the legal code, affected the status of women in Palestine. With regards to customary law, if disputes fall outside either the civil or religious courts, then issues are handled according to tradition. Palestinian society, much like most of the Middle East, is a patriarchal and male-dominated society, where women usually encounter discriminatory treatment. Customary law affects several key issues pertaining to women, including family law, honor killings, education, and domestic violence. Since women are considered crucial in the maintenance of family honor, fathers or husbands exert an enormous amount of control over their lives, including whether or not they can work or get an education. Additionally, because of the importance of family honor, the practice of honor killings still exists but is rare in Palestine.

Under the Jordanian Penal Code, which is used in the West Bank, a man who witnesses his wife committing adultery and then murders her is exempt from punishment. In many cases, judges render arbitrary decisions with regards to prosecuting those charged with an honor killing. Likewise, men usually get light punishments if they rape a woman who was acting or dressed inappropriately. In fact, if a man agrees to marry the woman that he raped, judges have the authority to drop the charges. Custom has also led to an acceptance of domestic violence in Palestine and other parts of the Middle East. One poll found that 50 percent of Palestinian men felt that beating a woman is justified.[47] The history of the Palestinian territories has been fraught with violence and challenges both from external and internal players. Issues such as domestic violence are sometimes ignored or deemed secondary to the priority of solving the larger conflict and achieving independence. The Institute of Women's Studies at Birzeit University, located in the West Bank, reaches out to women in the Gaza Strip and in refugee camps through distance learning. The Institute works with organizations such as the United Nations Development Program to ameliorate conditions for women in these conflict areas.[48]

In 1947, the United Nations partitioned the area of British Mandated Palestine into Jewish and Palestinian states. For a variety of reasons beyond the scope of this work, the Jewish state of Israel was born after its War of Independence with the Arab states and the Palestinian territories were taken over by other Arab states. Egypt took control of the Gaza Strip, while Jordan gained control of the West Bank. In the West Bank, the sharia courts were combined with the Jordanian ones and were controlled by Jordan's Chief of Islamic Justice. Personal status issues in the West Bank fell under the Jordanian Family Law of 1951.[49] Following the Six Day War in 1967, when Israel gained control of the Gaza Strip and the West Bank, the West Bank continued to apply Jordanian Family Law. In 1976, Jordan passed a new family law that was applied in the West Bank.

The Gaza Strip, administered by Egypt, presented a different case than the West Bank with regards to family law. Egypt did not extend Egyptian law into the region and, in 1954, the Egyptian governor in Gaza issued a Law of Family Rights that utilized Gaza's sharia courts for implementation. This law continued to be based on the Ottoman Law of Family Rights, although it contained several provisions that were similar to some Egyptian family laws.[50] After Israel's occupation in 1967, the Israelis took over administration of both the sharia and civil court systems. Because the West Bank's and Gaza's laws differed with respect to age of marriage, divorce, and custody issues, this fact challenged the Palestinian National Authority, which assumed administrative control of both territories following the Oslo Accords in 1993. A crucial aspect for the new Palestinian administration was how to unify these various laws. After some important work by women's organizations, which presented amendments to the personal status law, many clerics concentrated on unifying and consolidating the Islamic court system. Some Palestinians regarded the creation of a unified civil code that would apply equally to all Palestinians, since three percent of Palestinians in the West Bank and Gaza are Christian, as crucial. Several laws were changed to parallel the Jordanian laws, including raising the minimum age of marriage to 15 for girls and 16 for boys, and stipulating that a judge's permission was required for a girl between the ages of 15 and 17 to marry. Likewise, girls who reached the age of 18 would be able to decide for themselves whether or not to marry and did not require the approval of a guardian. If either parent objected to the marriage contract, a judge needed to rule on the objection. This proposal illustrated a recognition by the courts of a parent's views, but did not allow them the final word in the marriage.[51]

Likewise, since both Islamic and customary law contain provisions that are clearly discriminatory toward women, some Palestinian feminists supported a civil legal code to protect women's rights. The Palestinians drafted a Basic Law in 1997 that was intended to be an interim constitution until the final status of a Palestinian state was determined, and addressed key areas in relation to women's rights. Both documents afforded everyone equality under the law "without discrimination because of race, sex, color, religion, political views or disability." The Draft Constitution added provisions that directly discussed women's rights that were lacking in the Basic Law. The constitution provided that women shall have the right to participate in all aspects of political, economic, and social life and that they can have their own independent financial assets., yet another provision in both the Draft Constitution and the Basic Law stated that sharia law would be a major source for legislation.[52] This provision concerned many women and women's groups, as interpretations of sharia law can differ widely depending upon the judge and legal scholar. All issues of personal status are placed under one of the religious courts, which for the majority of the population, who are Muslim, means sharia law.

In January 2006, the Islamic Resistance Party, Hamas, won an unexpected victory at the polls. In a fairly free and fair election, Fatah, the more secular, nationalist party, could not muster the parliamentary seats to form a government. Hamas' victory shocked the world and caused extreme consternation in Israel and the United States as to how to proceed with the peace process and relations between the Palestinians and Israelis. Hamas refused to recognized Israel or the prior peace agreements stemming from the 1993 Oslo Accords and would not renounce violence. Hamas' platform includes the destruction of Israel and the creation of a Palestinian state in what was British mandatory Palestine, territory that includes modern-day Israel. As a group that champions Islamic values, many women's groups that were active in Palestine under both the Israeli occupation and Fatah's rule are concerned about the future of women's rights under a Hamas-led government.

Complicating an already confusing situation was Hamas' takeover of the Gaza Strip in June 2007; this resulted in a split Palestinian government, with Hamas controlling Gaza and Fatah ruling in the West Bank. Most of the international community continues to recognize Fatah as the only legitimate government of Palestine. Hamas promulgated an Electoral Platform in 2005, describing its vision and plan for a Hamas-led Palestinian state. The document held that sharia law should be the principal source of legislation. This view differs somewhat from the Basic Law's discussion of sharia law as a major source of legislation, but not the principal one. With regards to women, the Electoral Platform states that a woman should have "an Islamic education, make her aware of her religious rights and confirm her independence which is based on purity, modesty and commitment."[53] The Palestinian Authority is still exploring issues such as the rights of non-Muslim women.

SAUDI ARABIA

The roots of the modern Saudi Arabian state are based upon a merger between the warrior Al-Saud family and the religious fervor of Muhammad ibn-Abdel Wahab in the 18th century. Saudi Arabia follows a strict interpretation of Islamic law, and, as such, there are no civil courts, only religious ones. Even though Saudi Arabia implemented a Basic Law in 1992, the Basic Law holds that Saudi Arabia's constitution is the Qu'ran and the hadith. The law stipulates that the state shall protect human rights according to Islamic law, which is open to the interpretation of the Council of Senior Ulama. It is through its connection with religion that the Saudi regime maintains its legitimacy. However, in earlier periods in Saudi Arabia, women's roles in society, whether segregated or not, reflected a more flexible approach and depended upon various accepted interpretations of Islam.[54]

According to Saudi Arabian law based on an interpretation of the sharia, women are required to be completely covered with a black abaya, the traditional cloak, and a black veil that conceals their faces. As mentioned, the concept of complete veiling does not stem from the Qu'ran, but has its roots in pre-Islamic tribal society. Coupled with this concept of veiling is the law that women must be segregated from men in all public facilities including schools, restaurants, and transportation.[55] In Saudi Arabia, a law instituted in 1969 mandated the strict segregation of women and men in the workplace. That the Saudi government passed such a law reflected a belief that women could work outside the home.[56] In Saudi Arabia, and in the capital city of Riyadh specifically, women are involved in the public realm, not just the domestic sphere, despite the fact that many public spaces are restricted to them.

The Saudi family structure is a traditional one and women are clearly subordinated to men. Over the last few decades, the role of women in the workplace and in daily life has changed significantly, yet it has also developed in a segregated female sphere. The concept of women's roles in society has been used by many states in the Middle East as part of their political development. Turkey and other modernizing countries banned the veil, reflecting a political trend toward modernization. Saudi Arabian laws segregating women and mandating veiling signal both a conservative view and the crucial role that Islam holds in that society. In 1995, during the Fourth World Conference on Women in Beijing, many issues of family law regarding Muslim women were discussed and what emerged were some key contradictions. The Platform for Action, which affirmed legal equality and universal human rights for women, was contradicted in many cases by family law in particular countries. For example, the child of a Saudi Arabian woman is not a Saudi if the father is a foreign national, and her husband cannot get Saudi citizenship by following a similar path as that of a foreign woman married to a Saudi man. This makes it very difficult for the child of a Saudi woman whose father is not Saudi to be a citizen and to receive the rights that accompany that status. Likewise, women achieve citizenship differently from men. Saudi law, which is based on Islamic law, deals more with issues of the community, rather than individual rights. As such, when viewed by Western standards, different rules regarding men and women connote unequal treatment.

The women's movement is significantly constrained in Saudi Arabia. Women are subject to strict guardianship rules where a father, husband, or brother has the right to make certain decisions for her such as whether or not she can travel abroad. Additionally, male relatives must escort a woman overseas or in many places within Saudi Arabia. Saudi Arabian women are not permitted to drive and, as such, have restricted freedom of movement, which hampers their ability to shop, work, and function on a daily basis. In 1990, some women, many with their husbands' permission, protested the driving ban by getting behind the wheel and driving through downtown Riyadh.

With regards to family law, in the past, a father or male guardian contracted a marriage on behalf of his daughter, although this custom is becoming more flexible. However, women still have more constraints put on them in marriage decisions than do men. A woman must get permission to marry a non-Saudi man and is usually denied marriage to a non-Muslim man. Polygyny is allowed, and simple repudiation exists for a man to divorce a wife. As in many other Muslim countries, women need to go through legal channels to initiate a divorce, and they are often unsuccessful.[57] In 2003, Crown Prince Abdullah, who became king in 2005, began a series of national dialogues to discuss a variety of issues of import to the kingdom. As part of these national dialogues, women's issues were discussed and recommendations were passed on to the Crown Prince. Abdullah lent his support to many of the recommendations, including reaffirming the primary duty of both women and men as the maintenance of the family unit, while simultaneously supporting a woman's right to work. The recommendations also ask for more specific institutions for women to correspond with the broadening of public spaces for women, albeit in a segregated context.[58] The importance of the dialogue has been to make a discussion of women's issues a legitimate one in Saudi politics. The Saudi regime has also appointed women to the consultative council. In 2006, six women joined the council; they are mainly relegated to exploring issues that pertain to women.

NOTES

1. Nabia Abbott, "Women and the State in Early Islam," *Journal of Near Eastern Studies* 1 (January 1942): 107.

2. A. A. Engineer, *The Rights of Women in Islam* (New Delhi: Sterling Publishers Private, 1992), 57.

3. Nora Alarifi Pharaon, "Saudi Women and the Muslim State in the Twenty-First Century," *Sex Roles* 51 (September 2004): 355.

4. Bernard Lewis and Buntzie Ellis Churchill, *Islam: The Religion and the People* (Upper Saddle River, NJ: Wharton School Publishing, 2009), 113.

5. Nikki R. Keddie, *Women in the Middle East: Past and Present* (Princeton, NJ: Princeton University Press, 2007), 37.

6. Lewis and Churchill, *Islam: The Religion and the People,* 114.

7. Amira Mashhour, "Islamic Law and Gender Equality-Could There Be a Common Ground? A Study of Divorce and Polygamy in Sharia Law and Contemporary Legislation in Tunisia and Egypt," *Human Rights Quarterly* 27 (2005): 572.

8. Mashhour, "Islamic Law and Gender Equality-Could There Be a Common Ground?," 573.

9. Mashhour, "Islamic Law and Gender Equality-Could There Be a Common Ground?," 572.

10. Fereydoun Hoveyda, "Arab Women and the Future of the Middle East," *American Foreign Policy Interests* 27 (2005): 422.

11. James Reilly, "Women in the Economic Life of Late-Ottoman Damascus," *Arabica* 42 (March 1995): 91–92.

12. Ziba Mir-Hosseini, "How the Door of Ijtihad Was Opened and Closed: A Comparative Analysis of Recent Family Law Reforms in Iran and Morocco," *Washington and Lee Law Review* (Fall 2007): 1503.

13. Nesta Ramazani, "Women in Iran: The Revolutionary Ebb and Flow," *Middle East Journal* (Summer 1993): 410–11.

14. Mir-Hosseini, "How the Door of Ijtihad Was Opened and Closed," 1504.

15. Azadeh Kian, "Women and Politics in Post-Islamist Iran: the Gender Conscious Drive to Change," *British Journal of Middle Eastern Studies* (1997): 95.

16. Lord Kinross, *Ataturk: The Rebirth of a Nation* (London: Weidenfeld and Nicolson, 1964), in June Starr, "The Role of Turkish Secular Law in Changing the Lives of Rural Muslim Women, 1950–1970," *Law and Society Review* 23 (1989): 502.

17. Starr, "The Role of Turkish Secular Law," 505–7.

18. Yesim Arat, "Feminists, Islamists, and Political Change in Turkey," *Political Psychology* 19 (March 1998): 120.

19. Zana Çitak and Özlem Tür, "Women between Tradition and Change: The Justice and Development Party Experience in Turkey," *Middle Eastern Studies* 44 (May 2008): 456–57.

20. Çitak and Tür, "Women between Tradition and Change," 463–64.

21. Mashhour, "Islamic Law and Gender Equality-Could There Be a Common Ground?," 578.

22. Mashhour, "Islamic Law and Gender Equality-Could There Be a Common Ground?," 580.

23. Keddie, *Women in the Middle East,* 123–25.

24. Farida Deif, "Divorced from Justice," *Journal of Middle East Women's Studies* (Fall 2005): 108–10.

25. Josep Lluís Mateo Dieste, "Demonstrating Islam: The Conflict of Text and the Mudawwana Reform in Morocco," *The Muslim World* (January 2009): 135–36.

26. Fatima Sadiqi and Moha Ennaji, "The Feminization of Public Space: Women's Activism, The Family Law and Social Change in Morocco," *Journal of Middle East Women's Studies* (Spring 2006): 100–102.

27. Adrien Katherine Wing and Hisham A. Kassim. "The Future of Palestinian Women's Rights: Lessons from a Half-Century of Tunisian Progress," *Washington and Lee L. Review* (2007): 1557.

28. Mashhour, "Islamic Law and Gender Equality—Could There Be a Common Ground?," 585.

29. Hafidha Chekir, "Women, the Law and the Family in Tunisia," *Gender and Development* 4 (June 1996): 45.

30. Keddie, *Women in the Middle East,* 142.

31. Chekir, "Women, the Law and the Family in Tunisia," 44–45.

32. Noga Efrati, "Negotiating Rights in Iraq: Women and the Personal Status Law," *Middle East Journal* (Autumn 2005): 587–90.

33. Lucy Brown and David Romano, "Women in Post-Saddam Iraq: One Step Forward and Two Steps Back?" *NWSA Journal* 18 (Fall 2006): 52.

34. Victoria Stanski, "Linchpin for Democracy: The Critical Role of Civil Society in Iraq," *Journal of Third World Studies* 12 (2005): 209.

35. Isobel Coleman, "Women, Islam and the New Iraq," *Foreign Affairs* (January/February 2006): 26.

36. Efrati, "Negotiating Rights in Iraq," 586–89.

37. Brown and Romano, "Women in Post-Saddam Iraq," 57.

38. Brown and Romano, "Women in Post-Saddam Iraq," 54.

39. Coleman, "Women, Islam and the New Iraq," 27.

40. Coleman, "Women, Islam and the New Iraq," 29.

41. Keddie, *Women in the Middle East,* 153.

42. Anna Würth, "Stalled Reform: Family Law in Post-Unification Yemen," *Islamic Law and Society* 10 (2003): 13–14.

43. Maxine Molyneux,. "Women's Rights and Political Contingency: The Case of Yemen, 1990–1994," *Middle East Journal* 49 (Summer 1995): 419.

44. Würth, "Stalled Reform: Family Law in Post-Unification Yemen," 15–16.

45. Würth, "Stalled Reform: Family Law in Post-Unification Yemen," 20–21.

46. Würth, "Stalled Reform: Family Law in Post-Unification Yemen," 25–26.

47. Adrien Katherine Wing and Hisham A. Kassim, "Hamas, Constitutionalism, and Palestinian Women," *Howard Law Journal* 50 (2007): 483–85.

48. Cheryl Toman, "The Link Between Women's Studies Programs and Grassroots Organizations," *Arab Studies Quarterly* (Spring 2003): 64.

49. Lynn Welchman, "In the Interim: Civil Society, the Shar'a Judiciary and Palestinian Personal Status Law in the Transitional Period," *Islamic Law and Society* 10 (2003): 39–40.

50. Welchman, "In the Interim," 41.

51. Welchman, "In the Interim," 61–62.

52. Wing and Kassim, "Hamas, Constitutionalism, and Palestinian Women," 490.

53. Wing and Kassim, "Hamas, Constitutionalism, and Palestinian Women," 506.

54. Amelie Le Renard. "Only for Women: Women, the State and Reform in Saudi Arabia," *Middle East Journal* 62 (Autumn 2008): 613.

55. Sifa Mtango, "A State of Oppression? Women's Rights in Saudi Arabia," *Asia-Pacific Journal on Human Rights and the Law* (2004): 55.

56. Renard, "Only for Women: Women, the State and Reform in Saudi Arabia," 614.

57. Mtango, "A State of Oppression? Women's Rights in Saudi Arabia," *Asia-Pacific Journal on Human Rights and the Law* (2004): 60–62.

58. Renard, "Only for Women: Women, the State and Reform in Saudi Arabia," 619.

SUGGESTED READING

Dieste, Josep Lluís Mateo. "Demonstrating Islam: The Conflict of Text and the Mudawwana Reform in Morocco." *The Muslim World* (January 2009): 134–54.

Ghabra, Shafeeq. "Voluntary Associations in Kuwait: The Foundations of a New System? *Middle East Journal* 45 (Spring 1991): 119–215.

Mashhour, Amira. "Islamic Law and Gender Equality-Could There Be a Common Ground? A Study of Divorce and Polygamy in Sharia Law and Contemporary Legislation in Tunisia and Egypt." *Human Rights Quarterly* 27 (2005): 562–96.

Mir-Hosseini, Ziba. "How the Door of Ijtihad Was Opened and Closed: A Comparative Analysis of Recent Family Law Reforms in Iran and Morocco." *Washington and Lee Law Review* (Fall 2007): 1499–1511.

Molyneux, Maxine. "Women's Rights and Political Contingency: The Case of Yemen, 1990–1994." *Middle East Journal* 49 (Summer 1995): 418–31.

Rehman, Javaid. "The Sharia, Islamic Family Laws and International Human Rights Law: Examining the Theory and Practice of Polygamy and Talaq." *International Journal of Law, Policy and the Family* 21 (2007): 108–27.

Stanski, Victoria. "Linchpin for Democracy: The Critical Role of Civil Society in Iraq." *Journal of Third World Studies* 12 (2005): 197–225.

Starr, June. "The Role of Turkish Secular Law in Changing the Lives of Rural Muslim Women, 1950–1970." *Law and Society Review* 23 (1989): 497–523.

Süral, A. Nurhan. "Legal Framework for Gender Equality at Work in Turkey." *Middle Eastern Studies* 43 (September 2007): 811–24.

5

◆◆◆

Women and Politics

Women have possessed both private and public power throughout the Middle East and North Africa. Some scholars argue that, despite the inequities that have existed in the Middle East and North Africa, women wield power in a variety of ways. When the prophet Muhammad received his revelations in 610 C.E., some women converted to Islam while their husbands did not. Others pledged their support to the Prophet and even joined him in battle. Throughout history, women held informal power that influenced their husbands, sons, and fathers. Muhammad's first wife, Khadija, played a significant role in the Prophet's life and was well respected within her community in Medina. During this early period, women were usually not segregated and were permitted to pray in mosques and attend public gatherings. In the period after Muhammad's death in 632 C.E., Muhammad's successors limited women's freedom, although some elite women played crucial public roles in charitable and social works.

The later Ottoman period, in the 1800s, ushered in liberalizing policies that affected women. Debates about their role in society ensued and by the early 20th century women began to participate in nationalist movements across the Middle East and North Africa.

Women participated in organizations, movements, and other forms of civil society that cut across both social and economic class to unite women on particular issues. The chapter moves from the early period of Islam in the seventh century to the present and analyzes the significant changes in women's public and political participation. Most Middle Eastern countries today allow women to contribute to the political system, but the 2002

United Nations Development Report underscored the fact that women occupied only 3.5 percent of seats in Arab legislatures. However, some important changes have been afoot. Since 2002, both Kuwait and Qatar have granted women the vote and allowed them to run for parliament. Qatar appointed the first female minister in the region and is continuing to open its political system to women. Other countries are starting to follow suit.

THE ISLAMIC PERIOD

At the beginning of the Islamic period, in the early seventh century, it was clear that women enjoyed certain freedoms, as evidenced by the fact that some women converted to Islam even if their father, brother, or husband did not opt to do so. In one case, Muhammad's cousin, Ramlah, accepted Islam while her husband remained a Christian. In other instances, the men converted to Islam, while the women in their lives refused to do so. Muhammad's first wife, Khadija, played an important role in his life and was instrumental in convincing others to convert to the new faith. Muhammad himself recognized the important influence that women could have over others. In one early case, Muhammad sanctioned an early convert to Islam, Umm Waraqah bint Abd Allah, to be the imam (religious leader) for both men and women in her household.[1] Although there is no case of a woman leading the community in a mosque, Umm Waraqah's case illustrated a belief that women could be active leaders in the public realm. Muhammad also listened to women's requests and attempted to oblige them. Some early female converts to Islam approached the Prophet to complain that many of the revelations were addressed only to men. Later revelations remedied this particular grievance by addressing both men and women. For example, a verse in the Qu'ran reads:

> The self-surrendering men and the self-surrendering women, the believing men and the believing women, the obedient man and the obedient woman, the truthful men and the truthful women, the enduring men and the enduring women, the submissive men an the submissive women, the almsgiving men and the almsgiving women, the fasting men an the fasting women, the continent and the continent women, the Allah-remembering men and the Allah-remembering women- for them Allah has prepared forgiveness and a might reward.[2]

Women's position in society during Muhammad's early years reflects the fairly free position that Arab women held in pre-Islamic Arabia. According to scholars, in pre-Islamic Arabia women were allowed to select their marriage partners, initiate divorce, and interact with men.[3] Following this example, Muhammad allowed women to participate in public life by praying in the mosque, attending his public speeches, praying over the dead, and making the pilgrimage to Mecca's shrines. Clearly, at this point in history, the segregation of women was not required.

When Muhammad made the journey to Medina from Mecca and sought protection and an alliance with the Medinians, two women were present for the secret meetings at Aqaba, in what is present-day Jordan. The men concluded a defensive alliance with the Prophet and, along with the women, took the "women's oath." Once Muhammad was in Medina, other women approached him to take the "women's oath," reflecting their allegiance to Islam. Although women were exempt from military service, several took a pledge that proclaimed their loyalty to fight to the death. There are records of women fighting alongside men, the most famous case being Umm Umarah, who participated in many battles and lost her hand in the Battle of Aqrabah.[4] Additionally, Muhammad's third wife, Aisha, led men to war during the Battle of the Camel. Although women participated in battle, there is little stated in the Qu'ran about any type of political role that women might take in a state. In the later years of Muhammad's life, he experienced some upheaval with his wives that led him to institute the practice of seclusion for them. Coupled with the influence of his close companions, Muhammad began to hold a more unfavorable attitude toward women. This change set the stage for later interpretations extending the rule of segregation that was meant only for the Prophet's wives to all women.[5]

THE GOLDEN AGE OF ISLAM

After Muhammad's death in 632, one of his earliest companions, Abu Bakr, became caliph. Abu Bakr's reign was short and his attitude toward women did not change much from that of Muhammad's. Abu Bakr was preoccupied with internal revolts from those who believed that Muhammad's death signaled the end of their loyalty to Islam. Some women led revolts against the new Muslim community, including Salma bint Malik, indicating that women had a role in the political life of the community.[6] Umar followed Abu Bakr as caliph and began to limit women's public role, especially in public worship. There was some backlash from his own wife and son against the idea of forcing women to pray at home, so he then segregated the sexes in public and appointed an imam for each group. Umar forbid women from making the pilgrimage to Mecca and used the Prophet's widows as an example of this new restriction. However, he reversed this decision in his last year of power and accompanied the Prophet's wives on the pilgrimage, although they were secluded and guarded at all times.[7]

When Uthman became caliph in 644 C.E., he loosened some of Umar's restrictions and permitted women to pray with men. However, the seeds had been planted for a more passive and restrictive life for women, especially in the public realm. Despite the curbing of their public responsibilities, during the Abbasid period (750–1258), several women played key roles as advisors to their husbands or sons who held power. Khayzuran was born a slave girl in Yemen and attracted the attention of the second Abbasid caliph, Al Mansur, who took her from Yemen to marry his son, Muhammad al Mahdi, who became the third caliph. Khayzuran's two sons, Musa al Hadi and Harun al Rashid's (706–809), became the fourth and fifth caliphs. Throughout the reigns of her husband and sons, Khayzuran participated in many aspects of political life, including the appointment of the caliphs' advisors, the administering of justice, and overseeing an extensive system of social works. She also owned a large amount of property, making her extremely wealthy. Her niece, Zubayda, who was also married to her son, al Rashid, sponsored an elaborate system of wells that followed the hajj trail from Iraq to Mecca.[8] Her investment in public works is legendary in Islamic history. After Harun al Rashid's death, a battle over succession occurred, pitting Zubayda's son, Muhammad Amin, against another one of her husband's children. Amin, with Zubayda's influence and backing, emerged victorious.

As the Muslims conquered more land and were influenced by other empires, such as the Sasanian and Byzantine Empires, and other religions, such as Christianity and Judaism, more negative views of women were accepted. A symbiotic relationship between the rulers and conquered developed. The rulers adopted trends and traits that fit with the new territories and the newly conquered peoples adopted the language and religion of their Arab rulers. Consequently, customs that did not initially stem from Islam became associated with the religion. Women retreated from the roles they had held during the Islamic period and were less visible in public life. Discussions of women from this period stems from hadiths and literature with a more negative perspective coming to the forefront.[9] During the Abbasid period, the seclusion of women became official policy, as evidenced by Caliph Mansour's (754–775) building a separate bridge for women over the Euphrates River.[10] Whereas the elite of Muslim society practiced the seclusion of women, by the end of the Abbasid period, it had become common practice for many cities across the Middle East.

Turks began arriving in the Middle East in the ninth century and with them came their ideas about the role of women. Women had important functions in tribal councils due to their economic contributions in pastoral society. Mongol society also afforded women a larger, more public role in politics than in the Muslim world. Prior to the Turkish or Mongol integration into their conquered lands, Turkish and Mongol women's status was similar to what it had been in their native lands. Over time, as they assimilated into their new homes and both the Turkish and Mongol invaders converted to Islam, the Islamic norms influenced the status of both the Turkish and Mongol women as they became confined to their roles in the home. According to some scholars, some nomadic women maintained some of their previous power.[11]

THE OTTOMAN PERIOD

Great changes with regards to women's issues emerged during the Ottoman period, and especially during the Tanzimat era (1839–1876), which set the stage for liberal reforms. During this period of modernization, more schools were built for women and more females were trained as teachers and midwives. Additionally, debates on gender and women's place in society were becoming more commonplace.[12] Prior to this period, for the most part, Ottomans practiced Islamic traditions that kept women from the public realm.[13] The Young Turk movement, which championed a constitution for the country, overthrew Sultan Abdul Hamid II and ushered in a period of social change. The number of women's associations increased and more women attended university and entered the workforce.

In the 19th century, women were active in promoting women's rights and participating in political protests across the Middle East. For governments that were pursuing modernization, such as Egypt, Iran, and Turkey, a woman's status in society measured the level of their society's modernity. Intellectuals and elites debated issues such as secularism, the rule of law, and the role of women in society, all issues that have a significant impact on women's status. Many women's rights advocates, especially from the middle class, promoted women's education since a woman's primary role in the household is as an educator for her children, especially the boys. During this period, women were not passive actors, but actively pursued avenues to further their cause.

One tactic that women used to advance their ideas was to develop their own presses. Turkey and Egypt led the way in separate women's presses, followed by Iran and Syria.[14] In Egypt, Algeria, and Iran, women from both rural and urban sectors participated in bread and other riots to demand rights. In 1891, when the British gained a tobacco concession from Iran, the mullahs, who disagreed with the concessions, declared a boycott on tobacco. To further support this protest, women from the ruling household refused to smoke. In 1905, Iran underwent a constitutional revolution and women defended the movement by protesting against foreign intervention in Iran. During the growth of nationalism in the Middle East, women performed significant functions for the movement, although in many instances their contributions to the national movement were overlooked.[15]

Western colonialism had a strong impact on the growth of national consciousness in the Middle East. In part, Arab nationalism arose as a reaction to Western colonialism and the growth of Turkish nationalism. These new movements significantly affected the role of women in the political realm and the growth of a feminist movement. Some argue that, because feminism arose as part of the national movement, it is a Western innovation and has no place in the Arab world. Others argue that although the feminist movement was influenced by groups outside the Arab world, the organization retains relevance for the Middle East. Interestingly, although many women throughout the Middle East participated in nationalist movements, many did not proclaim their goals as feminist. They stressed nationalist concepts and objectives while subordinating their goals to improve women's rights to the nationalist movement.[16]

The decline of the Ottoman Empire was one factor that contributed to the expansion of feminism in the Middle East and a push toward more power for women within the political, social, and economic realms. In the latter part of the 18th century, pressure from an increasingly strong Europe led to the Ottoman Empire's decline. The Ottomans controlled huge swaths of land in the Middle East and North Africa except for some portions of Morocco, the Sudan, and parts of Arabia. As its grip weakened, territories that were further from its center of power in Istanbul became more independent. Egypt was a case in point. Its Ottoman-appointed governor, Muhammad Ali, who ruled from 1805–1848, led Egypt to become a fairly autonomous state. The socio-economic changes that occurred under Muhammad Ali's tutelage impacted upon the subsequent growth of the feminist movement in Egypt. During that period, Egypt exported both grain and cotton to Europe; this increased capital went to the merchant class, increasing the middle class. As the middle class began to grow, Muhammad Ali modernized the education system while also reorganizing the state's administrative structures. He also introduced private property, thereby enticing people to work their land and undertake capitalist endeavors.[17] A growth of new classes and the transforming social structure led to changes for Egyptian women.

Under Muhammad Ali, growing urbanization increased competition and forced women out of the labor market and back home. During this time, elite women were able to get a private education, which suited their husbands, who, for the most part, maintained ties to the colonial powers and wanted their women to appear similar to the European women. Lower class women, however, could not afford an education and were needed by their husbands to run small family businesses. When the private property law was passed, issues arose with regards to inheritance for women, a matter whose resolution was frequently unfavorable for women. These economic and social changes increased women's discontent and led to unrest in Egypt. The women most prepared to articulate their demands were the upper class, educated women. As such, they were the ones to play a key role in the growth of the Egyptian feminist movement. Some male reformists raised the issue of women's rights in the 19th century, but mostly with

regards to education. Rifaa Rafi al Tahtawi, one of the most famous reformers during that period, held that Islamic ideals had been distorted and
that societies needed to return to the basic teachings of Islam. As such,
the early champions of women's rights framed their ideas in a religious
context. Qasim Amin, an Egyptian philosopher, believed that Egypt could
not progress without improving the position of women in society. Basing
his ideas less on religious concepts than philosophical ones espousing the
natural rights of human beings, Amin advocated legal reforms to improve
women's rights.[18] Elite women were in the forefront of the feminist movement in Egypt due primarily to their education and their ability to socialize with Europeans, granting them access to a separate view of a woman's
position in society. Interestingly, although Egyptian women were in the
vanguard of the women's rights movement in the region, other countries
such as Tunisia and Syria had more success achieving some of their goals,
such as curtailing polygamy and changing the rules of unilateral divorce. At
the start of the nationalist revolution against British rule in 1919, women's
political activity increased, with women's organizations participating in the
protests. Huda Sha'rawi was the leader of a feminist movement in Egypt
that called for respect of the individual.[19] Women also created an important
place for themselves within the Wafd party, a nationalist group that gained
partial independence from the British in 1922.

WORLD WAR I AND ITS AFTERMATH

During World War I, the British had made agreements with the Arab
states to grant them independence if they allied with the British to defeat
the Ottomans. British promises of an independent Arab state were ambigu-
ous and contributed to many current problems that exist with regards to
boundaries and control. While the British were negotiating with the Arabs
for their support, they were also dividing up control of the Middle East
with both the French and the Russians. It was this reinforcement of foreign
domination that motivated the indigenous populations to pursue their
independence.

After World War I and the postwar settlements that continued colonial power control of many Middle Eastern states, nationalist movements
arose contesting these arrangements. The rise of women's movements was
intertwined with the nationalist movements, and therefore must be understood within the context of that particular history. Although women
participated in these movements, they rarely attained positions of power
and retained their traditional roles in education and charity associations.
Women were encouraged to participate in the battle against colonialism,
but only on the margins of the movements. It was the men who held the
high positions necessitating public circulation and recognition. It was clear

that women's aspirations for equal rights were going to take a back seat to the fight for independence. In some cases, national groups held on to the traditional views of women despite their participation. This reflected an attempt to reject Western ways, which included a more public role for women in society. In Algeria, for example, the Front de Liberation Nationale (FLN) adopted many of society's reactionary views of women as a backlash to French influence. The nationalist movements sought independence, not the complete "transformation of society."[20] In fact, after the Algerian revolution, where over 10,000 women played some role, post-revolutionary rhetoric was steeped in traditional patriarchal concepts, including the role of Islam in society and the role of men as head of the household.[21] The nationalist and subsequent independence movements across the Middle East influenced the political development of countries throughout the region in a variety of ways. As states fought both external and internal battles for self-determination, the question of government structure floated to the surface. Along with debates on the type of regime that would develop, as states prepared for independence the controversial topic of women's status in the new governing structure emerged.

Algerian women filled a stadium in Oran in 1958 to demonstrate their support of the Algerian insurgent movement. The insurgent leaders formally constituted their new regime. (AP Photo)

TURKEY

The women's press in Turkey differed from its counterparts in Iran and Egypt, which limited their discussions to domestic issues rather than touch the more pertinent and controversial issues of society. In Turkey, articles criticized men for not fulfilling promises to liberate women after their participation in the nationalist movement. In 1908, following on the heels of significant changes in Turkish society, the first women's associations were formed. The Young Turk era lasted from 1908–1918 and led to key reforms for women. The Young Turk revolution had as its aim the end of an autocratic sultan and a retreat from the Westernizing influences of the Europeans. Women had participated in the Young Turk movement, pushing for Turkish nationalism in an era of growing discontent with Turkey's subordination to the West. In its quest to centralize control, the Young Turks revamped the educational and legal systems. The movement fostered reforms that stressed secularism and these modifications affected both the status of women and the public role that women could hold in Turkish society. In 1914, Istanbul University opened its doors to women. Even before the founder of modern Turkey, Mustafa Ataturk, abolished use of the veil in 1925, women in some Turkish cities had begun to remove them. After Turkey gained its independence in 1924, Ataturk's rigid adherence to secularism and Turkish nationalism cultivated equality for Turkish women. Ataturk's intention for secularization and modernization was to find his country's place in the modern world. Women's issues moved front and center and were deliberated outwardly during this early period of Turkish statehood. Reformers pressed for improvements in girls' education, the abolition of polygamy, and a replacement of Islamic law with a civil code. Many of these changes were implemented to allow women to participate in the building of the nation-state.[22] Despite the continuing patriarchal structure in Turkish society, the government pressed for sweeping adjustments with regards to women.

Changes in women's emancipation and views on feminism were moving rapidly in the 1930s. A debate was raging as to whether or not the women's groups that arose during this period were actually fostering real change for Turkish women in the political, economic, and social realm. Nezihe Muhiddin, who had been active in women's issues during the Ottoman period, founded the Turkish Women's Union (TWU) in 1924. One year prior, Muhiddin had founded the Women's Popular Party, but when the government rejected the formation of a separate women's party, she founded the TWU, a voluntary organization. To gain international appeal, the TWU aligned itself with the International Alliance of Women and focused on hosting the Twelfth Congress of that organization in Istanbul in 1935. As with most women's movements in Middle Eastern countries, the TWU began with elite, educated women. The mission of the organization was to gain political and social rights for women. In 1927, after public calls for women's suffrage, Muhiddin was targeted by the Republican People's Party—the only political party in Turkey at the time—and charged with mismanagement. After her resignation in 1927, the organization shifted roles and took on more charitable and philanthropic undertakings, although the TWU did not abandon its goal of suffrage and increased political rights. In 1930, women were granted suffrage in municipal elections, and they could vote in national elections by 1934. When the Congress of the IAW convened in Istanbul in 1934, Ataturk was viewed as a liberator of women.[23] In reality, the government was concerned about giving any group too much of an independent voice and shut down the TWU in 1935.

Whereas Turkey's transition to multi-party politics in the 1950s ushered in a fairly calm political period, the 1960s brought with it a challenging time for the country. During the 1980s, many educated women were influenced by the global feminist movement, especially from the West, and used the issue of domestic violence to unite a variety of women's groups and bring domestic problems into the public realm. As Turkey was undergoing domestic upheaval with a military coup suppressing groups on both the right and left of the political spectrum, women sought to reestablish their role in the public realm. Women organized large rallies to bolster public awareness of the issue and highlight the state's inattention to the problem. During the 1980s, women began asserting their own voices, rather than having the government speak for them under the pretext of improving society. Women began to define issues as they interpreted them and not as they were interpreted for them by the state.[24] An important event for women in Turkey and the Muslim world was Tansu Ciller's election as Turkey's first female prime minister in 1993. She was a university professor in economics and her election energized women who viewed this event as the ultimate achievement of women's liberation.[25]

In 2002, the Justice and Development Party (AKP) came to power in Turkey. The AKP stems from Islamist roots, although the party maintains its commitment to the secular nature of Turkey. The party describes itself as a "conservative democratic" one that champions "change with tradition." The AKP holds that addressing women's issues is a priority for the government. Some questions that the government wants to tackle include education for women, support for civil society organizations, and exploration of the economic and sexual exploitation of women, especially the practice of honor killings.[26] With regards to education, the government wants to entice the rural population to send their children, especially girls, to school. As such, the government has begun to pay mothers to send their children to school and offers increased payments for girls who attend school.

Tansu Ciller, former prime minister and leader of center-right True Path Party, speaks to her deputies in Parliament, 1998. (AP Photo/Burhan Ozbilic)

The AKP has organized Women's Branches across the country to entice women to join the party. Prime Minister Recip Tayyip Erdogan originally supported a quota for women within the political system, but eventually backed down from that stance. Selma Kavaf, the head of the AKP's women's branches, argued that quotas foster the perception that women who gained positions of power attained them because of the quota rather than through talent and hard work. With Prime Minister Erdogan's support of women in the party, Kavaf believes that increased representation will occur naturally.[27] Women currently hold 9.1 percent of parliamentary seats in Turkey.

IRAN

By the 1860s, under the Qajar Dynasty in Iran, a group of men interested in women's reform as part of an overall strategy to increase political liberalization and national strength emerged. These reformers believed in the

Conservative Turkish women protest against the country's top prosecutor's move to disband the governing Islamic-rooted party in Istanbul, 2008. (AP Photo/Ibrahim Usta)

family as an important unit of social progress and, as such, pursued programs that would ameliorate women's positions in society.[28] Iranian men who had studied in the West and witnessed social interactions between women and men along with education for girls influenced the feminist movement in their home country. During the Safavid period, from 1501–1722, most Iranians converted to Shia Islam; although Shiism is the main religion of Iran, Shias make up only 15 percent of the 1.3 billion Muslims worldwide. Some Shia laws, including those that pertain to women, differ significantly from those of the various Sunni schools.

Secret societies developed in 1905 to push for the creation of a constitution in Iran. In one such society, the Homeland Freedom Society, there were 60 female members. By 1906, women's organizations already existed concentrating mostly on promoting girls' education. One of the first women's magazines in Iran began in 1910, and women were instructed not to discuss issues of politics, thereby restricting themselves to domestic issues discussing home life, chores, childrearing, and the like.[29] Women participated in political activities during the Constitutional Revolution from 1906–1911 and published their first newspaper in 1911. Those in the forefront of the Constitutional Revolution were an eclectic association of merchants, landowners, clergy, and secular intellectuals who wanted to restrain the power of the monarch and protect Iran against Western encroachment. The Constitutional Revolution's vision of a democratic Iran included emancipation for women as a means to gain national independence and develop into a modern society. As such, women's emancipation became inextricably linked with national progress and "created a generic link between feminism and nationalism which has shaped the course of Iranian feminism ever since."[30] Constitutionally, however, women were not allowed to field candidates for parliament.

Women continued to participate in the independence movement. In 1910, after the Homeland Freedom Society was disbanded, the Women's Society emerged and eventually changed its name to the Homeland Ladies Association. This group participated in political demonstrations and also protested wearing the veil, although they refrained from overt criticism of Islam.[31] In 1913, Maryam Amid Mozayen al Saltaneh founded the *Shokufeh* newspaper, along with the Iranian Women's Society.[32] This group, along with others, was directed by predominately educated middle and upper class women who wanted to convince the government that women's issues were intricately connected to Iran's "national aspirations to claim its place in the international community of modern and 'civilized' countries."[33] In the 1920s and 1930s other prominent women's groups emerged, and their growth coincided with the end of the Qajar Dynasty.

When Reza Shah took power in 1921, ending the Qajar Dynasty's grip on power, he was heavily influenced by Ataturk and his secular reforms. After a visit to Turkey, Reza Shah returned home and enacted significant changes, especially in the area of public education for both boys and girls. Several women's movements began to expand during this period, bringing women's issues squarely into the public realm. One woman who was particularly active was Sediqeh Daulatabadi, who had founded several newspapers and women's groups. After her newspaper was banned, she went to Paris to study psychology and returned to Iran in 1927. In her absence, the Patriotic Women's League, headed from 1922 to 1925 by Muhtaram Iskandari, was recognized by most other women's organizations as representing Iranian women. Therefore, the League participated in the Second Eastern Women's Congress, held in Teheran in 1932, with the goal of reforming Iran's policies toward women by exposing them to the international perspective on women's rights. Although the League attempted to tow the Pahlavi regime line, occasional acts of confrontation led to the elimination of all independent women's groups. Many women joined the state-run Women's Society and continued to lobby for suffrage.[34]

To control the women's movement and end the independence of women's groups, the state-sponsored Women's Awakening project was created 1936. The project insisted that women remove their veils in public and, in exchange, granted them admittance to education and public employment. While the concept of male guardianship dictated that a male relative must supervise the modesty of women, another notion began to prevail during this period. State propaganda held that unveiled women were going to be "guarded" by their co-workers, supervisors, and teachers. What this policy of "state chaperoning" did not do was grant women true equality; rather, it continued to subordinate women to male control of some sort.[35]

Part of Reza Shah's legacy created resentment among the Islamic clergy with regard to many issues, not least of which were its liberal policies toward women. When Reza Shah abdicated power to his son, Mohammed Reza Shah, in 1941, he many of his father's modernization programs along with strong political repression. Clearly not a proponent of "women's lib," having declared to an Italian journalist that women are inferior to men, the Shah implemented policies to demonstrate that modernization was occurring in his country. Between 1941 and 1951 more than 70 political organizations emerged along with dozens of women's groups. The most influential women's group was the Women's Party, founded in 1943. Unlike many other women's groups across the Middle East during this period, which emphasized national goals rather than feminist ones, the Women's Party made feminist goals a priority. In 1943, two key players in the group received passports from the Iranian government to travel to Turkey to prepare the ground for women to participate in the Peace Conference. The Women's Party. along with the Women's committee of the communist-leaning Tudeh party, petitioned the government for women's suffrage. A member of the Tudeh party proposed women's suffrage in parliament and, although that proposal failed, women did eventually get the vote in 1963. A religious cleric, Ayatollah Ruhollah Khomeini, who was a formidable opponent for the Shah, denounced this move and declared that allowing women to vote ran counter to Islam. After the 1979 revolution, however, Khomeini retracted that view and endorsed a political role for women.[36]

In 1946, the Women's Party changed its name to the Women's Council to discount any notion that it was a political party and to widen its appeal to a variety of women's groups. Women's issues gained more attention; those involved in the debate over gender were supremely aware of the global implications. The activists' strategy reflected a belief that international legitimacy would force the Iranian regime to recognize women's rights, especially suffrage. Elites, who sought international recognition as "civilized states," led modernizing rulers to champion women's rights. Clearly, group members did have political aspirations because, in 1963, the year that women got the vote, Hajir Tarbiyat became one of the first eight female members of parliament, representing Teheran. Under the Shah, women's organizations were eventually centralized under a government sponsored Women's Organization of Iran (WOI), which supported the amended Family Protection Law of 1967, which was strengthened in 1975. The law widened the conditions under which women could seek divorce, limited polygamy and a man's grounds for divorce, and allowed women to get custody of children. Secular, not religious courts, would decide the outcome of these cases.[37]

Ayotollah Khomeini, taking advantage of the anti-Shah sentiment even within the secular community, encouraged women to protest during the 1978–1979 revolution. When the revolution occurred, many things changed for women under Khomeini's new theocracy. He enforced veiling, which was met with both protests against the move and a counter-protest supporting it. Eventually, the measure was enforced and it continues to be a source of debate in Iran. Khomeini abolished the Family Status Law and allowed girls to be married at age nine. Women were prohibited from becoming judges. As a way to engender women's support, however, Khomeini allowed them to enter the political and public realm, a concept that ran counter to the views of the conservative and traditional clerical establishment. Khomeini hoped that women would influence their husbands or fathers to support for the regime.[38] As such, in post-revolutionary Iran, women's civil and social rights were severely curtailed while their political rights were not. Even with these steps backwards in the personal status realm, women were granted some important rights as Khomeini encountered a backlash against some of his more conservative policies. They were allowed to go to work and study, provided that they were segregated and covered. Despite the fact that they were required to wear the veil, they did not, like women in Saudi Arabia, have to cover their entire faces. Women were permitted to cover only their hair. Interestingly, women who had protested the Shah while veiled to signal discontent with his policies and Westernization resented the forced Islamic dress Khomeini's regime imposed.

During the protracted Iran-Iraq war, from 1980–1988, women participated in the war effort as volunteers and as members of the Iranian Revolutionary Guard Corps. Despite this public contribution to the war, their major roles were that of mother and wife, supporting their men as they went to the battlefield. Issues affecting women, such as their social and political status, were ignored during these eight years.

During the first three governments after the revolution, women held only 1.5 percent of parliamentary seats, and most of these politically active women emerged from established religious families.[39] As more conservative women, they worked on improving women's rights within the private, family realm, contending that a woman's most important role is in the home. Consequently, it made sense that the issue of divorce was one of the first women's issue addressed by the first parliament. After the revolutionary period and the death of Khomeini in 1989, more women served in parliament. By 1992, women comprised 3.3 percent of the representatives, bringing the number of women members of parliament to nine. These women were better educated and younger than their predecessors. The representatives, however, appeared to be out of touch with many Iranian women who wanted to see real change take place with regards to the social, economic, and political position of women in the Islamic Republic.

Women came out in large numbers for the March-April 1996 legislative elections. Several of the female candidates projected a new view for women's rights and believed that working through the political system was the most important issue. They differed from the previous female members of parliament who held a more traditional view about the role of women. Women were seeking real changes in employment opportunities and in the civil code. To mobilize women during these elections, President Hashemi Rafsanjani's older daughter, Fatimeh, argued that women, who would confront women's issues, should occupy half the seats in parliament. In 1997, Faizeh Rafsanjani, another daughter of the Iranian president, won the second highest number of votes in Tehran in the parliamentary elections of April 1996. As an activist for women's rights, Faizeh wanted to use the political system to alter women's status in Iran. She gained support from young females who believed that she related to their plight. A gradual cultural change has been occurring in Iran as younger, more vocal female parliamentarians are willing to blatantly confront key women's issues. Additionally, male members of parliament have been recognizing that women have issues separate from those of men.[40]

Several women's magazines, which are basically moderate Islamist in nature, are now being published in Iran. Although the magazines have an Islamist leaning, secular women also contribute to the editions since both groups work toward ameliorating conditions for women within Iran. These magazines have invited criticisms by the more traditional elements of society, but they have also had an impact on Iranians' views of women.

EGYPT

Women found a voice in society with the advent of women's publications such as Hind Nawfal's *The Young Women,* published in 1892 in Alexandria, Egypt. The publications were instrumental in leading to the development of women's associations and organizations. Egypt had one of the earliest and strongest women's movements in the region. In 1924, an Egyptian feminist, Huda Shaarawi, removed her veil in public and her photo made the front pages of Egyptian newspapers. This event followed Egypt's admission of women to universities. Shaarawi headed the Egyptian Feminist Union (EFU), a secular group that pushed for social, economic, and political rights for all Egyptian women regardless of religion. Disagreeing with Egypt's increased Westernization, Hassan al Banna founded the Muslim Brotherhood in 1928. Al Banna, who was a teacher in the Suez region of Egypt, was appalled by the treatment of Egyptian laborers in comparison to the treatment that foreigners received. He began preaching for an Islamic

education to strengthen the Muslim world in order to repel foreign intervention. He gained female supporters as he pushed for women's education
and extensive social work as a way of bringing Islamic values back into
society. In response to the secular nature of the EFU, and influenced by
the views of the Muslim Brotherhood, Zaynab al Ghazali formed the Muslim Women's Society in 1936, which engaged primarily in welfare work.[41]
She founded the society to convince women of their important role in the
Islamic movement as both devoted mothers and wives and active participants in the Islamic community. She partnered with Hassan Al-Banna and
fostered education as a key mechanism to bring women into the Islamic
fold. She also supported the idea that Islam provided for equal rights for
women, although governments did not always implement these rights.[42]

Women's political activity continued to grow into the 1940s when the
Egyptian Feminist Party was established. In 1948, Doria Shafiq founded a
women's organization seeking more political participation and rights for
women and used the press to fight for these rights. After the Free Officer's
Revolution in 1952 brought Gamal Abdel Nasser to power, many women's
organizations were shut down, including the EFU and Bint al-Nil, so as not
to become opposition parties for the government. Despite the organizations' closing, women continued their public battle for equal rights. In 1954,
Shafiq staged a sit-in at the Cairo headquarters of the journalists' union
to underscore her impatience with the government's lack of response to
women's demands. By 1957, Nasser introduced a new constitution granting women suffrage, and, in that same year, two women were elected to
parliament.[43] Nasser encouraged women to participate in the political
system and to work in economic production. He pushed for new female
leadership, and in 1962 the Ministry of Social Welfare was created to specialize in women's affairs, particularly those dealing with labor practices.
Women also gained entrance to the ruling party, the Arab Socialist Union,
and were placed on several popular committees, while also being assigned
five percent of the total membership of the party. Despite these changes,
traditions held women back from both registering to vote and participating
in the political system.[44]

In Egypt, after the Free Officer's revolution in 1952 which eventually
brought Nasser to power, the women's movement experienced both a setback and slight progress. When Nasser moved against his leftist opponents
to consolidate power, the feminist movement suffered along with those
groups. Although Nasser's government did implement reforms to ameliorate education, employment opportunities, and healthcare for women, they
were still not given a role in the top echelons of power. During Nasser's
rule, women entered leadership positions in education granting them much
greater visibility and access in the public realm. When Anwar Sadat took
power in 1970 after Nasser's death, he allied with some Muslim groups to

gain their support. The growth of Islamic radicalism became much more evident in the 1970s when newly urbanized men mixed with modern, un-veiled women in universities both in Egypt and across the Middle East. The traditional values that the men carried with them from rural society, cou-pled with an antagonism to Western ways, put them squarely into conflict with the women.

In 1977, Sadat broke with these Islamic groups and began to enhance women's political power by applying quotas to give women more positions in parliament and in regional councils. Jihan Sadat, Anwar Sadat's wife, was an important force and voice for women's issues in Egypt. She pushed through liberal marriage and family laws, which were later repealed follow-ing protests by more conservative women. Sadat also established several women's groups to deal with family planning, education, and child wel-fare. During Sadat's reign, feminist movements gained influence by writing books and articles, which, although eventually banned by the government, reached a large audience. In the 1970s, feminist Nawal El Saadawi ignited a discussion on authoritarianism and the violence toward women.[45] She edited a journal and organized the Arab Women's Solidarity Association, which was banned in 1991.

When Hosni Mubarak assumed power after Sadat's assassination in 1981, he reversed some of the gains that women had made. He abolished the women's quota for parliament, resulting in fewer women involved in government. Additionally, both Sadat and Mubarak attempted to curtail the growth of an already bloated bureaucracy. As the number of people in government jobs decreased, women were hit hard, since many were con-centrated in these positions. The Arab Women's Solidarity Association, which formed in 1984 to promote equal rights and democracy, was shut down in 1991 due to its opposition to Egypt's participation in the first Gulf War. President Mubarak viewed some women's movements as similar to other opposition movements that existed in Egypt at the time and cracked down on them.

As Egypt's economy slowed and opportunities arose elsewhere, Egyptian men went to work in the oil rich Gulf States with the intention of sending remittances home to their families in Egypt. A significant social change occurred during the men's absence, especially in rural society. Women assumed responsibility for the home and the farms, granting them more independence and power in both the domestic and public realms. Women continued to participate in politics. In 1984, women had 34 of the 458 seats in parliament, but the number in 2005 had declined to only nine. In 2009, new legislation passed setting a quota for women in Egypt's parlia-ment to allot them 64 out of 518 seats. This new legislation has caused debate with other minorities groups, such as Coptic Christians, requesting a quota for their representatives in parliament.[46]

MOROCCO

The women's movement in Morocco began in the 1940s during Morocco's fight for independence from the French when women helped their male relatives hide and transport arms. When King Mohammad V's daughter, Lalla Aicha, appeared unveiled in 1947, her father wanted to send the message that the era of women's emancipation had begun. During that same period, several women's organizations emerged, but these were groups that mostly performed charitable functions and assisted in the struggle for independence. After Morocco gained independence in 1956, most activists were demobilized and the women's movement was less active.

In 1961, the Union Progressite des Femmes Marocaines (UPFM) emerged out of the only trade union at that time and worked toward creating a more equitable work environment for women. The UPFM, however, trickled out and did not accomplish its goals due to a lack of competent leadership and political battles. One big proponent of women's rights in the workplace and throughout Morocco was the king. In 1969, he pushed women to form a union that eventually emerged in May of that year. The Union Nationale des Femmes Marocaines' (UNFM) purpose was to bring women's issues to the public's attention and to make sure that any reforms remained within the realm of Islam. A key challenge for the UNFM was that it did not attract a broad spectrum of Moroccan women, primarily because it was founded by royal women and did not appeal to the majority of the population. By the 1970s, women's groups were not independent, but were organized within political parties. The female base of these parties was limited, with most female members having ties to prominent party members.[47] Finally, in 1985, the Democratic Association of Moroccan Woman, the first women's organization independent of a political party, was formed.[48] Numerous women's organizations formed in the 1980s and 1990s, due primarily to the liberalization of Moroccan politics. Many opposition parties formed and took up the mantle of the marginalized members of the population. Very few political organizations were independent of the Moroccan state in the 1970s. The Istiqlal party did have a women's section, and a separate women's organization was eventually developed in 1987. A confluence of events during the 1980s led to increased activity and interest in women's movements.[49]

In 1992, the Democratic Association of Moroccan Women led a campaign to collect 1 million signatures to establish more equitable family laws prompting a response by Islamist groups. The Islamic activists collected 3 million signatures to oppose the campaign. Eventually, the women who began the campaign opted to present their demands to the king. This incident illustrates the growing strength of the Islamist groups and the necessity of more secular groups to adapt to some of their demands. In 1993, King Hassan made some small reforms, but it was not until King Mohammad's ascension to the throne in 1999 that more profound reforms were planned. However, the Islamist groups again put pressure on the government to halt reforms and, in March 2000, the king backed down on his plan to make laws more egalitarian and to integrate women into the nation's development. The king, however, continued to work for gender equality and worked with the parliament to set aside 30 seats for women in the national elections of September 2002.[50] Despite succumbing to pressure from the Islamist groups, the king managed to convince parliament to pass amendments to the family law in 2004, bringing it closer to Tunisia's more egalitarian code. Similar to Tunisia, the king used Islamic concepts to justify his stance on women's rights.[51]

KUWAIT

After World War I, the British and local emirs controlled Kuwait. Prior to signing an agreement of protection with the British in 1899, Kuwait was ruled by the Al-Sabah family, who remain the country's ruling family. Under the agreement with the British, Kuwait was a self-governing state with British protection from other foreign powers. In the 1950s, with the growth of the oil industry, women entered the workforce to increase the number of Kuwaitis in the economy and decrease the growing number of foreign workers in Kuwait. Although a very traditional society, a group of men educated in Egypt pushed for reform contending that progress entailed flexibility. As such, they argued that the practice of seclusion needed to be revamped if Kuwait was going to modernize. It was during this period that women's groups emerged and, in 1963, the Women's Cultural Social Society (WCSS) was formed to provide upper class women an opportunity to participate in charity work. For women and more traditional members of society, performing charity work could be understood as a logical extension of women's role in the private realm as caregivers.[52] Also in 1963, middle class women established the Arab Women's Development Society (AWDS) and concentrated on more controversial issues than those pursued by WCSS, such as equal rights and citizenship rights. During the 1960s and 1970s, other women's groups formed, yet they were plagued by divisions between upper and middle class women and eventually by Islamist elements of society.[53]

The AWDS forced the 1973 parliament to explore an equal rights bill. The bill concerned polygamy, equality in employment, and family law. Opponents to the bill outweighed supporters, for many feared that restructuring society would modify the patriarchal nature of Kuwait, thereby lessening men's grip on power. To avoid a challenging conflict, the members of parliament did not vote on the bill and referred it instead to another governmental group for further study.

Government concern broadened as feminist groups pushed for changes, while the regime, under pressure from Islamist groups, sought to preserve traditional values. In several statements by the emir, he emphasized the Islamicization of society and the importance of maintaining the traditional family structure. The Personal Status Law was enacted in 1978 and codified the control of men over women. In this law, imprisonment for women who had premarital sex increased from 5 to 10 years. In 1975, upper class women established the Girl's Club to compel the government to give women a voice on laws that affected women, along with suffrage. At the same time in Kuwait, secular opposition groups were clamoring for increased rights and the government decided to crack down on opposition by banning several groups. To increase its control over the AWDS, in 1978, the government appointed a women to assume leadership of the organization. Many members, however, showed their discontent by refusing to cooperate with the new leader, and eventually the government disbanded the organization, dealing a blow to women's groups in Kuwait.[54]

The nature of the women's movement then took a traditional and conservative turn. By the 1980s, several Islamic women's groups emerged, along with a return to veiling, and these groups espoused the view that women played an important role in society by remaining in the home. Neither the WCSS nor the Girls' Club would assume the feminist mantle and oppose the government. They tacitly accepted that patriarchal structure yet continued to work toward women's suffrage. The WCSS petitioned the government to appoint women to senior government positions. Despite disappointments for women, by the late 1980s women comprised over two thirds of university students, leading to a higher GPA requirement for women than for men in certain fields. One reason that women made up a large number of university students was also related to the fact that men were able to study abroad more easily than women, which could account, in part, for the discrepancy between male and female students.[55]

The Gulf War in 1991 affected women's issues and organizations in several ways. Women's groups shifted their focus from equal rights and political power to community issues. In 1994, the Federation of the Kuwaiti Women's Associations (FKWA) was established and headed by Sheikha Latifa al Fahad al Salem al-Sabah, who was married to the Crown Prince. The FKWA became the umbrella organization for all women's groups and was the sole representative of women's positions in Kuwait. The assumption of women's issues by the elite of Kuwaiti society left a segment of society without a voice or a mechanism by which the could address issues of importance to their lives. The Gulf War also increased the number of female-run households. Additionally, the government's negative perception of foreigners deepened after the war, and children who were the offspring of a Kuwaiti woman and a foreign man were denied rights given to

male citizens such as housing, welfare, and other types of government support.[56] These women united to lobby for citizenship to be passed through
the mother as well father.

Although women's groups in Kuwait have been hijacked by the FKWA,
which does not fight for women's rights but accepts the traditional view of
women's role in society, the WCSS has tried to revamp its image. A new
president took control of the organization in 1994 and recruited educated
women from both the middle and upper classes to raise awareness of wom-
en's issues and their rights in Kuwaiti society.

In the political realm, in 2002, the Emir of Kuwait supported wom-
en's suffrage and had gained support from the Council of Ministers. The
measure was struck down by the more conservative parliament. In 2006,
women gained the right to vote, and 27 candidates stood for elected office.
Although no women were elected, the election indicated some progress for
Kuwaiti women in the political realm. Additionally, in 2005, the first female
minister was appointed to Kuwait's cabinet.

Almost all voluntary associations in Kuwait are controlled and funded
by the state, more specifically by the Ministry of Social Affairs and Labor.
Women's groups fall under this category, and this provides them with a
legitimate outlet for public expression. However, the fact that the organization is controlled by the state, which can dissolve it at any time, inhibits
the growth of a real feminist movement. Upper class women have aligned
themselves with the state and have come to an agreement as to what the
ideal role entails: conforming to a more traditional definition of a woman's
role. As such, real change in the status of women and their role in society
have been difficult to achieve.

IRAQ

In the early 20th century, the Iraqi leadership began to encourage wom-
en's education and was even supported by some traditional families that
believed an educated woman had better marriage prospects than an uneducated one.[57] When the Hashemite kingdom was founded in 1921, despite
the lack of democracy, it fostered the growth of civil society through ethnic inclusiveness and civic participation.[58] King Faisal I rewarded talented
female students by permitting them to attend college. Women, however,
were not fully accepted as equal students to men. Sabiha al Shaykh Daud
became the first female student to study at Iraq's College of Law, in 1936,
but she was forced to sit in a box to separate her from her male counterparts. Despite some difficulties, women's education had significant male
supporters, most specifically male poets. One poet, Jamil Sidqi al-Zahawi,
pushed women's education along with abolition of the veil, which he
viewed as "calamitous."[59] He also held that men should not have privileges

in divorce and that forced marriage should be abolished. Likewise, another poet, Ma'ruf al-Rusafi, published a poem in an Iraqi paper criticizing women's treatment. This poem led to the Islamic clerics issuing a fatwa (religious edict) against him.[60]

Taking its cue from the Egyptian literary movement, by 1923 a Palestinian woman, Paulina Hassoun, published the first woman's publication in Iraq, *Leila*. Although the publication lasted only two years, it set the stage for other women's movements to emerge. In 1925, the poet al Zahawi's sister, Asma Zahawi, began a women's association in Iraq called the Awakening Club. It taught classes in child care, literature, and hygiene and also sponsored social projects. Nazik al Mala'ika, the daughter of two poets, began to publish poems in newspapers and magazines. In 1947, she published a poem on the cholera epidemic in Egypt that won national acclaim due to its style. She went on to earn a degree from Princeton University and then went to Kuwait to teach in the university.

Some prominent families also participated in pushing for education and women's rights. Sheik Ahman al-Sheik Da'ud, who was the Minister of Religious Endowments and an Iraqi member of parliament in 1928, supported girls' education and sent his daughters to the first state school for girls. As mentioned, his daughter became the first female student at the Iraqi School of Law, and his wife was an active participant in the first Iraqi women's organization. The Women's Awakening Club began in 1923 and was open to women of all religions, but was comprised primarily of upper and middle class women. The initial functions of the organization were to educate orphaned girls, provide literacy classes, and teach sewing. King Faisal took an interest in the organization and invited members to meet him and his wife.[61] Despite the king's support, the organization aroused some dissent by ulema, and by the end of the 1920s the club's activities were dwindling. Other groups, many missionary or religious ones, also operated during this period, including the Jewish Women's Charitable Society, founded in 1927 that concentrated on helping the blind. It also taught poor women handicrafts to assist them in making a living.[62]

Another aspect of the women's political awakening was their role in the nationalist movement. Similar to women in other Middle Eastern and North African countries, Iraqi women were in the forefront of the independence movement.[63] Their hope was that, by participating in the state's independence, women would be granted equal rights during the process of state building. In 1920, when the San Remo conference granted Britain a mandate over the territory including Iraq, women joined the protests. Some scholars hold that, in the rural areas, women accompanied men as they revolted against the British and carried equipment, provided supplies, and yelled encouragement, much as women did during the time of Muhammad. Notwithstanding women's support of the national movement, the new constitution promulgated after Iraq's independence in 1932 denied them the right to vote and run for public office. Women's organizations continued to flourish and there was a surge during the 1940s in response to the Cairo Women's conference in 1944 and issues associated with World War II.[64]

Women's groups began to push for political rights, as opposed to just providing charitable works and advocating for education. In 1952, the League for Defense of Women's Rights was formed along with the Iraqi Women's League. The Iraqi Women's League was disbanded in 1968, along with all organizations not under Ba'athist control. During this period, only the government-sponsored Ba'athist General Federation of Iraqi Women was permitted to operate. The Ba'athist party defined the nature of all expression in Iraq and, although the Federation offered job training and pressed for changes in the personal status law, all aspects of the organization were controlled by the government. The Iraqi Women's League went underground and continued to function.[65]

Under Saddam Hussein's rule (1979–2003), women held 20 percent of seats in parliament, compared to an average of 3.5 percent in the region during that same period. Despite the fact that the only real power lay with Hussein, women were involved in the political system to the extent permitted. They gained the vote in 1980 and held cabinet level positions. However, Hussein could nullify any law passed in Iraq and frequently abused women using rape and torture to extract information from male dissidents. In the 1990s, after Hussein's invasion of Kuwait precipitating the Gulf War, women's position in society deteriorated. Hussein sought support from more conservative elements of society and used women's rights as a bargaining chip. He rolled back on many personal status laws that were favorable to women. United Nations sanctions on Iraq exacerbated poverty in that country, and women and girls bore the brunt of the challenges.

The Kurdish population in the north fared much better than the rest of the Iraqi people after the war in 1991. A democratic, albeit imperfect, government was formed, and held parliamentary elections, opened new schools, and promoted political tolerance. Women's groups emerged and led to the formation of the Women's Network, a coalition of 20 women's organization that united to press their issues. Since its creation in 1991, women have become representatives and judges in the Kurdistan Regional Government.[66] Women's groups, with help from international organizations, promoted women's participation in all levels of government and attracted women from all ethnic groups and across the political spectrum. Numerous new women's organizations also formed, such as the National Council of Women, Iraqi Women's Higher Council and the Women's Alliance for Democratic Iraq (WAFDI). These groups and others were meant to inform women about their political rights. Additionally, new publications emerged including women's magazines and newsletters. Women became editors of two papers, *Habeux Bouz* and *As-Saah,* both dealing with general and women's issues.[67]

After the United States' invasion in 2003, Iraqi women were concerned about their position in a future, potentially more conservative Iraq. Under the Transitional Administrative Law that was issued in 2004, women were required to make up at least 25 percent of the National Assembly, although in the 2005 elections, women captured 31 percent of the seats. Initially, however, women were almost totally excluded from the Iraqi Governing Council. Only three women were members of the 25-person council, despite the fact that women made up about 55 percent of the population. The new Iraqi constitution provides that 25 percent of seats in parliament are reserved for women, which is one of the highest percentages in the world. Despite this initial success, women were still worried about their future. According to the Iraqi constitution that was approved on October 15, 2006, Iraqis are equal before the law "without discrimination because of sex," although the constitution also states that no law can be passed that contradicts "established rulings" of Islam.[68] Some women have interpreted this ambiguity as detrimental to women's rights, yet Islamic modernists contend that, due to a wide variety of Islamic interpretations, the constitution does not necessarily portend doom for Iraqi women. If a progressive interpretation of Islam is adopted, then women's rights will be protected. Striking the right balance between tradition and equality in the Muslim world has been challenging and, if Iraq finds a workable path, it can be a model for other countries struggling with the debate on women's rights.[69]

QATAR

Qatar is a small country in the Middle East that became part of the Ottoman Empire in 1872. After World War I when the Ottomans evacuated their former strongholds in the Middle East, the British negotiated a treaty with the ruling al-Thani family, making the country a protectorate. Qatar did not gain its independence until 1971. Although Qatar borders one of the most conservative regimes in the Middle East, Saudi Arabia, the country is now considered one of the more progressive Middle Eastern countries with regards to many issues, including women's rights.

Under the leadership of the emir, Sheikh Hamad bin Khalifa al Thani, who ousted his conservative father in a coup in 1995, Qatar has transformed its social and political system in ways that would have seemed impossible just several years prior. Sheikh Hamad allowed migrant workers to build a church, championed women's rights, and established the Al-Jezeera television network.[70] An influential cleric, Youssef al-Qaradawi, who was originally from Egypt but settled in Qatar, backed the emir in his changes. Conservative Qatari society has been slow to embrace these social changes, including the lifting of restrictions on women and alcohol consumption, something that is forbidden in Islam. Easing this transition is the fact that the emir has stifled opposition to his reforms, a paradoxical move in the face of his support of increased liberalization.

A turning point for Qatari women was in 1998 when they were granted suffrage for municipal elections. Qatar did not have a parliament at that time. Women were not only allowed to vote, but they were also permitted to run for office. Although some segments of traditional Qatari society objected to the change, the emir decided to allow women to participate in politics. Prior to the 1999 elections, the government invited specialists to discuss the issue of voting and political participation and appealed to women as well. During the election, 45 percent of the voters were women and, although six women were candidates, none were elected.[71] Despite this setback reflecting traditional values that men could do a better job in public life than women, women did vote and began a more active political role in the small Gulf state. Qatar became the first Gulf Cooperation Council country to appoint a female minister in 2003. Sheikha Ahmad al Mahmud

Moza al-Malki, the only female candidate in District 2 in Doha, looks on as election authorities seal a ballot box during Qatar's municipal elections, 1999. (AP Photo/Leila Gorchev)

became the Minister of Education and worked to place more women in higher positions of authority.[72]

During the second municipal election, in 2003, one woman was elected to the council. Interestingly, voter turnout was lower during this election, primarily because, after four years of having an elected council, people perceived its role as more advisory than active in formulating policy. In 2004, a new constitution was promulgated to replace Qatar's temporary one; it allowed for universal suffrage for all people over 18 years old. To date, Qatar still does not have parliamentary elections.

ISRAEL

As a liberal democracy, Israel has given women equal rights with men since its independence in 1948. Founded by mostly educated European Jews, women fared well in Israeli society. With that said, on four occasions since Israel's creation, some women attempted to gain political power—in the form of electoral representation—by presenting a separate women's list in the parliamentary elections. The concept of a separate women's list predated the creation of the state of Israel and can be found in the 1918 elections to the Representative Assembly that existed during the British mandate period over Palestine.[73] Cross-culturally, women have tried to raise their profiles and numbers in legislatures by creating separate women's parties. Clear examples of this are in Canada and Europe. In pre-state Israel, women's parties participated in the Assemblies of Delegates, an elected body that governed the Jews as they attempted to establish a Jewish state. From 1920–1944, women were elected to this body and comprised 15 percent of the Assembly.[74] Despite this history, a debate has ensued as to whether women's parties hamper or help women achieve their objectives. By having separate parties, women can increase awareness of key issues that might get short shrift in integrated parties. These parties can also test new ideas that might eventually be incorporated into the larger parties. Some Israeli women viewed separate parties as useful prior to Israel's independence, but assumed that, with Israel's creation, women would be included in all political parties. Other scholars claim that women's lists foster segregation that is detrimental to women and the issues they advance.[75]

For a variety of complex reasons, Israel does not have a written constitution, but maintains a series of basic laws that address the issue of equal rights. Women are guaranteed equality in Israel's proclamation of independence. Additionally, Israel was founded on the principle of socialist Zionism best exemplified through its kibbutz system, a philosophy that fosters equal rights. Furthermore, service in the Israeli Defense Force (IDF) has been mandatory for both men and women since Israel's creation. All of these factors would appear to negate the need for separate women's parties to integrate women completely and equally into the fabric of Israeli society.

Despite these factors, women have played a smaller role in Israeli politics than would be expected. Since 1948, only 11 women have held cabinet positions in the Israeli government. In 2008, women held only 3 out of 26 cabinet positions, although these were high profile and power positions. Tzipi Livni was both the Foreign Minister and Deputy Prime Minister, and Yuli Tamir was the Minister of Education. In 2006, only 17 out of 120 members of parliament in the 17th Knesset (14%) were women. In comparison to other Western countries, this number is low. In 2009, 17 women served in the U.S. Senate (34%), while 74 served in the U.S. House of Representatives (17%).

In Israel, women remain underrepresented in politics due to a political structure that hinders their advancement. The major avenues to progress in national politics are through local politics, the army, and political parties. Although women serve in the IDF, they serve for two years, and mainly in non-combat roles, while men serve for three years and are required to do annual reserve duty. Israel was founded on an egalitarian ethos and thus became one of the only Western states with mandatory conscription for women, but early on it was clear that women did not have equal roles to men in the military. Prior to 1948, some women trained for battle to participate in the war for Israel's independence. Approximately 15 percent of

Israeli Foreign Minister Tzipi Livni, 2006. (AP Photo/Alexander Zemlianichenko)

armed units that opposed the British were women.[76] After Israel became a state, women were removed from combat units and had to serve in the Women's Corps and were trained as nurses, teachers, and social workers. Married women and mothers were exempt from service. With just a glance at key political leaders, one can recognize "parachuting," or the connection between high-level military jobs and politics.[77]

Despite the fact that legislation in Israel promotes gender equality, there remains a gender gap in most realms of Israeli society. Again, the society places a great amount of emphasis on the military and the importance of that institution. As many elements in Israeli society are seen through a security lens and the necessity to deal with external threats, the military, predominantly a male institution, gains increased importance. The military constitutes the public sphere and is male-dominated, while family life is associated with women and falls into the private realm. It is this aspect of culture that institutionalizes the gender division of labor found in Israeli society. In states that are under threat and where the family assumes a key role in this society, women's roles are subsumed to those of men.[78] Women are responsible for perpetuating the family through reproduction and educating the future generation. As such, their role in the private sphere is emphasized. Military service is also perceived as a measure of one's loyalty to the state, which translates into political, economic, and social access.[79]

Women were incorporated into pre-state security structures. Hashomer, a Jewish self-defense organization, was established in 1908 while the country was under Ottoman control. Although the Ottomans were responsible for the security of towns, some of the more remote communities arranged for their own security to protect crops, settlements, and people. Women participated in Hashomer, but rarely joined in the more dangerous tasks, such as the pursuit of attackers or raids on Arab villages; instead, they became cooks, nurses, and bookkeepers.[80] In one incident in 1909, when Hashomer members were going to fight for a piece of land near Mount Tabor, the women's role was to prepare a picnic. When the British gained the mandate to Palestine in 1918, the Jewish leadership disbanded Hashomer and then created the Hagana to protect the Jews in Palestine. As the Jewish community became more socialist, it granted more rights to women, yet men continued to dominate in most realms. However, in 1941 when the British feared a German invasion into Palestine, they allowed the Jews to organize assault companies, called the Palmach, and women were permitted to join. Women made up about 15 percent of the organization and were fully integrated members. When the German threat subsided, the British no longer supported the Palmach and it was forced underground. Jewish men and women, however, were encouraged to join the British Army to get some needed military experience and help the British fight the

Germans in other arenas. Women served, but were once again relegated to traditional female jobs, such as nurses, cooks, and chauffeurs.

On the eve of Israel's War of Independence after the United Nations voted to partition Palestine in 1947, a mixed gender unit of the Palmach, now operating without British permission, was attacked by a group of Arabs in the Negev Desert and brutally slaughtered. After that gruesome attack, the Hagana headquarters ordered all women removed from combat units, although some women remained during the first months of fighting.[81] By the time the War of Independence occurred, women were no longer integrated into military units with men and their ability to be in combat declined rapidly. When the IDF was established on May 30, 1948, women were put into a separate women's corps serving in supporting roles. Additionally, officer training courses were separated by gender and were not integrated until 2003. At the end of the war in 1949, the newly formed government decided on compulsory conscription for men and women. Despite some opposition from religious groups in Israel, the government upheld its decision to draft women, yet have them fulfill supporting roles, while leaving men available for combat. Married and pregnant women were exempt from service.

Women served mainly in support positions until 1973, when the number of Military Occupation Specialties (MOS) for women began to expand. However, the Israeli Army was an anomaly as a society that gave women enormous rights compared with its neighbors, yet discrimination and exclusion characterized men's attitude toward women in the military. In the 1980s, more slots were opened to women and they served as military police, intelligence, surveillance, medical professionals, and as trainers.[82] By 1995, after pressure from female politician and Israel's Supreme Court, a few combat roles were opened to women. In 1997, the air force was forced by Israel's Supreme Court to admit female trainees for pilot school, and in 2004 a light infantry battalion was established that was comprised of 70 percent women who patrolled the Jordanian-Israeli border.[83] Despite these changes, real combat is still men's territory and this factor has impacted upon women's roles in Israeli politics.

Furthermore, women's representation in Israeli politics remains fairly low due to a variety of cultural factors, including the belief that people should subordinate group interests to those of the nation. With external threats facing Israel, the population is encouraged to concentrate more on national than particular group concerns. Israel also remains a traditional society with an emphasis on family life. Although the socialist kibbutzim were supposed to provide for gender equality, studies have shown that women have been pushed into the more traditional tasks, including cooking, childcare, and laundry.[84] In 1951, the Women's Equal Rights Law was passed prohibiting discrimination against women. Interestingly, in Israel, issues of personal status (marriage, divorce, and death) are all under rabbinical court jurisdiction. Since only Orthodox Judaism is recognized, laws pertaining to these areas tend to be more conservative. To explore some of the issues present in Israeli society with regards to women, Prime Minister Yitzhak Rabin appointed a Commission on the Status of Women in 1975. The commission's findings led to some changes in the government structure to promote women's equality.

In 1977, a group of Israeli feminists met with the goal of sending more women to the Knesset by forming a women's party. Despite the debates over whether forming a women's party would be successful, the consensus was that the party would try to raise awareness about women's concerns rather than win votes. The importance of the Women's Party was that it brought key women's issues to the nation's attention and forced the major parties to explore them more closely. By pushing women's issues to the forefront, other parties also recognized that they would have to appeal to women as a separate group. As such, women have worked through women's wings of integrated political parties to gain access to the national stage. The most successful of these women's wings has been *Na'amat* (Movement of Working Women and Volunteers), a group that is part of the Labor party. The Israel Women's Network, founded in 1984, is one organization that has pushed for more political power for women.[85] Women's parties in Israel, although not always credited, have proven a catalyst for women's political participation and for improving the lagging representation of women.[86]

NOTES

1. Nabia Abbott, "Women and the State in Early Islam," *Journal of Near Eastern Studies* 1 (January 1942): 107–11.

2. Surah 33:35 in the Qu'ran, as quoted in Abbott, "Women and the State in Early Islam," 110.

3. Jane I. Smith, "Women in Islam: Equity, Equality, and the Search for the Natural Order," *Journal of American Academy of Religion* 47 (December 1979): 520.

4. Abbott, "Women and the State in Early Islam," 117.

5. Abbott, "Women and the State in Early Islam," 124.

6. Nikki R. Keddie, *Women in the Middle East: Past and Present* (Princeton, NJ: Princeton University Press, 2007), 26.

7. Abbott, "Women and the State in Early Islam," 114–15.

8. Marshall G. S. Hodgson, *The Venture of Islam: Conscience and History in a World Civilization* (Chicago: University of Chicago Press, 1974), 294.

9. Keddie, *Women in the Middle East: Past and Present,* 30.

10. Jacob Lassner, "Why Did Caliph al-Mansur Build ar-Rusafa?" *Journal of Near Eastern Studies* 24 (January 1965): 95–99.

11. Guity Nashat and Judith Tucker, *Women in the Middle East and North Africa* (Bloomington: Indiana University Press, 2006), 57–59.

12. Mervat F. Hatem, "Modernization, the State and the Family," in *A Social History of Women and Gender in the Modern Middle East* (Boulder, CO: Westview Press, 1999), 68.

13. Yesim Arat, "From Emancipation to Liberation: The Changing Role of Women in Turkey's Public Realm," *Journal of International Affairs* (Fall 2000): 107–23.

14. Ellen L. Fleischmann, "The Other 'Awakening': The Emergence of Women's Movements in the Modern Middle East, 1900–1940," in *A Social History of Women and Gender in the Modern Middle East*, eds. Margaret Meriwether and Judith Tucker (Boulder, CO: Westview Press, 1999), 101.

15. Fleischmann, "The Other 'Awakening,'" 107.

16. Nawar Al-Hassan Golley, "Is Feminism Relevant to Arab Women?" *Third World Quarterly* 25 (2004): 521.

17. Golley, "Is Feminism Relevant to Arab Women?" 530.

18. Golley, "Is Feminism Relevant to Arab Women?" 531–32.

19. Fatema Mernissi, *Islam and Democracy* (Cambridge, MA: Perseus Publishing, 2002), 160.

20. Beverly Milton-Edwards, *Contemporary Politics of the Middle East* (Boston, MA: Polity Press), 191–92.

21. Milton-Edwards, *Contemporary Politics of the Middle East*, 193.

22. Kathryn Libal, "Staging Turkish Women's Emancipation: Istanbul, 1935," *Journal of Middle East Women's Studies* 4 (Winter 2008): 34–35.

23. Libal, "Staging Turkish Women's Emancipation: Istanbul, 1935," 36–38.

24. Arat, "From Emancipation to Liberation," 114–20.

25. Nilgun Anadolu-Okur, "The Demise of the Great Mother: Islam, Reform, and Women's Emancipation in Turkey," *Gender Issues* (Fall 2005): 25.

26. Zana Çitak and Özlem Tür, "Women between Tradition and Change: The Justice and Development Party Experience in Turkey," *Middle Eastern Studies* 44 (May 2008): 456.

27. Çitak and Tür, "Women between Tradition and Change," 458.

28. Camron Michael Amin, "Globalizing Iranian Feminism: 1910–1950," *Journal of Middle East Studies* 4 (Winter 2008): 16.

29. Fleischmann, "The Other 'Awakening,'" 101.

30. Parvin Pardar, "Feminism and Islam in Iran," in *Taking Sides: Clashing Views on Controversial Issues in Anthropology* (Guildford, CT: McGraw Hill, 2003), 201.

31. Pardar, "Feminism and Islam in Iran," 201.

32. Keddie, *Women in the Middle East: Past and Present*, 84.

33. Amin, "Globalizing Iranian Feminism: 1910–1950," 18.

34. Amin, "Globalizing Iranian Feminism: 1910–1950," 18–22.

35. Amin, "Globalizing Iranian Feminism: 1910–1950," 8.

36. Azadeh Kian, "Women and Politics in Post-Islamist Iran: The Gender Conscious Drive to Change," *British Journal of Middle Eastern Studies* (1997): 76.

37. Nikki Keddie, "Women in the Middle East: Progress and Backlash," *Current History* (December 2008): 435.

38. Kian, "Women and Politics in Post-Islamist Iran," 76.

39. Kian, "Women and Politics in Post-Islamist Iran," 78–79.

40. Kian, "Women and Politics in Post-Islamist Iran," 89.

41. Lisa Blayedes and Safinaz El Tarouty, "Women's Electoral Participation in Egypt: The Implications of Gender For Voter Recruitment and Mobilization," *Middle East Journal* 63 (Summer 2009): 366.

42. Geneive Abdo, *No God But God* (Oxford: Oxford University Press, 2000), 148.

43. Ghada Hashem Talhami, *The Mobilization of Muslim Women in Egypt* (Gainesville: University Press of Florida, 1996), 17–18.

44. Talhami, *The Mobilization of Muslim Women in Egypt*, 19–21.

45. Mernissi, *Islam and Democracy*, 161.

46. Ramadan Al Sherbini, "Egypt Approves Parliament Quota for Women Amidst Protests," June 16, 2009 accessed at www.Gulfnews.com/region/Egypt.

47. Laurie Brand, *Women, the State and Political Liberalization: Middle Eastern and North Africa Experiences* (New York: Columbia University Press, 1998), 48–49.

48. Keddie, *Women in the Middle East*, 145.

49. Brand, *Women, the State and Political Liberalization*, 48–50.

50. Fatima Sadiqi and Moha Ennaji, "The Feminization of Public Space: Women's Activism, The Family Law and Social Change in Morocco," *Journal of Middle East Women's Studies* (Spring 2006): 105.

51. Keddie, "Women in the Middle East: Progress and Backlash," 434.

52. Haya Al-Mughni, "Women's Organizations in Kuwait," *Middle East Report* 198 (January–March 1996): 33.

53. Keddie, *Women in the Middle East*, 157.

54. Al-Mughni, "Women's Organizations in Kuwait," 34.

55. Keddie, *Women in the Middle East*, 157.

56. Al-Mughni, "Women's Organizations in Kuwait," 35.

57. Judith Colp Rubin, "Women in the New Iraq," *Middle East Review of International Affairs* 12 (September 2008): 33.

58. Victoria Stanski, "Linchpin for Democracy: The Critical Role of Civil Society in Iraq," *Journal of Third World Studies* 12 (2005): 208.

59. Rubin, "Women in the New Iraq," 33.

60. Noga Efrati, "The 'Other' Awakening in Iraq: The Women's Movement in the First Half of the Twentieth Century," *British Journal of Middle East Studies* (November 2004): 155–56.

61. Efrati, "The 'Other' Awakening in Iraq," 156–59.

62. Efrati, "The 'Other' Awakening in Iraq," 162.

· 63. Lucy Brown and David Romano, "Women in Post-Saddam Iraq: One Step Forward and Two Steps Back?" *NWSA Journal* 18 (Fall 2006): 52.

64. Efrati, "The 'Other' Awakening in Iraq," 164–66.

65. Swanee Hunt and Cristina Posa, "Iraq's Excluded Women," *Foreign Policy* 143 (July/August 2004): 42.

66. Brown and Romano, "Women in Post-Saddam Iraq," 54–56.

67. Stanski, "Linchpin for Democracy," 212–14.

68. As quoted in Isobel Coleman, "Women, Islam and the New Iraq," *Foreign Affairs* (January/February 2006): 24–32.

69. Coleman, "Women, Islam and the New Iraq," 32.

70. Yaroslav Trofimov, "Lifting the Veil: In a Quiet Revolt, Qatar is Snubbing Neighboring Saudis," *Wall Street Journal*, October 24, 2002, A1.

71. Andrew Rathmell and Kirsten Shultze, "Political Reform in the Gulf: The Case of Qatar," *Middle Eastern Studies* 35 (October 2000): 55.

72. Louay Bahry and Phebe Marr, "Qatari Women: A New Generation of Leaders? *Middle East Policy* 12 (Summer 2005): 111.

73. Leah Simmons Levin, "Setting the Agenda: The Success of the 1977 Israel's Women's Party," *Israel Studies* 4 (Fall 1999): 40.

74. Ester Hertzog, "Women's Parties in Israel: Their Unrecognized Significance and Potential," *Middle East Journal* 59 (Summer 2005): 440.

75. Levin, "Setting the Agenda," 42.

76. Martin Van Creveld, "Armed But Not Dangerous: Women in the Israeli Military," *War in History* (2000): 82.

77. Levin, "Setting the Agenda: The Success of the 1977 Israel's Women's Party," 44.

78. Hanna Herzog, "Homefront and Battlefront: The Status of Jewish and Palestinian Women in Israel," *Israel Studies* 3, no. 1 (Spring 1998): 61–63.

79. Orna Sasson-Levy and Sarit Amram-Katz, "Gender Integration in Israeli Officer Training: Degendering and Regendering the Military," *Signs* 33 (2007): 109–10.

80. Creveld, "Armed But Not Dangerous," 83.

81. Creveld, "Armed But Not Dangerous," 85–86.

82. Creveld, "Armed But Not Dangerous," 91–95.

83. Sasson-Levy and Katz, "Gender Integration in Israeli Officer Training," 114.

84. Levin, "Setting the Agenda," 42.

85. Levin, "Setting the Agenda," 46–47.

86. Hertzog, "Women's Parties in Israel," 450.

SUGGESTED READING

Abbott, Nabia. "Women and the State in Early Islam." *Journal of Near Eastern Studies* 1 (January 1942): 106–26.

Al-Ali, Nadje. *Secularism, Gender and the State: The Egyptian Women's Movement.* Cambridge: Cambridge University Press, 2000.

Amin, Camron Michael. "Globalizing Iranian Feminism: 1910–1950." *Journal of Middle East Studies* 4 (Winter 2008): 6–30.

Anadolu-Okur, Nilgun. "The Demise of the Great Mother: Islam, Reform, and Women's Emancipation in Turkey." *Gender Issues* (Fall 2005): 6–28.

Arat, Yesim. "Feminists, Islamists, and Political Change in Turkey." *Political Psychology* 19 (March 1998): 117–31.

Blayedes, Lisa and Safinaz El Tarouty. "Women's Electoral Participation in Egypt: The Implications of Gender For Voter Recruitment and Mobilization." *Middle East Journal* 63 (Summer 2009): 364–80.

Brand, Laurie A. *Women, the State and Political Liberalization: Middle Eastern and North African Experiences.* New York: Columbia University Press, 1998.

Charrad, Mounira. *States and Women's Rights: The Making of Postcolonial Tunisia, Algeria and Morocco.* Berkeley: University of California Press, 2001.

Kar, Mehrangiz. "Focusing on Women in the Internal Politics of Iran." *Brown Journal of World Affairs* 15 (Fall/Winter 2008): 75–86.

Meriwether, Margaret and Judith Tucker eds. *A Social History of Women and Gender in the Modern Middle East.* Boulder, CO: Westview Press, 1999.

Naghibi, Nima. *Rethinking Global Sisterhood Western Feminism and Iran.* Minneapolis: University of Minnesota, 2007.

6

—⚬⚬⚬—

Women and Culture

Although immortalized by 18th- and 19th-century travel writers as erotic belly dancers, women in the Middle East have had a long and varied history as entertainers, singers, artists, and authors. This chapter explores the roles that women have played in the cultural evolution of the Middle East and North Africa and how class and status influence the type of arts in which women participate. For illiterate women, oral folk poetry has long been an important part of Middle Eastern and North African cultural and religious traditions. As such, women have played an important role in transmitting and maintaining oral histories of their respective communities. Not only have women been active in the arts, they have also been portrayed in literature, music, and pop culture. Women, in their roles as wives and mothers, transmit cultural practices to successive generations that reinforce solidarity and loyalty to the family. Women have also played an important role in making traditional handicrafts and other items that are closely associated with life in the region. In each major culture, here identified as Arab, Turkish, Iranian, and Israeli, and in minority cultures, women have had a role in continuing the traditions that define each cultural group. The Arab, Turkish, and Iranian cultures emerged from great Islamic empires and trace their histories, languages, and practices to those civilizations. In ancient and early Islamic times, women were more likely to be the subjects of poems, stories, and myths rather than the authors of those works. However, scholars believe that women perpetuated their culture by telling stories, reciting poetry, and conveying these important oral histories to their children. Early works of literature, passed down from one generation to the next, give scholars clues about societal views of women. In these works, women were often portrayed as heroines or villains depending on their level of conformity to society's expectations. Ancient and early Islamic women also perpetuated special rites of passage and religious practices that provided community members with a sense of belonging and cultural distinctiveness.

Given the high rates of illiteracy across the region, it was not until after World War I that Middle Eastern women's written work was published in journals and other types of print media. The early 1900s also marked a period when women were increasingly active in public entertainment. In cities like Cairo, women performed in coffee shops and in theatrical productions for paying audiences. Some women even recorded their music and enjoyed a large fan base in certain regions. In terms of literary accomplishments, several feminist writers who emerged after World War II challenged the prevailing view of women's role in society. Over the years, female scholars, authors, entertainers, and actresses have embarked upon successful careers in the arts, often expressing their unique roles in Middle Eastern and North African culture.

Women's contributions to the cultural landscape of the Middle East and North Africa are also evident in how they approach their daily tasks. For instance, an ancient Zoroastrian tradition that endures is its basic philosophy of cooking. In some parts of Iran, people regard food as either "hot" or "cold" in nature, having a distinct effect on those who consume it. Therefore, some foods are believed to cause lethargy, while others cause excitement. Women, who prepare meals, will try to balance these two qualities while using spices in moderation; Iranian dishes often emphasize contrasting flavors like sweet and sour. As purveyors of culture, women taught their daughters how cook traditional meals that serve as a source of comfort and continuity for generations. In fact, a traditional proverb states that the way to win someone's favor is to share one's food with him or her. As such, food and the preparation of family meals served as a means to reinforce family solidarity and cultural identity.[1] Women are critical in maintaining and passing on these traditions to successive generations.

LANGUAGE, POETRY, AND SYMBOLISM

One important aspect of major cultural groups in the Middle East and North Africa is their shared language. Scholars suggest that language is a vehicle that carries culture from generation to generation. In pre-modern times, mothers played an important role in teaching their children the words that they would use to communicate with the world around them. The Arabs, who many believe descended from Ishmael, Abraham's son by his Egyptian maid Hagar, spoke Semitic languages and are kin ancestors of the Hebrews, Assyrians, and Arameans. The use of language was key means of expression. Pre-Islamic Arabs favored the use of poetry as a way to communicate and keep an oral record of their shared history. Their poetry embodied the Arab code of virtue and related to the most important aspects of life before the rise of Islam, including strict adherence to tribal values. For example, poems expressed the importance of loyalty to the tribe, bravery in battle, protection of the weak, and other moral principles associated with the maintenance of order in tribal nomadic conditions. Most poems expressing tribal solidarity were handed down from one generation to the next. These oral traditions and folktales provided future generations with an understanding of the tribe's history and culture. Scholars believe that poetry was so important to pre-Islamic Arabs that they would stop fighting and raiding other tribes for several weeks to focus on reciting and composing new verses. In many ways, pre-Islamic Arabs' use of poetry shaped the Arabic language and culture.[2] Women perpetuated key aspects of their society's cultural identity by fostering these oral traditions and practices.

Like pre-Islamic Arabs, most pre-Islamic Persians memorized and recited poetry. Rural and lower class people were largely illiterate, so they relied upon the oral traditions conveyed by elders to understand their shared history. Only a small, mostly elite segment of society could read and write. Hence, much of the Persians' pre-Islamic poetry was written for and by elites. The language and script used in Persian literature went through a variety of changes. New or modern Persian is but one of several Iranian languages that evolved over time. Scholars suggest that the roots of the language came from pre-Islamic Sasanids. The Persian language also borrows from Arabic, Turkish, and European languages. Likewise, Persian speakers did much to shape the Arabic language by incorporating it into their literature and often speaking Arabic in certain regions. For reasons still not understood, during the 9th and 10th centuries, a form of New Persian written in Arabic script emerged as the literary language in the region. As Persian is written in Arabic script, people often assume that the two languages are related, but they are not. Arabic is a Semitic language, while Persian is an Indo-European language. In Eastern Iran, Persian became known as Dari or Parsi. Dari is considered "court" Persian in Afghanistan; Parsi, or Farsi, is the main dialect spoken in Iran today. In Persian, there is no way to distinguish gender in verbs, nouns, and pronouns, hence Persian words often have multiple meanings and are thus subject to different interpretations.[3] This makes Persian poetry interesting, as the subject of a verse can be male, female, or both.

Mecca, the land of Muhammad's birth and the place where he received his first revelations, was an important economic, religious, and cultural center in Arabia. Across the region, people used poetry to express themselves throughout Muhammad's lifetime. In addition to being an important caravan station and pilgrimage site for its holy shrines, people also came to Mecca for its annual poets' fair near a place called Ukaz.[4] Poetry remained the most important genre in Arabic literature for generations.[5] Scholars suggest that Muhammad's detractors used poetry to express their dissatisfaction with his message. At one point, Muhammad fired back at those who used poetry to mock him, indicating that they used poetry merely as a way to make social commentary.[6] However, poetry and the poetic use of language and rhythm were not limited to Muhammad's critics. The Qu'ran is written in rhymed prose and sounds lyrical, if not musical, when chanted by an individual who has trained specifically to recite its Arabic words. Although there is little evidence available, scholars suggest that it is entirely reasonable to believe that women had a role in composing and reciting poetry.[7] Clearly, women had a role in transmitting Muhammad's message, which was often delivered in the form of rhythmic verses of worship and prayer. However, women's role in culture evolved with the times. Later, as successive caliphs conquered new lands and built sizable harems, slave women became their source of entertainment. In the Islamic world, non-Muslim female slaves were trained to be dancers and singers because entertainment was not considered an appropriate role for Muslim women.

Muhammad's female relatives had an important role in society, and this was reflected in artwork, jewelry, and other types of artistic symbolism. Throughout the Muslim world, depictions of Fatima's hand have symbolic and artistic significance. As the Prophet Muhammad and his first wife Khadija's daughter, Fatima's enduring image has come to symbolize the desirable attributes of a woman who devoted her life to family and faith. In religious art, the hand is often associated with affection. Evidence suggests that Mesopotamian amulets in the shape of hands offered people a sense of protection.[8] In the Islamic world, the Hand-of-Fatima in art is a ubiquitous symbol of protection against evil spirits and the evil eye. The folk belief in the danger of the "evil eye" is pre-Islamic in origin. People believed that Fatima's hand protected them from the effects of bewitchment that could lead to spiritual and physical maladies ranging from malice and envy to sickness and even miscarriage. After the rise of Islam, people believed that an open right hand had the power to distract and repel evil spirits. These symbols and beliefs were especially powerful for women who sought intercession and divine favor while pregnant, while lactating, or while trying to get pregnant. Shia women frequently hung silver representations of Fatima's hands around their children's necks to protect them from evil. Scholars suggest that women took comfort in this visual symbol of female power and protection, as they were frequently at risk for a number of spiritual, physical, and emotional maladies.[9]

LITERATURE

During the Age of the Rightly Guided Caliphs, in the seventh century, there was an ample amount of Persian literature, especially poetry. Women were often the subjects of Persian poetry as the objects of affection or the sources of unrequited love. Again, scholars believe that women had a role in composing and performing poetry despite few remaining records of such activities. However, it is clear that writing poetry remained an elite activity, reserved for the few who could read and write. Poets were frequently paid for their skills. In areas where poets were part of a patronage system, those with unique talents were rewarded handsomely. Most patrons favored poems that lavished praise upon rulers for their noble qualities, triumphs in battle, and other positive attributes. Perhaps the greatest poem of this period, written by Abo'l-Qasem Ferdowsi (C.E. 940–1020), is the Shahnameh or the "Book of Kings." This epic poem, about four times the length of *The Iliad* and the *Odyssey* combined, took Ferdowsi about 30 years to write and contains 60,000 verses. As a whole, the Shah-nameh serves as Ferdowsi's version of Iranian history. While some parts of the Shah-nameh are true and reflect actual events as they happened, much is mythical and folkloric.[10]

Today, scholars believe that women played an important role in driving the Shah-nameh's narrative flow. For instance, women or feminine symbols in the Shah-nameh arbitrate or mediate all significant transfers of power. In one example, a rebel military general named Bahram-i Chubina receives women's clothing from the king as an affront to his power. Bahram decides to wear the clothing in front of his troops who convince them to rebel against the king. Before the rebellion, his decision is reaffirmed when he meets with his "fortune," who assumes the form of a beautiful woman.[11] Hence, his transition from a loyal military leader to a rebel leader is through feminization. Female entities even stand at the transition between life and death in the Shah-nameh.[12] Perhaps this reflects women's role in carrying children and giving birth. It also reflects people's transformation when they marry and eventually become parents. Both transitions involve women whose relationships with men change their identity. Scholars also argue that, in patriarchal societies, all men experience some sort of encounter with a powerful woman. Mothers, for instance, have a certain amount of power over their children, who can be a source of great comfort or frustration. Therefore, in the Shah-nameh, patriarchal power is disrupted at transitional moments by powerful women or feminine symbols.[13] In this epic account of Iranian history, women have critical roles during transitions in Ferdowsi's characters' lives. Today in Iran, restaurant patrons can enjoy a meal while listening to a performer recite or sing parts of the Shah-nameh, often to the beat of a drum.

Another important piece of literature from the region, *The Thousand and One Nights,* is actually a collection of folktales that were transmitted orally from ancient times. Known in the West as *Arabian Nights,* the work was first printed in the Middle Ages. In this work, female characters have important roles reflecting their place in society. Shahrzad serves as the main storyteller and disobeys her father's wishes by marrying a king who weds a new virgin every night only to execute her the next day. The king, who engages in this practice after his first wife was unfaithful, meets his match when he marries Shahrzad. Rather than accept her fate, Shahrzad skillfully puts the king to sleep each night with a new story so that, in the morning, he will let her live another day. Shahrzad brilliantly and creatively weaves together innovative stories to keep the king entertained.[14] She also includes stories about other women. Some are presented as role models, while others are portrayed as unfaithful seductresses.[15] Women who are revealed in a positive light care for their families and remain faithful to their husbands. Those who cheat on their husbands represent the least desirable attributes of a wife and mother.[16] Shahrzad's storytelling and creative abilities paid off. After 1,001 nights, the king changed his mind about women and spared Shahrzad's life. She later became queen and had three sons.

Like the fictitious character Shahrzad, women have had important roles as poets, storytellers, and oral history custodians throughout the Middle East. Since early Islamic times, women guarded the heritage of Arabic storytelling by transmitting stories orally from one generation to the next. For instance, Al-Khansa (575–664) was the first Arab woman poet and literary critic who participated in public poetry readings and critiques in Arabia.[17] Women's unique role as purveyors of oral history reflects their role in the family and the fact that most women were illiterate, leaving very few women with the opportunity or ability to write their own literary works. In many ways, women's roles in the culture were closely tied to their role in religion. Religious texts were also communicated orally and passed down from successive generations through family members.

Through the end of the 18th century to the early 19th century, middle class women engaged in several cultural activities. Some frequented baths where women could socialize and catch up on news. Others made pilgrimages to saints' shrines and attended various types of performances. Although slaves continued to serve as entertainment for certain segments of the population, there were fewer slaves available to provide such services.[18] Toward the end of the 19th century, more women gained access to an education. With education came increased literacy, granting women new opportunities to contribute to culture. While women in the lower classes tended to transmit traditions orally, a few literate women became authors. One outlet of female expression was in print media. Some women contributed to journals devoted to poetry, short stories, and social commentary.

Before World War I, Egypt had about 25 different journals dedicated to publishing women's literary work for a primarily female audience. Women's journals circulated throughout major capital cities and often broached topics such as women's status in other countries, issues of marriage and family, and the even the differences between the sexes.[19] Scholars are still researching and uncovering women's roles in Middle East literature. A recent study revealed that, in 1906, a Lebanese woman named Afifa Karam wrote the first novel in Arabic literature. Prior to this study, it was widely accepted that an Egyptian man penned the first novel in 1914. Through the years, female authors have delved into some of the most challenging and controversial issues of their times. After World War II, a small group of Arab women started writing about gender discrimination and inequality. For instance, in the 1950s, a Syrian woman named Widad Sakkakini published her work detailing the injustices that women suffered in a male-dominated society. She also wrote a biography of Rab'ia, the first female Sufi mystic. In the 1960s, several authors wrote feminist books and articles exploring politically and religiously sensitive gender issues. Many of these female authors challenged traditional assumptions about a woman's place in society by refuting her status as the weak or inferior sex.[20]

Jewish women have always had important responsibilities in Israel's struggle for survival amid multiple threats to its existence. Their roles were

Palestinian women speak to an Israeli border police officer as they wait to cross a checkpoint on their way to pray for the holy fasting month of Ramadan at the Al Aqsa Mosque in Jerusalem's Old City, in the West Bank town of Bethlehem, 2009. (AP Photo/Nasser Shiyoukh)

particularly interesting in 1948 when Israel became independent and was immediately engulfed in armed conflict. At the height of the war in 1948, Jewish women wrote columns in two newspapers, *Ha'aretz* and *Ma'ariv*, showcasing women's contributions during the conflict and forging new roles for themselves as authors writing specifically for female readers. Several of these articles emphasized women's involvement in the war effort. Women fulfilled numerous roles that, while not directly involved in combat, still supported the nation's struggle to survive. Some articles offered advice and often included stories and letters related to women's domestic practices including cooking, sewing, dressing fashionably, and providing comfort. These articles reflect women's role in perpetuating their culture in a time of crisis and mobilizing their skill sets in support of the war effort. Female authors also introduced new heroines, saviors, and victims, giving people a unique glimpse into the lives of Israeli women as part of the nationalist movement in a war torn country.[21] Women authors also encouraged readers to use their practical skills and abilities in support of the newly born nation's struggle for survival. For instance, some authors encouraged readers to knit khaki items and comfort neighbors as a way to contribute to the community. In writing about their experiences, women forged networks and expressed themselves in new and inventive ways in a time of crisis and instability. They also contributed to the literary landscape of women authors using creative outlets to share their experiences with one another, and with the world.

Palestinian women have also used writing to express themselves in times of hardship and tragedy. Female Palestinian novelists comprise a relatively new group of feminist authors. One of the most famous feminist authors is Sahar Khalifeh (1941–) who uses reading, writing, and painting as a way to escape her tragic life in the West Bank town of Nablus. Born to a middle class family disappointed to have a girl, Sahar Khalifeh's work reflects her feelings of worthlessness and sorrows associated with her gender. Feeling unwanted from a young age, Sahar's disappointments continued when her father abandoned her family for a younger wife. Her life deteriorated when she entered an arranged marriage with an abusive husband. After divorcing, she published her first novel, earning acclaim for her use of colloquial language that appealed to readers in the lowest socioeconomic class. She also published several other novels dealing with topics ranging from the plight of migrant Palestinian laborers in Israel to the complexities of everyday life under Israeli occupation.[22] Both Israeli and Palestinian women have used literature to share their culture and their struggles with their readers.

REGIONAL CUSTOMS AND PRACTICES

Throughout Middle Eastern history, Sufi women used poetry and special rituals to forge a unique cultural and religious identity. Classical Persian poetry was often shaped by the author's involvement in mystical Sufism. As such, the Sufis' use of poetry stems from their emphasis on an individual's pursuit of a relationship and communication with divinity. Sufis also used metaphors to veil aspects of their relationship with divinity. Authors commonly referred to their mystical experiences in terms of a lover and the beloved, the consumption of wine and intoxication, the positive feelings associated with music and dancing, and the celebration of the beauty.[23] Across several different cultural groups, women contributed to Sufi cultural traditions and practices. Over time, their involvement and activities in Sufi culture steadily increased. Originally, when women were the subjects in Sufi biographic literature, they often remained nameless, whereas men were identified by name. Furthermore, although attributed to male authors, women might have authored some Sufi literature. Scholars suggest that it was much easier for a work to gain acceptance if people believed that the author was male.[24] In their roles as teachers and purveyors of Sufi traditions, women used oral poetry to preserve religious knowledge, much of which was never recorded in writing. Sufi oral poetry often focused on an individual's personal history and religious experiences. Women were particularly fond of telling stories about Muhammad's female relatives like Zaynab, his granddaughter, and Sayyida Nafisa, his great-granddaughter. Sufi women also enjoy ritual visits to their shrines in Cairo. In North Africa, Sufi women have had significant leadership roles in certain cultural rituals and practices and are no longer on the margins of Sufism. For example, women lead spirit possession ceremonies characterized by songs praising Muhammad. Sufism remains a spiritual outlet accessible to the poor and uneducated.[25] Women's continued presence in Sufi practices is shaping an important part of their cultural identity.

Despite the manner with which women were largely restricted to their homes and families, Middle Eastern women often found unique ways to have rich and meaningful lives filled with cultural practices. In 14th century Egypt, women's superstitions formed their own unique cultural identity. For instance, women believed that burning incense on special occasions would ward off the evil eye and that purchasing milk on the eve of the Islamic New Year would bring prosperity. When a man left the house, women refrained from housework because they alleged that doing so might keep him away for good. Some women even designated certain days of the week to perform specific tasks, for fear that deviation from a particular schedule invited bad luck.[26] Cairene women in Egypt had a unique set of rituals and celebrations reserved for the birth of a child. Babies were welcomed with songs, dancing, and even trumpets to notify the neighbors of the birth. Then, seven days after the child's birth, when the baby's potential for survival was more likely, families held a great celebration. To welcome the child into the family, friends and family brought special foods such as nuts and sweets. People would also wrap the infant's head in cloth inscribed with Qu'ranic verses written with saffron. As another way to ward off evil spirits, for 40 days, new mothers carried with them the knife that had been used to cut the umbilical cord.[27]

DANCERS, SINGERS, AND ENTERTAINERS

In Ottoman Turkey, women's cultural roles in society were tied to their socioeconomic class. The majority of Turkish women were deprived of education and intellectual training, although a few elites had private tutors. Therefore, few women contributed to literary works of the time. However, some women were involved in music and dance, even training other women in this form of artistic expression. Without access to formal religious institutions or instruction, Turkish girls and women often studied the Qu'ran informally, sometimes reciting lengthy verses from memory.[28] In Turkish society, female servants and wage laborers had an active role in entertaining elites. Groups of female entertainers comprised a unique sub-culture largely considered separate from the rest of women in society. Due to their interaction with men, many looked down upon entertainers, regarding them as similar to prostitutes. Some went so far as to allege that they were not Muslim, but "Roman or Tsigane," or members of other religious and ethnic groups.[29]

Egyptian women have played important roles in celebrating their distinctive and ancient culture. Historically, Arab women have served as singers and professional musicians throughout the region, yet few male critics and commentators considered women "professional" performers. In fact, some associated performers with members of the lower class and with vices such as prostitution, drunkenness, and gambling.[30] However, in the late 1800s and early 1900s, women assumed new roles in the Egyptian musical entertainment scene as professional singers, musicians, and managers.[31] Many of these women shared common characteristics. Most were Muslim and came from families who performed for a living; some even started out reciting the Qu'ran. A study of these entertainers found that most came from lower class backgrounds and used their careers in entertainment as a way to gain access to wealth and notoriety. Most women began their careers performing for private functions and then moved on to coffee shops and other small venues. Eventually, some women entertained large audiences and secured their own recording contracts. Life as an entertainer was challenging, as many entertainers had to deal with unruly crowds who were frequently intoxicated.[32]

In the early 19th century, Egyptian women traveled with other musicians who played for special events such as weddings and saints' days. Performers often traveled with their families and worked several nights each week. Eventually, performers established their own trade guild. Those with

Bedouin maiden dancing the sword dance in the early 20th century.
(Courtesy of Library of Congress)

unique talents were rewarded for their services, often gaining attention by word of mouth. Modestly dressed, some women performed in coffee shops and other public venues. Small theaters developed in urban areas, such as Cairo, where women were part of the growing commercial entertainment industry. Some professional guilds of female singers contracted their work through agents who organized their workload and scheduled events.[33]

Twentieth century women continued to play active roles in the Egyptian entertainment industry. Musical theater gained popularity across the Arab world, and in Egypt patrons visited the theater to glimpse stars, who were often women. The Egyptian government also encouraged the arts, as did the growing urban elite with the means to support female entertainers. Women also assumed managerial roles in the entertainment industry. Several women, such as Badi'a Masabni, born in Syria in 1890, spent her life singing and dancing in music halls in Syria, the Levant, and Egypt. She starred in a theatrical troupe until the 1940s, when she opened her own wildly successful music and dance hall where she chose the performers and personally taught them how to dance. Badi'a was also a lively personality who reportedly threatened to shoot anyone who published information about her colorful past.[34]

The most important Egyptian singer of the early 20th century was Umm Kulthum. Scholars suggest that her life and career were critical in establishing female singers as talented and accomplished individuals in Egyptian society.[35] Her father, who recited the Qu'ran, supplemented his income by singing for weddings and other special events. Upon recognition of her special voice, he incorporated her into his performing arts business. After gaining a local following, Kulthum's family moved to Cairo to support her career. Once in Cairo, members of the upper class discovered her talents and abilities and she was soon in high demand. Kulthum also had detractors and critics who found her style and subject matter folksy and out of date. Nevertheless, her mentors showed her how to update her style and songs. At her peak, she performed for groups numbering 800. While her performance schedule was demanding, Kulthum experienced her biggest financial success after making commercial recordings. Phonographs were popular in Egypt at the time and, because she performed for so many people, others wanted to hear her music, often marking a special moment in their lives.[36] She even portrayed other female entertainers in movies, such as one about Sallamah, a Syrian slave woman with a superb voice who performed for the Umayyad court in Damascus.[37] As a performer and businesswomen, Umm Kulthum used her talents to foster a tremendously successful career that changed public perceptions of women in the entertainment industry.

Syria has also had a long history of music, dance, and literature. As in other countries discussed in this chapter, women often entertained elites in a system of royal patronage. Classical Syrian dancers were well trained and traveled in troupes to amuse the ruling elite. Their dances were choreographed to music and often performed at parties and other special events. The dancers used their movements to tell a story and express emotion during their performances. Women also frequently performed belly dances, which scholars suggest are a modern manifestation of rhythmic temple dances that drew criticism from the prophets in the Old Testament. By observing their mothers, young girls learned how to shake their hips, shoulders, and torsos to the beat of drum music. Belly dances were often performed at weddings and other celebrations leading some scholars to suggest that the belly dance was used to teach young brides how to consummate their marriage.[38]

Female dancers, singers, and performers often strayed from what was considered appropriate behavior for women. Around the same time that women assumed active roles in the music scene in Cairo, a few Syrian women also made their livings as entertainers, traveling from city to city to perform for paying audiences. A noteworthy musical duo of the early 1900s was a Druze brother and sister, Farid and Amal al-Atrash. Like other female performers of the time, Amal had a colorful life filled with travel, romantic relationships, and a bit of controversy. Amal and Farid's mother encouraged them to learn the 'ud, a pear shaped stringed instrument, from an early age. After the Syrian Revolt of 1925, Amal and Farid moved to Cairo, where they pursued their musical careers, often lending their voices to films. In 1944, Amal mysteriously died amidst a series of allegations that she was a British spy. She had a series of husbands, the last of which tried to kill her prior to their divorce. In a mysterious accident, Amal drowned in the Nile after her car was run off the road. Later, allegations surfaced that Umm Kalthum, jealous of Amal's success, was involved with the accident. Others believed that the Germans or the French had her killed.[39] Amal, like her contemporaries, went against social norms throughout her life. She married non-Druze men, earned a living as an entertainer, and died in an untimely and controversial way. Still, her work and example changed expectations of female performers in the Middle East.[40]

RITES OF PASSAGE

One of the most important cultural markers of a people is the way they celebrate important rites of passage. Often these events reflect societal views of gender and identity. For example, after the establishment of the Islamic Republic in Iran in April 1979, people started to mark the coming of age of nine-year-old girls with a publicly celebrated ritual. Likewise, since the 14th century, Israeli boys have had a bar mitzvah ceremony at age 13 to mark their acceptance of adult responsibilities in Judaism. It was not until 1922 that families celebrated similar rituals for Jewish girls.[41] In Tunisian communities, women host visitors in their homes for important rites of passage in their immediate families. Special rites of passage include, but are not limited to, completion of the *hajj* (pilgrimage to Mecca), marriage, the birth of a child, a birthday, or the purchase of a major item, like a car. When women visit one another, they often bring gifts that will best meet the receiver's needs. For instance, if a woman has a baby, her female friends and family might bring money, food, or other items that will help the entire family. Guests often bring food to feed other guests so that the family does not have to bear the cost of feeding visitors. Those who contribute time and resources expect reciprocal treatment in the future. When Tunisians experience a death in the family, women in the local community cook, clean, and perform other tasks to allow for a period of bereavement, sometimes lasting several days.

For most women in the Middle East and North Africa, weddings are the single most important rite of passage. As a woman transitions from her nuclear family and role as daughter and sibling, marriage marks the transition to wife and mother. In Tunisia, women normally receive money on their special day to begin life as a married woman with her own financial resources.[42] In Kuwait, women used to have fairly simple wedding ceremonies that were frequently segregated by gender and celebrated at the bride's home. In this traditional arrangement, only close family members were invited to the modest gathering, where they might listen to a few musicians. Guest typically brought gifts of small household items. While some of these smaller affairs endure, elite brides-to-be are marking the transition to wife and mother with more elaborate events. Today, some Kuwaiti women enjoy lavish weddings in five-star hotels, followed by a honeymoon. Wealthy brides might wear designer wedding dresses made of the finest materials. Although gender segregation is still practiced, the bride is often ushered into a hall as guns are fired to mark the event, pigeons are let loose, and as onlookers throw confetti.[43] These changing cultural traditions and manners with which Kuwaiti women mark special rites of passage reflect larger socioeconomic trends within the Middle East. Cultural aspects of women's lives are changing with the influx of wealth associated with Kuwait's significant petroleum reserves and contact with Western ideas and practices.

IRANIAN WOMEN'S TRADITIONS AND CRAFTS

Contemporary Iranian culture remains an amalgamation of several linguistic, ethnic, tribal, and national minority groups. Each group has its own unique rituals, practices, and traditions. Persian, or Farsi, the official language in Iran, is widely spoken, but other minority groups such as Turks, Kurds, Baluch, Arabs, and Lurs speak their own languages and identify primarily with their own cultures. While the majority of Iranians are Shia Muslims, some tribal and other minority groups include Sunnis, Baha'is, Zoroastrians, and Jews. Some tribal and nomadic groups practice their own cultural traditions that differ drastically from those of urban dwellers living in major cities like Tehran. After the Iranian Revolution, Iran's ruling clergy tried to force Shia beliefs and practices on minority groups by spreading Islamic education in Arabic to schools. Despite the central government's efforts, some tribal communities maintain the social and cultural practices of their ancestors. One Shia Turkish-speaking tribe, the Qashqa'i in southwestern Iran, maintains its unique, semi-nomadic lifestyle. The Qashqa'i tribe migrates annually to maintain its flocks of sheep and goats. This group also sells animal products such as meat, wool, milk, and especially woven products, which are made primarily by women. Men and women of the Qashqa'i are aware of the Islamic Republic's rules and regulations prescribing dress and appropriate behavior, but many do not adhere to these standards as they live in remote locations, far from the reach of government. This allows tribeswomen to interact with men in their community, especially when celebrating special events characterized by music, dance, song, poetry, and sport.[44]

Historically, women and children have had a prominent role in weaving and selling Persian carpets. Persian carpets and their makers are one of Iran's most distinguished and distinctive manifestations of culture and art.[45] Persian literature makes reference to the labor-intensive nature of carpet-making that requires the weaver to make millions of knots, leading some girls to finger and other injuries while working long hours in adverse conditions.[46] While some Persian rugs have a high monetary value, they are also culturally valuable in that they have a strong presence in people's homes, offices, palaces, shrines, and places of worship. As carpet weavers, women take their inspiration from nature, history, religion, and myths. In early times, women made carpets from wool, cotton, or silk that they dyed with colors from local flowers and plants, giving Persian rugs a distinctive look from their particular region. In fact, rugs are named for their region or for the people who made them. As such, Persian rugs reflect the culture and lifestyle of the maker. Some tribeswomen typically make rugs without a predetermined design. Rather, women will weave triple hand-knotted rugs according to their own taste and imagination. Unlike mass produced factory carpets, tribal women often fill their works with simple geometric shapes, pictures of animals, trees, and flowers. Their carpets are typically

Bedouin women weaving in the 1940s. (Courtesy of Library of Congress)

coarser and richer in color. Certain groups have their own distinctive styles, like the Baluchis, who favor flower motifs.

Carpets and rugs vary in size and function. For example, carpets describe hand-woven floor coverings larger than 6.5 feet, while smaller pieces are considered rugs. Some types of rugs tend to have recurring themes. For example, prayer rugs are smaller and are usually adorned with flowers or calligraphy. Women take extra care to keep these special rugs clean, as they are specifically designated for prayer and worship. Some people take their prayer rugs with them on the pilgrimage to Mecca, or to have them sanctified in holy shrines.[47] As carpet-weavers, women have played tremendously important roles as artists who contribute their immeasurable skills and talents to this distinctive cultural tradition.

Another vital aspect of women's contributions to Iranian culture is in Persian literature. Female authors contributed a variety of works to the genre that has evolved over time reflecting the rich experiences of the Iranian people and their beliefs. One of the most influential and unique contemporary Iranian poets was Forugh Farrokhzad (1935–1967), who achieved notoriety for her success in a male-dominated field. Her life and example broke with Iranian norms, as did her work. After quitting school, marrying, and divorcing against her parent's wishes, Farrokhzad attempted suicide while in a psychiatric hospital. After this series of traumatic events, she began to write poems about her experiences. Her work reflected a lifelong frustration with societal and cultural demands on women. One of her early works was entitled *Rebelliousness,* perhaps an appropriate title for a work about a woman whose life did meet societal expectations. For instance, she had a series of romantic affairs with men, rendering both her behavior and her work controversial. Due to her unconventional lifestyle and subject matter, her work was banned for a decade, after the Islamic Republic declared her ideas contrary to those espoused by the new clerical government. Later, the ruling clergy surrendered to pressure from people's interest in her work, creating an industry devoted to the promotion of her work, life, and art. One of her protégés, Simin Behbahani, was nominated for the Nobel Prize in Literature in 1997 for her poetry, which combines contemporary literature and theatrical subjects.[48] After the Iranian Revolution, other female authors emerged with an aggressive agenda to address a variety of subjects ranging from their personal experiences to the triumphs and tribulations associated with life as an Iranian woman.

Initially, women who excelled in the arts came from elite families. Prior to the 20th century, only the wealthy could afford private tutors for their wives and daughters since women were excluded from most Iranian schools. However, it appears that, since early times, women have made certain important cultural products, including carpets and rugs, thus contributing to their cultural identity and heritage. Today, Iranian women are very active in the public arena with several working in the film industry, literary field, and mass media.[49] Women continue to figure prominently in literary works, especially with increased access to technology, travel, and communication.

SYRIAN WOMEN'S CULTURE AND BELIEFS

Syria is known as a cultural crossroads where different groups have brought their traditional and urban crafts to trade and share with one another. Consequently, women have served as master craftswomen, making beautiful objects for sale and for everyday use. In places like Damascus, women play an important role in making jewelry, inlaid trays, boxes, small cabinets, and tables. In other more traditional areas, women specialize in embroidery, weaving, and basketry. Village and Bedouin crafts are closely associated with women's work, whereas urban crafts are more often a male-dominated enterprise. Women's artistic talents are especially evident in their embroidery and weaving.[50] Like weavers in Iran, Syrian women's crafts reflect their distinctive style, materials, and places of origin. Hence, village women have their own specialties. For example, women in northern villages are known for their elaborate embroidery, while women from southwestern Syria are known for their colorful straw basketry. For special events, women use special straw baskets that are edged with ostrich feathers and colored with wool yarn.[51] Syrians also specialize in a specific type of embroidery, known as *ghabani*. This specific style is identified by looped embroidery patterns that appear on everything from caftans to men's turbans. Today, *ghabani* patterns are made on a machine, but prior to the advent of sewing machines, women hand-stitched these patterns into cotton garments. Artisanal work was often a family affair, with men, women, and children assuming specific roles in the production of unique and specialized crafts. Jewish families typically made inlaid silver items, often with Qu'ranic verses written Arabic calligraphy.[52] Historically, Syrian cities are known for their silk and cotton textiles where women made and bought popular items such as *hamsiyah* scarves. Bedouin women from Syria, Turkey, Iraq, and Saudi Arabia wear these scarves that are made of silk or artificial silk treated with lime and printed with decorative designs.[53]

As consumers, women's preferences reflect their socioeconomic status and culture. Historically, Bedouin and village women tended to favor silver jewelry, while urban women favored gold. Over time, all women have come to prefer gold earrings, necklaces, and bracelets. Certain types of jewelry and adornments are thought to date from ancient times. Rural Syrian women still wear pieces that resemble those worn by women in the first centuries c.e. Some women wear accessories that are specific to a certain region or socioeconomic class. For instance, Bedouin women might adorn their temples or headscarves with jewelry, or they might wear decorative headbands. Rural Syrian, Jordanian, and Saudi Arabian women wear chains called *jnad* that go over one shoulder and under the other, reaching the wearer's waist. The chain typically has coins, bells, and balls interspersed throughout its length. Some Kurdish women from Northern Syria sew silver disks adorned with coins and small silver objects to the top of their headdresses. Throughout the region, women and children wear charms on different pieces of jewelry or clothing. Some of these charms have special meanings, including the blue bead, believed to ward off the evil eye; the fish, used to symbolize fertility; or the frog and salamander, commonly associated with long life. Even colors have symbolic meaning: blue offers protection from the evil eye; red is for good health; white helps with lactation.[54] Recently, women's ability to sell and export their traditional crafts has been undercut by the introduction of cheaper, machine-made items. Women who continue their traditional work serve as a bulwark for their culture by passing their artistry on to successive generations.

Late 19th-century Arab woman wearing jewelry.
(Courtesy of Library of Congress)

CONTRIBUTIONS TO CULTURAL IDENTITY TODAY

Despite the manner with which modernization threatens certain cultural traditions, Middle Eastern women are finding new ways to contribute to their communities' cultural identity. Across the region, women have important roles in the arts, culture, and literature. While elite women still have more access to roles outside the home, many continue to face pressures to stop working once they have children. However, several women are finding new ways to express themselves by writing and serving in influential positions in cultural matters. For instance, in Syria, Najah al-Attar served as the Minister of Culture for several years.[55] In other parts of the Middle East, women have access to new and innovative means of communication, giving them increased opportunities to express themselves creatively. Women also enjoy improved access to information and technology. With the advent of satellite television, the 24-hour news cycle, and Internet access, states are finding it difficult to censor the media and other forms of communication. The Jordanian town of Irbid probably has the most cybercafés per capita of any city in the world.[56] Today, women can remain connected to one another, and to their leaders, through online forums and mobile technologies. Even the most conservative states offer women outlets to express themselves artistically. In Saudi Arabia, female journalists cover issues ranging from family matters to fashion, but are not restricted to covering women's issues. In fact, women's magazines have multiplied a dozen-fold over the past decade.[57] These media outlets, and other information technologies, offer women a host of venues to express themselves across a wide variety of disciplines and issue areas.

NOTES

1. Elton L. Daniel and Ali Akbar Mahdi, *Culture and Customs of Iran* (Westport, CT: Greenwood Press, 2006), 150–51.

2. Arthur Goldschmidt Jr., *A Concise History of the Middle East* (Cambridge, MA: Westview Press, 2002), 25.

3. Daniel and Mahdi, *Culture and Customs of Iran,* 77.

4. Goldschmidt, *A Concise History of the Middle East,* 26.

5. Bouthaina Sha'aban, "Arab Women and Literature: An Overview," in *Arab Women Between Defiance and Restraint,* ed. Suha Sabbagh (Brooklyn, NY: Olive Branch Press, 1996), 235.

6. Goldschmidt, *A Concise History of the Middle East,* 41.

7. Nikki R. Keddie, *Women in the Middle East: Past and Present* (Princeton, NJ: Princeton University Press, 2007), 44.

8. Diane Apostolos-Cappadona, "Discerning the Hand-of-Fatima," in *Beyond the Exotic, Women's Histories in Islamic Societies,* ed. Amira El-Azhary Sonbol (Syracuse: Syracuse University Press, 2005), 354–55.

9. Apostolos-Cappadona, "Discerning the Hand-of-Fatima," 356–61.

10. Daniel and Mahdi, *Culture and Customs of Iran,* 71–73.

11. Mahmoud Omidsalar, "Waters and Women, Maidens and Might: The Passage of Royal Authority in the Shahnama," in *Women in Iran from the Rise of Islam until 1800,* eds. Guity Nashat and Lois Beck (Urbana: University of Illinois Press, 2003), 182.

12. Omidsalar, "Waters and Women, Maidens and Might: The Passage of Royal Authority in the Shahnama," 171.

13. Omidsalar, "Waters and Women, Maidens and Might: The Passage of Royal Authority in the Shahnama," 183.

14. Guity Nashat and Judith Tucker, *Women in the Middle East and North Africa* (Bloomington: Indiana University Press, 1999), 60.

15. Keddie, *Women in the Middle East: Past and Present,* 44.

16. Nashat and Tucker, *Women in the Middle East and North Africa,* 59.

17. Sha'aban, "Arab Women and Literature: An Overview," 235.

18. Keddie, *Women in the Middle East: Past and Present,* 65.

19. Bouthaina Sha'aban, "Arab Women and Literature: An Overview," 250 and 252.

20. Sha'aban, "Arab Women and Literature: An Overview," 237.

21. Shira Klein, "An Army of Housewives: Women's Wartime Columns in Two Mainstream Israeli Newspapers," *NASHIM: A Journal of Jewish Women's Studies and Gender Issues* (2008): 88, 89, and 102.

22. Samih K. Farsoun, *Culture and Customs of the Palestinians* (Westport, CT: Greenwood Press, 2004), 95–96.

23. Daniel and Mahdi, *Culture and Customs of Iran,* 70.

24. Valerie J. Hoffman, "Oral Traditions as a Source for the Study of Muslim Women," in *Beyond the Exotic, Women's Histories in Islamic Societies,* ed. Amira El-Azhary Sonbol (Syracuse: Syracuse University Press, 2005), 366–67.

25. Hoffman, "Oral Traditions as a Source for the Study of Muslim Women," 374.

26. Huda Lufti, "Fourteenth Century Cairene Women," in *Women in Middle Eastern History: Shifting Boundaries in Sex and Gender,* eds. Nikki R. Keddie and Beth Baron (New Haven, CT: Yale University Press, 1991), 105.

27. Lufti, "Fourteenth Century Cairene Women," 112.

28. Ian C. Dengler, "Turkish Women in the Ottoman Empire," in *Women in the Muslim World,* eds. Lois Beck and Nikki R. Keddie (Cambridge, MA: Harvard University Press, 1978), 231.

29. Dengler, "Turkish Women in the Ottoman Empire," 233.

30. Virginia Danielson, "Female Singers in Cairo during the 1920s," in *Women in Middle Eastern History: Shifting Boundaries in Sex and Gender,* eds. Nikki R. Keddie and Beth Baron (New Haven: Yale University Press, 1991), 303.

31. Danielson, "Female Singers in Cairo during the 1920s," 292.

32. Danielson, "Female Singers in Cairo during the 1920s," 301.

33. Danielson, "Female Singers in Cairo during the 1920s," 295.

34. Danielson, "Female Singers in Cairo during the 1920s," 297.

35. Danielson, "Female Singers in Cairo during the 1920s," 305.

36. Danielson, "Female Singers in Cairo during the 1920s," 298–300.

37. John A. Shoup, *Culture and Customs of Syria* (Westport, CT: Greenwood Press, 2008), 137.

38. Shoup, *Culture and Customs of Syria,* 146.

39. Shoup, *Culture and Customs of Syria,* 141–42.

40. Shoup, *Culture and Customs of Syria,* 142.

41. Rebecca Torstrick, *Culture and Customs of Israel* (Westport, CT: Greenwood Press, 2004), 36.

42. Paula Holmes-Eber, *Daughters of Tunis: Women, Family, and Networks in a Muslim City* (Boulder, CO: Westview Press, 2003), 116–19.

43. Fahad Al Naser, "Kuwait's Families," in *The Handbook of World Families,* eds. Bert N. Adams and Jan Trost (Thousand Oaks, CA: Sage Publications, 2005), 521–22.

44. Julia Huang, "Tribeswomen of Iran," (New York: I.B. Publishers, 2009), 7 and 18.

45. Daniel and Mahdi, *Culture and Customs of Iran,* 137.

46. Daniel and Mahdi, *Culture and Customs of Iran,* 141.

47. Daniel and Mahdi, *Culture and Customs of Iran,* 139.

48. Daniel and Mahdi, *Culture and Customs of Iran,* 82.

49. Daniel and Mahdi, *Culture and Customs of Iran,* 163.

50. Shoup, *Culture and Customs of Syria,* 96.

51. Shoup, *Culture and Customs of Syria,* 97.

52. Shoup, *Culture and Customs of Syria,* 91.

53. Shoup, *Culture and Customs of Syria,* 93.

54. Shoup, *Culture and Customs of Syria,* 94–95.

55. Keddie, *Women in the Middle East: Past and Present,* 139.

56. Donna Lee Bowen and Evelyn Early, *Everyday Life in the Muslim Middle East* (Bloomington: Indiana University Press, 2002), 8.

57. Nora Alarifi Pharaon, "Saudi Women and the Muslim State in the 21st Century," *Sex Roles* 51 (2004): 364.

SUGGESTED READING

Davis, Susan S. *Patience and Power: Women's Lives in a Moroccan Village.* Cambridge, MA: Schenkman Publishing Company, 1983.

Esfandiari, Haleh. *Reconstructed Lives, Women and Iran's Islamic Revolution.* Washington, DC: Woodrow Wilson Center Press, 1997.

Holmes-Eber, Paula. *Daughters of Tunis: Women Family and Networks in a Muslim City.* Boulder, CO: Westview Press, 2003.

Keddie, Nikki R. *Women in the Middle East: Past and Present.* Princeton, NJ: Princeton University Press, 2007.

Kreyenbroek Philip G. and Christine Allison, eds. *Kurdish Culture and Identity.* London: Zed Books, 1996.

Makhlouf, Carla. *Changing Veils: Women and Modernization in North Yemen.* London: Croom Helm Publishers, 1979.

Rubenberg, Cheryl A. *Palestinian Women Patriarchy and Resistance in the West Bank.* Boulder, CO: Lynne Rienner Publishers, 2001.

Wikan, Unni. *Behind the Veil in Arabia.* Baltimore, MD: Johns Hopkins University Press, 1982.

Glossary

Abaya: Women's traditional black coat, which is part of Islamic dress for countries in the Arabian Peninsula

Baraka: Holiness or divine grace emanating from people, places, or relics

Caliph: Title given to successors of the prophet Muhammad

Da'iyat: Missionaries

Divan: Collection of poetry

Fatwa: Religious edict

Fitna: Moral or social disorder

Hadith: Communications about sayings and actions of the prophet Muhammad

Hajj: Pilgrimage to Mecca (in present-day Saudi Arabia) that Muslims are supposed to make at least once in their life; one of the five pillars of Islam

Hanafi: Sunni legal school

Harem: From the Arabic word for "forbidden"; refers to the place in the home where women are segregated from men

Hijab: Head covering worn by Muslim women

Ijtihad: Independent legal reasoning

Imam: Muslim religious leader

Jihad: Muslim's internal struggle to follow the precepts of Islam. It can also refer to a holy war against infidels.

Knesset: Israeli parliament

Madrasa: Muslim religious school

Mahr: Similar to a dowry that the groom's family pays to the bride's family or to the bride

Majlis: Iranian parliament

Mudawwana: Moroccan personal status law

Mullahs: Islamic clerics in Iran

Mut'a: Temporary marriage in **Shi'a** Islam

Patrilocality: Practice where women move to their husband's home when they marry

Pir: Sufi spiritual guide or master

Polygyny: Marriage of a man to more than one woman

Qiwamma: "In charge." The Qu'ran set forth familial roles, placing men in charge, so as to strengthen the family

Ramadan: Ninth month of the Islamic calendar. Fasting, from sunrise to sunset, during Ramadan is one of the five pillars of Islam

Sahwa: Islamic revival

Sharia: Islamic law made up of the Qu'ran, **hadith,** and **sunna**

Shia: Islamic sect; Shi'a Muslims believe that Ali, Muhammad's cousin and son-in-law, should have succeeded Muhammad

Sufi: Muslim mystic

Sunna: Traditions of the prophet Muhammad

Sunni: Largest denomination of Islam. Differs from Shias with regards to succession.

Tanzimaat Period (1839–1876): Period of Ottoman rule in which the government implemented reforms to centralize power. Non-Muslims were allowed to serve in the military and had equal status with Muslims.

Twelver: Branch of **Shi'a** Islam

Ulema: Muslim religious scholars

Umma: Islamic global community that should transcend loyalty to states

Waqf: Charitable trust dedicated to Islamic purposes

Zawiya: Sufi lodge or sanctuary

Zoroastrianism: Monotheistic religion that originated in the 700s B.C.E. in what is now Iran

Selected Bibliography

Abbas, Shemeem Burney. *The Female Voice in Sufi Ritual.* Austin: University of Texas Press, 2002.

Abbott, Nabia. "Women and the State in Early Islam." *Journal of Near Eastern Studies* 1 (January 1942): 106–26.

Abbott, Nabia. "Women and the State on the Eve of Islam." *American Journal of Semitic Languages and Literatures* 58 (July 1941): 259–84.

Abdo, Geneive. *No God But God.* Oxford: Oxford University Press, 2000.

Abisaab, Malek. "Unruly Factory Women in Lebanon: Contesting French Colonialism and the National State, 1940–1946." *Journal of Women's History* 16 (2004): 55–82.

Adams, Bert N. and Jan Trost, eds. *The Handbook of World Families.* Thousand Oaks, CA: Sage Publications, 2005.

Al-Ali, Nadje. *Secularism, Gender and the State: The Egyptian Women's Movement.* Cambridge: Cambridge University Press, 2000.

Al-Hail, Ali. "Why Women Use Email Disproportionately in Qatar: An Exploratory Study." *Journal of Website Promotion* 1 (2005): 99–104.

Al-Hassan Golley, Nawar. "Is Feminism Relevant to Arab Women?" *Third World Quarterly* 25 (2004): 521–36.

Al-Jawaheri, Yasmin Husein. *Women in Iraq: The Gender Impact of International Sanctions.* Boulder, CO: Lynne Rienner Publishers, 2008.

Al-Mughni, Haya. "Women's Organizations in Kuwait." *Middle East Report* 198 (January–March 1996): 32–35.

Altorki, Soraya. *Women in Saudi Arabia.* New York: Columbia University Press, 1998.

Amin, Camron Michael. "Globalizing Iranian Feminism: 1910–1950." *Journal of Middle East Studies* 4 (Winter 2008): 6–30.

Amrane-Minne, Danièle Djamila. "Women and Politics in Algeria from the War of Independence to Our Day." *Research in African Literatures* (Fall 1999): 62–77.

Anadolu-Okur, Nilgun. "The Demise of the Great Mother: Islam, Reform, and Women's Emancipation in Turkey." *Gender Issues* (Fall 2005): 6–28.

Arabsheibani Reza G. and Lamine Manfor. "From 'Farashia' to Military Uniform: Male-Female Wage Differntials in Libya." *Economic Development and Cultural Change* 50 (July 2002): 1007–19.

Arat, Yesim. "Feminists, Islamists, and Political Change in Turkey." *Political Psychology* 19 (March 1998): 117–31.

Arat, Yesim. "From Emancipation to Liberation: The Changing Role of Women in Turkey's Public Realm." *Journal of International Affairs* (Fall 2000): 107–23.

Bahry, Louay and Phebe Marr. "Qatari Women: A New Generation of Leaders? *Middle East Policy* 12 (Summer 2005): 104–19.

Bates, Daniel and Amal Rassam. *Peoples and Cultures of the Middle East.* Englewood Cliffs, NJ: Prentice Hall, 1983.

Bayes, Jane H. and Nayereh Tohidi, eds. *Globalization, Gender and Religion: The Politics of Women's Rights in Catholic and Muslim Contexts.* New York: Palgrave, 2001.

Beck, Lois and Guity Nashat, eds. *Women in Iran from 1800 to the Islamic Republic.* Urbana: University of Illinois Press, 2004.

Beck, Lois and Guity Nashat, eds. *Women in Iran from the Rise of Islam until 1800.* Urbana: University of Illinois Press, 2003.

Beck, Lois and Nikki R. Keddie, eds. *Women in the Muslim World.* Cambridge, MA: Harvard University Press, 1978.

Bennoune, Karima. "Between Betrayal and Betrayal: Fundamentalism, Family Law and Feminist Struggle in Algeria. *Arab Studies Quarterly* 17 (Winter/Spring 1995): 51–77.

Blayedes, Lisa and Safinaz El Tarouty. "Women's Electoral Participation in Egypt: The Implications of Gender For Voter Recruitment and Mobilization." *Middle East Journal* 63 (Summer 2009): 364–80.

Bowen, Donna Lee and Evelyn Early. *Everyday Life in the Muslim Middle East.* Bloomington: Indiana University Press, 2002.

Brand, Laurie A. *Women, the State and Political Liberalization: Middle Eastern and North African Experiences.* New York: Columbia University Press, 1998.

Briegel, Toni and Jaye Zivkovic. "Financial Empowerment of Women in the United Arab Emirates." *Journal of Middle East Women's Studies* 4, no. 2 (Spring 2008): 87–94.

Brooks, Geraldine. *Nine Parts of Desire, The Hidden World of Islamic Women.* New York: Anchor Books, 1995.

Bronson, Rachel and Isobel Coleman. "The Kingdom's Clock." *Foreign Policy* 156 (September/October 2006): 55–61.

Brown, Lucy and David Romano. "Women in Post-Saddam Iraq: One Step Forward and Two Steps Back?" *NWSA Journal* 18 (Fall 2006): 51–70.

Bunzl, John. *Islam, Judaism, and the Political Role of Religions in the Middle East.* Gainesville: University of Florida Press, 2004.

Carapico, Sheila. "Women and Public Participation in Yemen." *Middle East Report* 173 (November/December 1991): 15.

Carmody, Denise L. "Judaism." in *Women in World Religions,* ed. Arvind Sharma. Albany: State University Press of New York, 1987.

Charrad, Mounira. *States and Women's Rights: The Making of Postcolonial Tunisia, Algeria and Morocco.* Berkeley: University of California Press, 2001.

Chatty, Dawn. "Women Working in Oman: Individual Choice and Cultural Constraints." *International Journal of Middle East Studies* 32 (May 2000): 241–54.

Chekir, Hafidha. "Women, the Law and the Family in Tunisia." *Gender and Development* 4 (June 1996): 43–46.

Çitak, Zana and Özlem Tür. "Women between Tradition and Change: The Justice and Development Party Experience in Turkey." *Middle Eastern Studies* 44 (May 2008): 455–69.

Coleman, Isobel. "Women, Islam and the New Iraq." *Foreign Affairs* (January/February 2006): 24–32.

Crabtree, Sara Ashencaen. "Culture, Gender and the Influence of Social Change Amongst Emirati Families in the United Arab Emirates." *Journal of Comparative Family Studies* 38 (2007): 575–87.

Daniel, Elton L. and Ali Akbar Mahdi. *Culture and Customs of Iran.* Westport, CT: Greenwood Press, 2006.

Davis, Susan S. *Patience and Power: Women's Lives in a Moroccan Village.* Cambridge, MA: Schenkman Publishing Company, 1983.

Deif, Farida. "Divorced from Justice." *Journal of Middle East Women's Studies* (Fall 2005): 108–15.

Dieste, Josep Lluís Mateo. "Demonstrating Islam: The Conflict of Text and the Mudawwana Reform in Morocco." *The Muslim World* (January 2009): 134–54.

Doumato, Eleanor Abdella. *Getting God's Ear, Women, Islam, and Healing.* New York: Columbia University Press, 2000.

Efrati, Noga. "Negotiating Rights in Iraq: Women and the Personal Status Law." *Middle East Journal* (Autumn 2005): 577–95.

Efrati, Noga. "The 'Other' Awakening in Iraq: The Women's Movement in the First Half of the Twentieth Century." *British Journal of Middle East Studies* (November 2004): 153–73.

Eickelman, Christine. *Women and Community in Oman.* New York: New York University Press, 1984.

El-Azhary Sonbol, Amira, ed. *Beyond the Exotic, Women's Histories in Islamic Societies.* Syracuse: Syracuse University Press, 2005.

El-Husseini, Rola. "Women, Work and Political Participation in Lebanese Shi'a Contemporary Thought: the Writings of Ayatollahs Fadlallah and Shams al-din." *Comparative Studies of South Asia, Africa and the Middle East* 28 (2008): 273–82.

Emerson, Michael O. "Through Tinted Glasses; Religion, World View, and Abortion Attitudes." *Journal for the Scientific Study of Religion* 35 (March 1996): 41–55.

Esfandiari, Haleh. *Reconstructed Lives, Women and Iran's Islamic Revolution.* Washington, DC: Woodrow Wilson Center Press, 1997.

Farsoun, Samih K. *Culture and Customs of the Palestinians.* Westport, CT: Greenwood Press, 2004.

Firro, Kais M. *A History of the Druzes.* Leiden, The Netherlands: E. J. Brill, 1992.

Gellner, Ernest. *Muslim Society.* Cambridge: Cambridge University Press, 1981.

Gerber, Haim. "Social and Economic Position of Women in an Ottoman City, Bursa, 1600–1700." *International Journal of Middle East Studies* 12 (November 1980): 231–44.

Ghabra, Shafeeq. "Voluntary Associations in Kuwait: The Foundations of a New System?" *Middle East Journal* 45 (Spring 1991): 119–215.

Goldschmidt, Arthur, Jr. *A Concise History of the Middle East.* Boulder, CO: Westview Press, 2002.

Hambly, Gavin R. G. *Women in the Medieval Islamic World.* New York: St. Martin's Press, 1998.

Hassim, Shireen. "Family, Motherhood, and Zulu Nationalism: The Politics of the Inkatha Women's Brigade." *Feminist Review* 43 (Spring 1993): 1–25.

Helminski, Camille Adams. *Women of Sufism, A Hidden Treasure.* Boston, MA: Shambhala Publications, 2003.

Hertzog, Ester. "Women's Parties in Israel: Their Unrecognized Significance and Potential." *Middle East Journal* 59 (Summer 2005): 437–51.

Hodgson, Marshall G. S. *The Venture of Islam: Conscience and History in a World Civilization,* Vol. 1. Chicago: University of Chicago Press, 1958.

Hokal and K. E. Shaw. "Managing Progress Monitoring in United Arab Emirate Schools." *The International Journal of Education Management* 13, No. 4 (1999): 173–74.

Holmes-Eber, Paula. *Daughters of Tunis: Women Family and Networks in a Muslim City.* Boulder, CO: Westview Press, 2003.

Howard, Jane. *Inside Iran, Women's Lives.* Washington, DC: Mage Publishers, 2002.

Huang, Julia. *Tribeswomen of Iran.* New York: I. B. Tauris, 2009.

Hudson, Leila. "Investing by Women or Investing in Women? Merchandise, Money and Marriage and the Formation of a Prenational Bourgeoisie in Damascus." *Comparative Studies of South Asia, Africa and the Middle East* 26 (2006): 105–20.

Hunt, Swannee and Cristina Posa. "Iraq's Excluded Women." *Foreign Policy* 143 (July/August 2004): 40–45.

Huntington, Samuel P. *The Third Wave: Democratization in the late Twentieth Century.* Norman: University of Oklahoma Press, 1991.

Husseini, Randa. "Promoting Women Entrepreneurs in Lebanon: The Experience of UNIFEM." *Gender and Development* 5 (February 1997): 49–53.

Jamali, Dima, Yusuf Sidani, and Assem Safiedinne. "Constraints Facing Working Women in Lebanon: An Insider View." *Women in Management Review* (2005): 581–94.

Joseph, Saud, ed. *Intimate Selving in Arab Families: Gender, Self, and Identity.* Syracuse: Syracuse University Press, 1999.

Kabalo, Paula. "Leadership Behind the Curtains: The Case of Israeli Women in 1948." *Modern Judaism* (February 2008): 14–40.

Kagitcibasi, Cigem. "The Changing Value of Children in Turkey." *Current Studies on the Value of Children.* Honolulu, HI: The East-West Center, 1982.

Kar, Mehrangiz. "Focusing on Women in the Internal Politics of Iran." *Brown Journal of World Affairs* 15 (Fall/Winter 2008): 75–86.

Kark, Ruth, Margalit Shilo, and Galit Hasan-Rokem, eds. *Jewish Women in Pre-State Israel: Life History, Politics and Culture.* Waltham, MA: Brandeis University Press, 2008.

Kawar, Mary. "Transitions and Boundaries: Research into the Impact of Paid Work on Young Women's Lives in Jordan." *Gender and Development* 8 (July 2000): 56–65.

Keddie, Nikki R. "A Woman's Place: Democratization in the Middle East." *Current History* (January 2004): 25–30.

Keddie, Nikki R. *Women in the Middle East: Past and Present.* Princeton, NJ: Princeton University Press, 2007.

Keddie, Nikki R. and Beth Baron, eds. *Women in Middle Eastern History: Shifting Boundaries in Sex and Gender.* New Haven, CT: Yale University Press, 1991.

Khan, M. *Islam Rediscovered: Discovering Islam from its Original Sources.* New Delhi: Goodword Books, 2001.

Kian, Azadeh. "Women and Politics in Post-Islamist Iran: the Gender Conscious Drive to Change." *British Journal of Middle Eastern Studies* (1997): 75–96.

Klein, Shira. "An Army of Housewives: Women's Wartime Columns in Two Mainstream Israeli Newspapers." *NASHIM: A Journal of Jewish Women's Studies and Gender Issues* 15 (Spring 2008): 88–107.

Kreyenbroek Philip G. and Christine Allison, eds. *Kurdish Culture and Identity.* London: Zed Books, 1996.

Labidi, Lilia. "The Nature of Transnational Alliances in Women's Associations in the Maghreb: The Case of AFTURD and ATFD in Tunisia." *Journal of Middle Eastern Women's Studies* 3 (Winter 2007): 6–34.

Lassner, J. "Why Did Caliph al-Mansur Build ar-Rusafa?" *Journal of Near Eastern Studies* 24 (January 1965): 95–99.

Latreille, Martin. "Honor, the Gender Division of Labor and the Status of Women in Rural Tunisia-A Social Organizational Reading." *International Journal of Middle East Studies* 40 (2008): 599–621.

Layne, Linda. "Women in Jordan's Workforce." *MERIP* 95 (March/April 1981): 19–23.

Le Renard, Amelie. "Only for Women: Women, the State and Reform in Saudi Arabia." *Middle East Journal* 62 (Autumn 2008): 610–29.

Levin, Leah Simmons. "Setting the Agenda: The Success of the 1977 Israel's Women's Party." *Israel Studies* 4 (Fall 1999): 40–63.

Lewis, Bernard. *The Multiple Identities of the Middle East.* New York: Schocken Books, 1998.

Lewis, Bernard and Buntzie Ellis Churchill. *Islam: The Religion and the People.* Upper Saddle River, NJ: Wharton School Publishing, 2009.

Libal, Kathryn. "Staging Turkish Women's Emancipation: Instanbul, 1935." *Journal of Middle East Women's Studies* 4 (Winter 2008): 31–52.

Lindholm, Charles. *The Islamic Middle East, Traditions and Change.* Malden, MA: Blackwell Publishing, 2002.

Makhlouf, Carla. *Changing Veils: Women and Modernization in North Yemen.* London: Croom Helm Publishers, 1979.

Marcus, Abraham. "Men, Women and Property: Dealers in Real Estate in Eighteenth Century Aleppo. *Journal of Economic and Social History of the Orient* 26 (1973): 137–63.

Mashhour, Amira. "Islamic Law and Gender Equality-Could There Be a Common Ground? A Study of Divorce and Polygamy in Sharia Law and Contemporary Legislation in Tunisia and Egypt." *Human Rights Quarterly* 27 (2005): 562–96.

Masters, Bruce. *Christians and Jews in the Ottoman Arab World.* Cambridge: Cambridge University Press, 2001.

Mayer, Ann. "Developments in the Law of Marriage and Divorce in Libya since the 1969 Revolution." *Journal of African Law* 22 (Spring 1978): 30–49.

McElwee, Gerard and Rahma Al-Riyami. "Women Entrepreneurs in Oman: Some Barriers to Success." *Career Development International* (2003): 339–46.

Meriwether, Margaret and Judith Tucker, eds. *A Social History of Women and Gender in the Modern Middle East.* Boulder, CO: Westview Press, 1999.

Mernissi, Fatima. *Islam and Democracy: Fear of the Modern World,* 2nd ed. Cambridge, MA: Perseus Publishing, 2002.

Mernissi, Fatima. "Women, Saints, and Sanctuaries." In *Women and National Development: The Complexities of Change,* ed. Wellesley Editorial Committee, 101–12. Chicago: University of Chicago Press, 1977.

Meyer, Katherine, Helen Rizzo, and Yousef Ali. "Islam and the Extension of Citizenship Rights to Women in Kuwait." *Journal for the Scientific Study of Religion* 37 (March 1998): 131–44.

Mir-Hosseini, Ziba. "How the Door of Ijtihad Was Opened and Closed: A Comparative Analysis of Recent Family Law Reforms in Iran and Morocco." *Washington and Lee Law Review* (Fall 2007): 1499–511.

Moghadam, Valentine M. *Modernizing Women: Gender and Social Change in the Middle East,* 2nd ed. Boulder, CO: Lynne Rienner Publishers, 2003.

Moghadam, Valentine M. "Patriarchy in Transition: Women and the Changing Family in the Middle East." *Journal of Comparative Family Studies* (Spring 2004): 137–62.

Molyneux, Maxine. "Women's Rights and Political Contingency: The Case of Yemen, 1990–1994." *Middle East Journal* 49 (Summer 1995): 418–31.

Mostafa, Mohamed M. "Attitudes Towards Women who Work in Egypt." *Women in Management Review* (2003): 252–61.

Mtango, Sifa. "A State of Oppression? Women's Rights in Saudi Arabia." *Asia-Pacific Journal on Human Rights and the Law* (2004): 49–67.

Naghibi, Nima. *Rethinking Global Sisterhood Western Feminism and Iran.* Minneapolis: University of Minnesota, 2007.

Nashat, Guity. *Women and Revolution in Iran.* Boulder, CO: Westview Press, 1983.

Nashat, Guity and Judith Tucker. *Women in the Middle East and North Africa.* Bloomington: Indiana University Press, 1999.

Nasr, Vali. *The Shia Revival.* New York: W. W. Norton, 2007.

Okkenhaug, Inger Marie and Ingvild Flaskerud, eds. *Gender, Religion, and Change in the Middle East.* Oxford, UK: Berg, 2005.

Paidar, Parvin, "Feminism and Islam in Iran," in *Taking Sides: Clashing Views on Controversial Issues in Cultural Anthropology,* eds. Robert L. Welsch and Kirk M. Endicott, 200–209. Guilford, CT: Dushkin McGraw Hill, 2003.

Pharaon, Nora Alarifi. "Saudi Women and the Muslim State in the Twenty-First Century." *Sex Roles* 51 (September 2004): 349–66.

Ramazani, Nesta. "Women in Iran: The Revolutionary Ebb and Flow." *Middle East Journal* (Summer 1993): 409–28.

Rathmell, Andrew and Kirsten Schulze. "Political Reform in the Gulf: The Case of Qatar." *Middle Eastern Studies* 36 (October 2000): 47–62.

Rehman, Javaid. "The Sharia, Islamic Family Laws and International Human Rights Law: Examining the Theory and Practice of Polygamy and Talaq." *International Journal of Law, Policy and the Family* 21 (2007): 108–27.

Reilly, James. "Women in the Economic Life of Late-Ottoman Damascus." *Arabica* 4 (March 1995): 79–106.

Robinson, Glenn E. "Democratization in Jordan." *International Journal of Middle East Studies* 30 (August 1998): 387–410.

Rosenfeld, Peri. "Women in Green: The Contributions of Hadassah Nursing to Immigrant and Refugee Health in Pre-State and the Early Years of the State of Israel." *Nursing History Review* 13 (2005): 101–19.

Ross, Michael L. "Oil, Islam and Women." *American Political Science Association* 102 (February 2008): 107–23.

Rubenberg, Cheryl A. *Palestinian Women Patriarchy and Resistance in the West Bank.* Boulder, CO: Lynne Rienner Publishers, 2001.

Rubin, Judith Colp. "Women in the New Iraq." *Middle East Review of International Affairs* 12 (September 2008): 33–46.

Saadawi, Nawal El. *The Nawal El Saadawi Reader.* London: Zed Books, 1977.

Sabbagh. Suha, ed. *Arab Women Between Defiance and Restraint.* Brooklyn, NY: Olive Branch Press, 1996.

Sadiqi, Fatima and Moha Ennaji. "The Feminization of Public Space: Women's Activism, The Family Law and Social Change in Morocco." *Journal of Middle East Women's Studies* (Spring 2006): 86–114.

Saktanber, Ayse. *Living Islam.* New York: I. B. Tauris, 2002.

Salloum, Habeeb. "Women in the United Arab Emirates." *Contemporary Review* (August 2003): 101–04.

Sasson-Levy, Orna and Sarit Amram-Katz. "Gender Integration in Israeli Officer Training: Degendering and Regendering the Military." *Signs* 33 (2007): 105–33.

Schvaneveldt, Paul L., Jennifer L. Kerpelman, and Jay D. Schvaneveldt. "Generational and Cultural Changes in Family Life in the United Arab Emirates: A Comparison of Mothers and Daughters." *Journal of Comparative Family Studies* (Winter 2005): 77–91.

Sechzer, Jeri Altneu. "Islam and Women, Where Tradition Meets Modernity." *Sex Roles* 51 (2004): 263–72.

Seymour-Jorn, Caroline. "Etidal Osman: Egyptian's Women's Writing and Creativity." *Journal of Middle East Women's Studies* 2 (Winter 2006): 95–121.

Shehadeh, Lamia Rustum. "The Legal Status of Married Women in Lebanon." *International Journal of Middle Eastern Studies* 30 (November 1998): 501–19.

Shilo, Margalit. *Princess or Prisoner? Jewish Women in Jerusalem 1840–1914.* Lebanon: Brandeis University Press, 2005.

Shoup, John A. *Culture and Customs of Syria.* Westport, CT: Greenwood Press, 2008.

Smith, Jane I. "Women in Islam: Equity, Equality, and the Search for the Natural Order." *Journal of American Academy of Religion* 47 (December 1979): 517–37.

Smith, W. Robertson. *Kinship and Marriage in Early Arabia.* London: Adam and Charles Black, 1903.

Stanski, Victoria. "Linchpin for Democracy: The Critical Role of Civil Society in Iraq." *Journal of Third World Studies* 12 (2005): 197–225.

Starr, June. "The Role of Turkish Secular Law in Changing the Lives of Rural Muslim Women, 1950–1970." *Law and Society Review* 23 (1989): 497–523.

"Step by Step for Middle East Women." *The Christian Science Monitor,* 101, (2009): 8.

Sümer, Sevil. A Comparative Study of Higher Educated Women from Urban Turkey and Norway." *Acta Sociolgica* 41 (1998): 115–29.

Süral, A. Nurhan. "Legal Framework for Gender Equality at Work in Turkey." *Middle Eastern Studies* 43 (September 2007): 811–24.

Talhami, Gahda Hashem. *The Mobilization of Muslim Women in Egypt.* Gainesville: University Press of Florida, 1996.

Taraki, Lisa. "Jordanian Islamists and the Agenda for Women: Between Discourse and Practice." *Middle East Studies* 32 (January 1996): 140–59.

Teitelbaum, Joshua. "Dueling for Da'wa: State vs. Society on Saudi Internet." *Middle East Journal* 56 (Spring 2002): 222–39.

Thompson, Elizabeth. "Public and Private in Middle Eastern Women's History." *Journal of Women's History* 15 (Spring 2003): 53–69.

Toman, Cheryl. "The Link Between Women's Studies Programs and Grassroots Organizations." *Arab Studies Quarterly* (Spring 2003): 55–67.

Toren, Nina. "Tradition and Transition: Family and Change in Israel." *Gender Issues.* 21 (Spring 2003): 61–76.

Toren, Nina. "Tradition and Transition: Family Change in Israel." *Gender Issues* (Spring 2003): 60–76.

Torstrick, Rebecca. *Culture and Customs of Israel.* Westport, CT: Greenwood Press, 2004.

Tremayne, Sonraya. "Modernity and Early Marriage in Iran: A View from Within." *Journal of Middle East Women's Studies* 2 (Winter 2006): 65–94.

Van Creveld, Martin. "Armed But Not Dangerous: Women in the Israeli Military." *War in History* (2000): 82–98.

Vivante, Bella, ed. *Women's Roles in Ancient Civilizations.* Westport, CT: Greenwood Press, 1999.

Weiner, Lauren. "Islam and Women: Choosing to Veil and other Paradoxes." *Policy Review* (October/November 2004): 49–66.

Welchman, Lynn. "In the Interim: Civil Society, the Shar'ia Judiciary and Palestinian Personal Status Law in the Transitional Period." *Islamic Law and Society* 10 (2003): 34–69.

Willoughby, John. "Segmented Feminization and the Decline of Neopatriarchy in GCC Countries of the Persian Gulf." *Comparative Studies of South Asia, Africa and the Middle East* 28 (2008): 184–99.

Wing, Adrien Katherine and Hisham A. Kassim. "The Future of Palestinian Women's Rights: Lessons from a Half-Century of Tunisian Progress." *Washington and Lee L. Review* (2007): 1551–68.

Wing, Adrien Katherine and Hisham A. Kassim. "Hamas, Constitutionalism, and Palestinian Women." *Howard Law Journal* 50 (2007): 480–513.

"Women in Pre-Islamic Arabia." Muslim Women's League, (1995). http://www.mwlusa.org/topics/history/herstory.html.

Würth, Anna. "Stalled Reform: Family Law in Post-Unification Yemen." *Islamic Law and Society* 10 (2003): 12–33.

Ya'ar, Ephraim. "Continuity and Change in Israeli Society: The Test of the Melting Pot." *Israel Studies* 10 (Summer 2005): 91–128.

Yonah, Yossi and Ishak Saporta. "The Wavering Luck of Girls: Gender and Pre-Vocational Education in Israel." *Journal of Middle East Women's Studies* 2 (Fall 2006): 71–101.

Yüksel, Metin. "The Encounter of Kurdish Women with Nationalism in Turkey." *Middle Eastern Studies* 42 (September 2006): 777–802.

Zaatari, Zeina. "The Culture of Motherhood: An Avenue for Women's Civil Participation in South Lebanon." *Journal of Middle East Women's Studies* 2 (Winter 2006): 33–64.

Zaghal, Ali S. "Social Change in Jordan." *Middle Eastern Studies* 20 (October 1984): 53–75.

Zuhur, Sherifa. "Women and Empowerment in the Arab World." *Arab Studies Quarterly* 25 (Fall 2003): 17–38.

Index

Abdullah (king of Saudi Arabia), 68, 70,
   151–52
Abu Bakr, 4, 105, 106, 157
Abu Talib, 2, 3
Adam and Eve, 101
Adultery, 129–30
Age of the Rightly Guided Caliphs and
   beyond: family, 56–62; literature, 193;
   overview, xxvii–xxviii; religion,
   107–12. *See also* Islam
Agricultural work, xvi, 6–7, 20
Ahmadinejad, Mahmud, 16
Aisha: family life, 52, 53, 56–57; religion,
   105, 107; work, 4–5
Al-Atrash, Amal, 200–201
Al-Atrash, Farid, 200–201
Al Banna, Hassan, 170–71
Algeria: family, 71, 73–74; politics, 162;
   work, 9, 21–22, 73
Ali, 4–5
Al-Qaeda in Iraq (AQI), 89
Amin, Qasim, 161
Arabian Nights, 194
Arab Women's Development Society
   (Kuwait), 174, 175
Arif, Abd al Salam, 142
Ashkenazis, 17
Ataturk, Mustafa, 12, 64, 134–35, 163

Ba'ath party (Iraq), 24
Badi'a Masabni, 199–200
Bektashi order of Sufism, 114
Ben Ali, Zein el-Abedin, 21
"Book of Kings" (Ferdowsi), 193
Bourguiba, Hagib, 20–21, 140
Bursa (Anatolian city), 7

Children: custody of, 131; Israel, 92–93;
   Kuwait, 78; Lebanon, 75–76; Morocco,
   73; Palestinians in the West Bank,
   84–86; Turkey, 66–67. *See also*
   Family
Christianity, 100, 101, 123
Ciller, Tansu, 164
Code of Personal Status (Tunisia),
   139–40
Committee for the Promotion of Virtue
   and the Prevention of Vice (Saudi
   Arabia), 32–33
Constitutional Revolution (Iran), 80,
   166–67
Cooking, 190
Crafts: Iran, 203–4; Syria, 205
Culture, 189–207; contributions to
   cultural identity today, 207; dancers,
   singers, and entertainers, 198–201;
   Egypt, 197–98; Iran, 202–5; language,

190–91; literature, 193–96; overview, 189–90; poetry, 191–92, 193, 194, 196–97, 204; pre-Islamic society, xxv–xxvi; rites of passage, xxv, 201–2; Sufi, 196–97; symbolism, 192; Syria, 205–6
Custody of children, 131

Damascus (Syria), 8–9
Dancers, singers, and entertainers, 198–201; Egypt, 198–200; Syria, 200–201; Turkey, 198
Divorce: Iraq, 87–88; Islamic law, 130–31; Qu'ran, 130
Druze, 109

Education: Egypt, 18–19, 20; Iran, 13, 14; Iraq, 23–24, 25; Israel, 17; Jordan, 26; Kuwait, 77; Lebanon, 41, 42; Libya, 22–23; Oman, 36, 37, 38; Qatar, 38–39, 40; Saudi Arabia, 30, 31, 33; United Arab Emirates, 34; Yemen, 35
Egypt: culture, 197–98; dancers, singers, and entertainers, 198–200; education, 18–19, 20; law, 135–37; politics, 170–72; work, 8, 11, 18–20
Entertainers. See Dancers, singers, and entertainers
Erdogan, Recip Tayyip, 165

Fadlallah, Muhammad Hussein, 43–44
Faisal I (king of Iraq), 176, 177
Family, 49–93; Age of the Rightly Guided Caliphs and beyond, 56–62; Algeria, 71, 73–74; early Islam, 51–54; family patterns, 54–56; Iran, 78–81; Iraq, 86–89; Israel, 89–93; Kuwait, 76–78; Lebanon, 74–76; marriage, 54–56; Morocco, 71–73; North Africa, 70–74; Ottoman period, 59–62; overview, 49–51; Palestinian women in the West Bank, 83–86; pre-Islamic society, xvi–xvii, xviii–xx; Saudi Arabia, 67–70; Tunisia, 71, 74; Turkey, 64–67; Turkish and Mongol period, 59; World War I and its aftermath, 62–63; Yemen, 81–83
Farrokhzad, Forugh, 204
Fatima: religion, 105, 108–9, 115; symbolism, 192; work, 43

Fatimids, 108–9
Federation of the Kuwaiti Women's Associations, 175, 176
Ferdowsi, Abo'l-Qasem, 193

Gaza Strip, 148
Gender relations, in Qu'ran, 56
Ghazali, Zaynab Al, 171
Golden Age of Islam: politics, 157–59; work, 4–5. See also Islam

Hamad bin Khalifa al Thani, 179–80
Hamas, 149–50
Hashomer, 183
Hassan (king of Morocco), 138
Hind bint Utbah, 4
Hizbulla, 76
Hussein, Saddam, 24, 143–44, 178

Inheritance, 131–32
Internet, 69
Iran: culture, 202–5; education, 13, 14; family, 78–81; law, 132–33; literature, 204; marriage, 78–80; politics, 165–70; weaving, 203–4; work, 10, 11, 13–16
Iraq: divorce, 87–88; education, 23–24, 25; family, 86–89; law, 141–44; marriage, 87; patriarchy, 86–87; politics, 176–79; work, 23–25
Iraqi Women's League, 178
Islam: family, 51–54; overview, xxvi–xxvii; veiling, 116–19; women's role in, 99, 102–6, 107–9, 110–12. See also Age of the Rightly Guided Caliphs and beyond; Golden Age of Islam; Qu'ran; Religion
Islamic law, 127–32; divorce, 130–31; inheritance, 131–32; marriage, 129–30; property rights, 132
Islamic period: politics, 156–57; work, 2–4. See also Age of the Rightly Guided Caliphs and beyond; Golden Age of Islam
Islamic Revolution (Iran), 80
Islamic Salvation Front (Algeria), 22
Isma'ili Muslims, 108, 109
Israel: children, 92–93; education, 17; family, 89–93; Judaism, 121–22;

About the Authors

RUTH MARGOLIES BEITLER is a Professor of Comparative Politics, Department of Social Sciences, U.S. Military Academy, West Point, New York. She is the co-author of *The Fight for Legitimacy: Democracy Versus Terrorism* (Praeger, 2006) and the author of *The Path to Mass Rebellion: An Analysis of Two Intifadas* (Lexington Press, 2004).

ANGELICA R. MARTINEZ is Instructor of International Relations, Department of Social Sciences, U.S. Military Academy, West Point, New York.